And The Word Became...
A Sermon

'A serious and major work on expository preaching. Thorough, detailed, carefully researched material with many in-depth examples. For those engaged in the regular exposition of the Word there are many valuable and practical insights. A goldmine of Biblical resource material from a competent scholar enriched by his years of experience in cross-cultural ministry.'

David Ellis, OMF

'Derek Newton writes with experience of preaching both in the United Kingdom and abroad which makes the book rich. It is thoroughly practical and yet full of deep teaching on the whole theme of preaching within the biblical context. Evangelicals often pride themselves on preaching but experience teaches that in many ways there is a great lack of exposition even in those circles.

In some ways this book is as much a handbook for reference as a book to read for inspiration. There are selected passages as examples of how to treat scripture and these could be a stimulus and not a crib sheet. Every preacher, actual and potential, could find this book stimulating and a very useful guide.

Philip H Hacking

The obvious fruit of a dedicated teacher of preaching, this book, based on a taught course, demands much of the reader. However, it offers rich dividends for those who will submit to its suggested discipline of study and preparation. It is not a book for the timid or the dilettante but for the serious student.

Derek Prime

And The Word Became...
A Sermon

A Guide to Biblical
EXPOSITORY PREACHING

Dr Derek Newton

Mentor/OMF

ISBN 1 85792 767 2

© Derek Newton 2003

Published in 2003 in the
Mentor Imprint
by
Christian Focus Publications,
Geanies House, Fearn, Ross-shire,
IV20 1TW, Scotland
and
OMF, Station Approach, Borough Green,
Sevenoaks, Kent, TN15 8BG, England

www.christianfocus.com

Cover design by Alister MacInnes

Printed and bound by
Bell & Bain, Glasgow

Contents

Preface

No one can pretend that preaching is the most popular activity on much of planet earth today. At best the sermon is often considered an irrelevance – an opportunity to switch off, slumber or indulge in day-dreaming, as the preacher fills the inevitable time slot in the Sunday order of service. At worst the sermon is viewed as an interruption, an intrusion, even an invasion of privacy – an attempt by the preacher to tell people what to do. Imposing dogma or issuing instructions are not fashionable lines of communication in our postmodern, pluralistic world.

This depressing state of affairs, however, represents only one side of the coin. On the other side is the glorious truth that countless lives down the centuries have been transformed by the gospel of Christ and the Word of God. Alcoholics and drug addicts have been delivered from bondage; Christian hospitals have been built; business people have had their lives and values turned around and reset into the new direction of Christ's compass. By Word and Spirit, people are transformed – profoundly and permanently. This is undeniable.

Clearly there is a paradox and a problem here. Something is wrong. The fault lies not with the living and enduring Word of God, but rather with our communication of that Word. Part of the problem is that some preachers start out with their own agenda or method and then hunt around in search of a text, story or illustration to suit what they want to say. Others start out with a genuine desire to preach well but simply feel unsure how to proceed. The overall result is that the truth contained in Scripture is not handled adequately, is seldom fully unpacked, and people go away unmoved, unchallenged and unchanged. That is tragic beyond words.

The message of the Gospel *is* powerful. Paul realized that the Thessalonian believers had been chosen by God 'because our gospel came to you not simply with words, but also with power, with the Holy Spirit and with deep conviction' (1 Thess. 1:4-5). It is true that we are saved by the free grace of God but that grace cost God His only Son. Our preaching of God's Word will be demanding. It will involve considerable cost and self-denying sacrifice. It will demand our time, both to prepare sermons and to listen to them. That will not be easy for busy, over-stretched and increasingly urbanized twenty-first century people. It is precisely because of this limited time that preaching will demand self-discipline if we are to give it the energy and effort it deserves. Preaching will demand not only our physical resources but our willingness to think, sometimes long and hard, about sermon preparation and delivery. Not only this, but preaching will demand that we match the words of our lips with the walk and witness of our daily living.

Demanding, yes, but enormously exciting and rewarding, as we work hard, whilst trusting the continual intervention of the Holy Spirit at every stage. Without His help, *all* will be in vain. The living God wants to speak to His people and build them up in Christ through our exposition of His very own Word. Our careful, prayerful and Spirit-led exposition of God's Word will be used by God to bring comfort, challenge, conviction and change. Can there be anything more exciting than that?!

In part at least it is the heavy demands of preaching that make it tempting to seek out a short-cut to accomplish the task. I have not yet discovered such a route! There is no quick fix that works! Yet the situation is by no means hopeless for a number of helpful books are available to us. What I offer in the book you now hold is a practical, hands-on and systematic guide for the preparation and delivery of a biblical expository sermon. It is my strong conviction that relevant, applied and powerful exposition emerges from the vital foundation of careful exegesis of the biblical text. Exegesis and exposition are the inseparable couple in any truly biblical sermon. That is why the heart of this book consists of five steps for our exegesis and understanding of the text. A further five steps then unfold a method for shaping our exegesis into the form of an applied expository sermon. Each step is explained in such a way that it can be read, studied and used as part of your practical preparation of an actual biblical passage for your next sermon. This method seeks to provide a comprehensive treatment of each step. In other words the text is dealt with very fully and this means that the preacher will need to be flexible, according to available preparation time in the nitty-gritty of daily life and ministry.

The essence of this method was worked out during my six years of teaching at Asian Theological Seminary, Manila, Philippines, from 1996–2002. Two out of several courses were taken by full- and part-time pastors of the Worldwide Church of God which over the past ten years has sought to shed its painful past and has emerged from Armstrongism into a new understanding and experience of the gospel of grace. I am deeply grateful to all those English – and Filipino – speaking pastors, elders, Christian educators, theological students and missionaries for joining me on those journeys of learning exposition together. Helpful comments were made by such fellow travellers for the writing of this book.

My admiration and thanks at its deepest human level are for my wife Audrey Elizabeth and our two teenage sons, Michael James and Stephen Paul, who were so patient and understanding. Through many struggles, I believe the Lord God Himself sustained this writing and enabled its completion. My prayer is that He alone, and no one else, will be glorified through the reading, study and application of this guide to biblical expository preaching.

1

The Need for Exposition of the Word

Many are the books on preaching penned over the last century. Steady is the stream of sermons delivered across the world week by week. Yet amidst the flow of speech from the Church's pulpits, a frightening number of listeners remain essentially unfed and unchanged by what they hear. Few would be surprised by the claim that, in churches where the Word of God is not taken seriously and is not given top priority, there will be little grasp of spiritual truth. More worrying is my suggestion that even in churches that give strong recognition to the inspiration and authority of Scripture, the lives of many regular sermon hearers fail to show real evidence of transformation.

If we are to be honest in our evaluation of sermons, it must be admitted that a large proportion of them can be classified under one, or a combination, of the following categories.

1. HOBBY HORSE SERMONS
A 'hobby horse' is a favourite topic or an obsessive, fixed idea. In the context of preaching, a hobby horse can become a regular feature. Whether the subject is Christian giving, women's ordination or the future of Israel, it is remarkable just how frequently the preacher returns to that same theme. Actually, of course, it is not remarkable at all, for such preachers frequently begin with their own thoughts or

hobby horse and then attach those thoughts to Scripture or look for proof-texts, rather than allowing the Scripture to control their thinking.

2. ROCKET SERMONS
Such sermons leave their launching-pad from a particular biblical text but, sadly, in the early stage of the sermon's journey, it becomes evident that the preacher has no intention of returning to that text or even of using the text in any meaningful way. Those in the congregation who had opened their Bibles to trace the sermon's trajectory will quickly become discouraged and will close the Scriptures even before the sermon's boosters have fallen away.

3. HEART-ON-THE-SLEEVE SERMONS
The sincerity of such preachers may well be exemplary but, so often, what is spoken from the heart has no basis or even occurrence in the biblical text or passage itself. Thoughts which arise in the mind or heart of the preacher may or may not be valid but, if they are not rooted in the Word of God itself, we have no measuring stick with which to evaluate them.

4. SKYSCRAPER SERMONS
Some sermons consist of a patchwork quilt of stories and illustrations, albeit skilfully interwoven. Entertainment value can be high for the listeners, but in the end, all they can remember is a skyscraper shrouded in the mist — or as an American faculty colleague used to put it — one 'storey' piled up on top of another. Such sermons lack biblical substance.

5. GRASSHOPPER SERMONS
Recently I heard a sermon which took a modified rocket approach. The preacher launched out from Ephesians 5:2, taking the theme of the love of God. It quickly became apparent that the love of God was to be broken into ten sub-themes and that each of those was to be supported by at least half a dozen biblical verses. So began the tiring task of flicking backwards and forwards across the entire spectrum

of Scripture as the sermon spiralled across space, overloading the weary listeners. The preacher was undoubtedly sincere but I believe he was sincerely wrong in thinking that the more Bible verses you pack into a sermon, the better it is bound to be!

Sadly, none of the preaching styles thus far mentioned actually encourage sermon listeners to open their Bibles and give serious attention to the content and context of Scripture. More alarming still is the fact that such discouragement of the open Bible inevitably closes the door to the very text of Scripture by which preaching needs to be evaluated.

Even when preachers do try to base their sermons on a biblical text, the practice of merely extracting the three main points – often alliterated – can be a potentially dangerous one, if it fails to take account of the background issues, the aim and purpose of the biblical writer and the various contexts in which the passage is set. Lack of serious appraisal of contexts is, of course, a constant temptation to those who prepare topical sermons that touch upon a wide range and variety of biblical texts.

If it is true that much current preaching does indeed give cause for concern, then we must go to the Scriptures themselves to ask whether this is a new problem and whether Scripture itself gives us clear indications or guidelines regarding the principles and practice of preaching. Alongside, and indeed integral to this investigation, lies the fundamental issue of the nature of Scripture, the goals of preaching and the methods of attaining those goals. Where better to turn than to the authoritative revelation of the two testaments of the Bible that God gave to his Church?

2

The Old Testament's Argument
for Exposition of the Word

*E*ven a cursory reading of the Old Testament indicates the presence of a triangle whose three sides are constantly interacting with each other – the revelation of the Word of Yahweh, the responsibility of the people of God to be obedient to that Word, and the role of Israel's leaders in communicating divine revelation to the people. This ever-present triangle emerges most clearly through the voices of the prophets, as God pleads with his erring people.

AMOS

Originating in the southern kingdom of Judah, Amos exercised his ministry in the northern kingdom of Israel. His warnings revolve round the religious hypocrisy, political oppression and blatant social injustice that would lead inexorably to Assyrian military victory over Israel in 722 BC. In chapters 7–9, God still offers Israel the chance to return but eventually punishment becomes inevitable. One of the features of God's breaking off his covenant agreement with the northern kingdom of Israel, announced in chapter 3, was the scarcity of Yahweh's prophetic words. Such scarcity was an element of the curse which derived from the original covenant (Deut. 4:28-9, 32:20; Hos. 3:4) and had been a feature also of the late judges period when the Word of the Lord was rare (Judg. 21:25; I Sam. 3:1). Amos 8:11 records this famine of God's words and the following verse shows how the divine punishment will be manifested, namely, that the people will seek the Word of the Lord right across the Assyrian Empire but their search will be in vain, for the Lord will have withdrawn from them for a time.

The message is clear. God had revealed his Word through the prophetic revelation and the written law and expected the obedient response of his people. Disobedience to the Word, in terms of a refusal to hear and practise that Word, brought the judgment of God.

Hosea

Our picture of the triangle of God's revelation, human response and the role of leaders, is given a further dimension in the prophetic writings of Hosea who followed Amos in his appeals to the northern kingdom of Israel during the closing stages of its existence. God's covenant with Israel is portrayed as a marriage, which Hosea comes to understand more profoundly through his own broken marriage. Israel has deserted the Lord and has run after Canaanite gods, yet the Lord still longs for his disobedient and struggling people to return to him. The divine words through Hosea are very revealing as Yahweh brings his charge against Israel in chapter 4.

God's condemnation of his people is rooted fairly and squarely in their lack of knowledge (Hos. 4:6a). The responsibility for this is laid firmly at the door of the priests who apparently knew the law of Yahweh but chose deliberately to forget and ignore it (Hos. 4:6b). A cult which was once Yahwistic had now degenerated into one that exhibited syncretism and prostitution (Hos. 4:12-14). Covenant law ought to have been diligently and faithfully mediated between God and his people through the ministry of the priests (Hos. 4:4) who served the cult in the Jerusalem temple, assisted by prophets. The setting of Hosea's prophecy may have been Bethel, prior to 745 BC, and we know that the priesthood had grown wealthy and degenerate during the prosperous rule of Jeroboam II. The symptoms of that decay are plain to read in the text. The priests appear to have been taking sin offerings from the people in return for declaring them forgiven (Hos. 4:7-8). Thus the priests encouraged the people to sin, and the richer and more secure the priests felt, the more they abandoned God, compromised with the people and withheld the law of the Lord. The priests failed to encourage knowledge of and obedience to God, with the predictable results that the people lacked understanding (Hos. 4:11), were deceived by a 'spirit of prostitution' (Hos. 4:12), indulged in sinful practices (Hos. 4:13) and suffered devastating ruin (Hos. 4:14b). Other symptoms served to compound the dire nature of the problem: lack of truthfulness and lack of faithfulness in personal relationships, lack of mutual care for one another (Hos. 4:1); moral anarchy and violence (Hos. 4:2); national deterioration (Hos. 4:3).

Knowledge of the law is thus presented as being very practical – it involved an understanding of God's ways and his moral requirements. Doctrine and practice have always been inextricably linked in God's will. But why is the knowledge of the people toward their God so crucial? That knowledge is the foundation of God's eschatological blessing on Israel (Amos 2); it was the basis on which Yahweh delivered his people during and after the Exodus (Hos. 13:4), and it is more important than any sacrifice Israel could make (Hos. 6:6). In short, it is so central that the absence of that knowledge condemned Israel to destruction (Hos. 4:6). Not only that but it was the priests who were held primarily to blame for failing to instruct the people in the law of the Lord. So serious was this neglect regarded that it carried a triple punishment. God will ignore the children of the priests (Hos. 4:6b) in a cult where the priesthood was hereditary; he will forsake the priests along with the people (Hos. 4:9); he will condemn the priests and people to hunger and infertility (Hos. 4:10), because of their adultery with the Canaanite gods and embracing of Baal worship.

Knowledge ought to have led to an understanding of God's Word, a continual awareness of it and an obedient submission to that Word, leading to transformation in the people of God and in the life of society. The intended function of the priests was to obey this law themselves and to instruct the people in the requirements of that law (Deut. 31:9-13). In both respects, the priests failed abysmally and it is that failure which Hosea presents as being of utmost concern to the living God. As old as the hills, and as true as ever, is the fact that when the leaders fail to recognize true knowledge as coming from

God's law, then the domino effect becomes inevitable – ignorance of divine truth, immorality in society, instability of the state, impact of divine judgment.

ISAIAH

In spite of the impending disaster of the northern kingdom of Israel at the hands of the Assyrian military machine, neither Amos nor Hosea were devoid of hope. The exile of Israel to Assyria, and later of Judah to Babylon, will be accompanied by the promise of glorious restoration for the remnant of God's covenant people. In the sixth century BC, God was to make a way for the rebuilding of Jerusalem – city and temple – and for the restoration of the people to the promised land. Isaiah 40 affirms the mighty sovereignty of God and the eternality of his Word (Isa. 40:8). God confirms repeatedly his longing to speak his Word to his people through his servant (Isa. 42:2, 6; 50:4).

In Isaiah 42:1, 3-4 Yahweh's servant is presented to the court as the one who will implement among the nations (v. 1) and in the land (v. 4) the verdict that Yahweh has reached. That decision is to restore Zion and the news will be made known to the nations, land and coastlands. What God speaks, he invariably fulfils in history. Isaiah continually reaffirms that God does indeed speak his Word to the people and that his Word is absolutely guaranteed to be fulfilled for his purposes and eternal glory. This is our great assurance for all times, places and circumstances.

EZEKIEL

The first thirty-three chapters of Ezekiel's prophecy convey the message that Jerusalem will be captured by Babylon and the temple will be destroyed, though God's judgment of Israel will then be followed by comfort and restoration from exile in Babylon. Alongside the voice of God through true prophecy, there came the voices of the false prophets who had assumed the name of God and were predicting, contrary to divine prophecy, that there would be a speedy return from exile. False prophecy at this period of Israel's history featured a number of elements.

(a) False prophecy was coming out of the imagination of human beings (13:2). This inspiration was no better than ordinary human wisdom.

(b) Ezekiel describes the false prophets as 'foolish' (13:3), which in Wisdom Literature is used to describe those who are arrogant (Prov. 30:32) and spiritually and morally deviant (Job 2:10). They follow their own impulses and reveal only their own delusions of imagination. They lack divine insight and do not represent God in any way, shape or form.

(c) Instead of helping to rebuild the nation, the false prophets are like 'jackals among ruins' who actually seek to benefit from Israel's devastation (13:4).

(d) The false prophets should have been standing in the breach by denouncing evil and rebuilding the wall by demanding renewal of the covenant relationship. Instead they have sought personal gain and have condemned Israel to suffer the wrath of God against an unwarned and unprotected people (13:5). False prophecy has robbed the people of God's Word.

(e) False prophets used the name of Yahweh to give the impression that their words were divinely inspired. In prophesying peace, these fake messengers were declaring false hope (13:6-7). They proclaimed a message not unknown in the twenty-first century, namely a stress on God's readiness to forgive but an exclusion of his demand for true repentance.

(f) These prophets of falsity have led the people astray by producing an illusory complacency among the people of God (13:10). No attempt at false whitewash can prevent the imminent storm from destroying the society.

Into this dire situation Yahweh then announces, through Ezekiel, that the city, the walls and the false prophets will all be wiped away in judgment (13:8-9, 10-16). Indeed the false prophets are not even counted among the genuine covenant people of Yahweh. Ezekiel has made clear the demands and purposes of Yahweh through this prophecy and the lessons for us are frighteningly clear. The preacher may have undergone extensive training, may possess rhetorical gifts par excellence, may be endowed with a sparkling personality and may be widely experienced, but these characteristics alone do not qualify one for the preaching ministry. If we are to speak for God, our message must carry God's genuine signature. In short it must be that message of God revealed in the Scriptures. Only that message, rooted in the authority and total integrity of God, will exhibit the power to attain its life-giving divine purpose for church and world. Ezekiel is absolutely up to date in its message for us.

The message is vital but no less so is the life of the messenger. We dare not move on without noting that the call to proclamation, both for Ezekiel and for the modern preacher, is inseparable from the call to stand in the presence of God (1:28b–2:2). Ezekiel is promised only that ultimately God *will* fulfil his purposes through the proclaimed Word. God reassures his messenger that there is no cause for fear (2:6). All that is required is for the true prophet to declare the words of Yahweh (2:7, 3:4). Yet that is actually not all that is required, for the prophet is called upon to eat the scroll tendered by Yahweh (2:9ff.). The sweetness of the bitter parchment arises through Ezekiel's direct, personal encounter with the divine Word. The true preacher is the one who is fed, nourished, equipped and empowered by the divine Word and herein lies our overwhelming responsibility. We ourselves are, in short, to be a living testimony to the power and reality of the Word of God that we preach. Ezekiel was called by God (2:1) and equipped by the Spirit (2:2) but his priority in ministry was the divine Word, through life and lips – Ezekiel is told to listen to God's Word (2:8; 3:10), to ingest God's Word (2:8; 3:1, 3), to speak God's Word (2:7; 3:4, 10) and to realize that as he does so, God himself is manifesting his authority and power (2:4; 3:11). God expects nothing less from the twenty-first century ministers of his enduring and unchanging Word.

JEREMIAH

Ezekiel was not the only prophet called by God to announce the impending exile of Israel into Babylon. Called in 627 BC in the thirteenth year of the reign of Josiah son of Amon king of Judah, Jeremiah knew he would face an uphill task in his preaching ministry (Jer. 1:19). Opposition and personal suffering were to be the hallmarks of Jeremiah's prophetic calling, yet called he was and encouraged even in the early stages of his ministry by a vision from God which helped to authenticate his commission. That vision (1:11-12) involved the branch of an almond tree, which would have been familiar as the first tree to bud in spring. The word for 'branch' was very similar to 'watching' and through this vision, God assures Jeremiah that he is watching over this Word to bring it to rapid fulfilment, like the quickly and early-budding almond branch, even as the prophet proclaims that Word.

Tragically, Yahweh had sent his prophets to Israel with repeated and urgent warnings to live out her covenant relationship with her creator, but to no avail. The people of God had chosen to ignore the words of Yahweh, thereby sealing their judgment (7:25-6). Each occurrence of the term 'rising early and sending' underlined the frequency with which Yahweh's words came to the people, only to fall repeatedly on deaf ears (25:3-5; 26:4-6; 29:16-19).

Running like a golden thread through Jeremiah's prophecies is the constant theme that Yahweh reveals his will through the voice of true prophets and that the rejection of these words of Yahweh invariably guarantees judgment. In particular Jeremiah predicted the destruction of the city and temple of Jerusalem, a prophecy considered blasphemy by those who opposed him. Indeed it was around 609/8 BC that Jeremiah faced trial at the gate of Yahweh's house. His prophecy of destruction was considered blasphemous by priests, prophets and people, and worthy of the death penalty (Jer. 26). Some of the most severe divine indictments in Jeremiah's prophecies are reserved for the false prophets who sought to oppose Jeremiah and at the same time, functioned to accelerate divine judgment on Jerusalem. A study of the biblical text of Jeremiah 23 has yielded material that challenges all who claim to preach the Word of God.

(a) The Lord, through his prophet Jeremiah, condemns the shepherds who instead of caring for the sheep, are actually 'destroying and scattering them' (23:1). God says he will appoint other shepherds who *will* care for the sheep (23:1-8).

(b) God condemns prophets and priests for a number of reasons: they use power unjustly (v.10); they practise wickedness (v. 11); they prophesy by Baal and lead the people astray (v. 13); they commit adultery, immorality and evil (v. 14); they are the source of the evil which infects and affects other people (v. 15).

(c) The root of the problem was that there had been a massive failure on the part of the prophets to stand in the council of the Lord. The Word of the Lord had not been seen or heard. These prophets were not listening to the Word of the Lord and were not giving it to the people (v. 18). Instead they were giving false hopes (v.16) and lies (vv. 25-6, 32).

(d) The authority of the false prophets was (a) their own imagination (v. 16), their desire to please the people (v. 17), their claim to direct inspiration (v. 25), their borrowing from others (v. 30), and their own individual claim (v. 36). The result of this situation was a cheapening of the Lord's Word in which every prophet claimed to have the Word of the Lord. This made it difficult to hear the true Word when it came. The result of such individual claims to authority was a state of distortion and confusion – a situation as real for the twenty-first century AD as it was for the sixth century BC.

(e) On the other hand, the authority of the true prophet is seen in three ways. First, they are called to stand in the council of God (vv. 18, 22); second, they will proclaim God's words to God's people (vv. 22a, 28b); third, they will see that God's Word is not only powerful (23:29) but actually does produce changed lives (23:22).

Jeremiah's observations on the communication methods of true and false prophets are surely of profound challenge for all who aspire to pulpit ministry in the twenty-first century. We ignore them at our peril.

EZRA

The exile to Babylon in the sixth century BC was followed, as both Ezekiel and Jeremiah had predicted, by the restoration of Israel's remnant to the promised land. Through the intervention of Persian kings who had conquered Babylon, the way was opened for the rebuilding of the Jerusalem temple. Following that slow and painstaking work, an expert in the Jewish law, Ezra, was sent from Babylon to oversee the re-establishment of the community of God's people. Another priest, Nehemiah, organized the rebuilding of the walls round Jerusalem to ensure the security of the city. Nehemiah documents the activity of Ezra in bringing the words of the Lord to the newly resettled people of God. His record in Nehemiah 8, along with the accounts in the book of Ezra, make compelling reading and bring to our attention the two-pronged necessity for all who seek to communicate God's Word, namely adherence to the revealed biblical text, alongside holiness in the life of the expositor of that revealed Word. Three important features can be seen in the life and ministry of Ezra: (a) Ezra's commitment to Scripture (Ezra 7:10); (b) his display of humility (8:21); (c) his readiness to say 'Sorry' (9:3f, 10:1f.);

We can trace the impact of his ministry in Nehemiah 8[1]. The setting was a celebration of the Feast of Tabernacles in Jerusalem. The overwhelming emphasis, however, is not on the details of the Feast, but on the ministry of the Word of God. The Law read by Ezra was almost certainly familiar to the people already. It was not completely new. The initiative for the reading of the Law seems to have come from the people (Neh. 8:1). Every seventh year this reading of the law is believed to have been an integral part of the Feast of Tabernacles. What are some of the aspects of note in his sermon?

First, the expounded Word addressed the minds of his hearers (8:1-8); this was where the initial impact was made. Second, the expounded Word stirred their emotions (8:9-12); as he applied Scripture, great conviction and remorse came upon the people as they realized their failure to meet the practical demands of the divine Word. Third, the expounded Word moved the will (8:13-18).

The lay people, priests and Levites realized that they should build booths during the harvest Feast of Tabernacles. For the first time in centuries they gathered branches and set up booths throughout Jerusalem, proclaiming and recalling their experiences as the people of God during the wilderness wanderings that followed the exodus from Egypt (8:16-17). The people acted in response to the reading and exposition of ancient Scripture. The point is this – those who

---

1 The idea of using this passage came from my reading of Dennis Lane 'Preach the Word' Evangelical Press, 1979. He offers additional helpful material on pp 10-12 of his book

heard the exposition of the Law experienced the power of God's Word. Their minds were challenged and brought to fresh understanding (8:8b, 12b); their hearts and emotions were profoundly moved (8:9); their wills were stirred into practical action (8:16). They were obedient to the expounded Word and that very obedience led to an experience and outpouring of joy (8:12, 17). They now had an insatiable appetite for the Word because in a new way they were experiencing its power. The message of the experience of Ezra is that the expounded Word of God changes lives.

3

The New Testament's Argument for Exposition of the Word

*I*n the previous chapter we saw a triangle clearly emerging through the priests and prophets of the Old Testament: the revelation of the Word of Yahweh, the responsibility of God's people to be obedient to that Word, and the role of Israel's leaders in communicating divine revelation to the people. Let us now take a journey through the New Testament to find out whether that pattern is repeated or even amplified and extended. We need to take account of the chief apostolic witnesses of the New Testament writings, namely, Paul, Peter and John, but let us briefly examine Luke's contribution to the issue of our communication of God's Word.

LUKE

The setting of Luke 24:13-35 portrays a fascinating narrative in which Cleopas and another disciple, during their walk to Emmaus, were prevented from recognizing that it was Jesus who had just joined them[1]. These disciples had failed to believe that which they knew of biblical prophecy (Luke 24:25). They had taken on board the idea of the glory of Israel's Messiah but had failed to understand that the triumph and glory of God had to come in and through the appalling suffering of the Christ. The one thing that these disciples had noticed – and this is of huge significance – was that, although they labelled Christ 'a prophet' (Luke 24:19b), they recognized the unmistakable

---

1 The work of Dennis Lane (1979: 13-14) made me aware of the relevance of the particular passage as well as Acts 2:14-41. His book is worth consulting on these texts

partnership in Jesus' life of his words and his deeds. The two were perfectly matched and it was a powerful combination.

Recognizing the failure of the two disciples to grasp the Old Testament background to the cross, Jesus gave a systematic survey of the Scriptures, starting with Moses and going through all the prophetic references to himself (Luke 24:27). We can only assume that the impact of the exposition was sufficient for them to press Jesus to stay overnight (Luke 24:29) and once their eyes were opened – notice the passive voice – they realized the significance of what had just taken place. Jesus had opened the Scriptures, the meaning had become clear, and their hearts burned within them (Luke 24:32). Exposition had touched their minds and hearts with the result that they acted immediately. Their need to stay overnight was suddenly set aside and they rushed back to Jerusalem to share the news (Luke 24:33-5). It was then in Jerusalem that Jesus underlined to the disciples that he indeed was the fulfilment of the Law of Moses, the Prophets and the Psalms (Luke 24:44).

Of enormous significance is the following act of Jesus in opening up their minds so that they could understand the Scriptures (Luke 24:45). Jesus portrays himself as fulfilling Scripture in his death and resurrection, but also in the provision for repentance and the forgiveness of sins which are to be preached to the nations (Luke 24:46-7). Jesus had interpreted the Scriptures for the disciples on the Emmaus road by making understandable that which the hearers did not immediately understand. The message was based on Old Testament Scripture, centred on his own Person, the Christ, and it left the disciples' hearts burning within them. What made the difference? The words of God. Simply that. It was the written words of Scripture, alongside the spoken words of the resurrected Christ, that impacted the minds, hearts and wills of those two disciples on the Emmaus road. Our task as preachers is precisely that – to proclaim and explain the words of God, as Christ continues to give the enabling by that precious gift of the Holy Spirit (Luke 24:49). Small wonder that even in the midst of 'losing' Jesus at the ascension, the Lord's exposition wrought its continuing change in the lives of those disciples, yielding the fruits of joy, worship and praise (Luke 24:52-3).

This power of the Word of God to bring about change is one of the key ongoing themes of Luke's record in the Acts of the Apostles. Three brief examples can be pinpointed as illustration of this.

ACTS 2:14-41

Once the disciples had received the anointing power of the Holy Spirit at Pentecost, Luke records in some detail the impact that was made by a weak human being, Peter, who proclaimed and explained the Word of God in the power of the Spirit of God. Basically, we see the operation of the same dynamic that we encountered previously in Nehemiah 8. After making an initial commitment to explain the linguistic goings-on during Pentecost (Acts 2:14), Peter uses a prolonged explanation method, based upon three Old Testament passages (Joel 2:28-32; Ps. 16:8-11, 110:1). He expounds, with close reference to these texts, the key elements of the gospel – the death, resurrection and ascension of Christ, together with the coming of the Spirit and the glorious day of the Lord. Peter thus extensively addresses the minds of his audience until eventually the divinely inspired words began to impact the emotions of the crowd. Indeed they were 'cut to the heart' (Acts 2:37) and pleaded for further directions which Peter was pleased to give, as he mixed in the final four ingredients – repentance, baptism, forgiveness of sin and the gift of the Holy Spirit (2:38). Peter had powerfully trusted Word and Spirit to engage the mind and move the emotions. We know that he employed further words of warning and plea (2:40), such that eventually the Spirit of God stirred the wills of three thousand human beings to believe and be baptized. The transformation of their lives as recorded in 2:42-47 is simply staggering: the Word of God, powerfully expounded, had produced ongoing hunger for that Word, fellowship, breaking of bread, prayer, signs and wonders, generosity, concern for the brethren, gratitude, genuine living, praise, recognition among the people and church growth. That is the message of Acts 2 – the power of the Word and the Spirit operating to bring change of mind, heart and will on an enormous scale.

ACTS 13:13-52

Change came also to the hearers of God's Word at Pisidian Antioch when Paul and his friends took the opportunity to address both Jews and Gentiles. Following the reading of the Law and the Prophets (13:15), Paul accepted the invitation of the synagogue rulers and began to explain the biblical history of the people of God (13:16ff.). His account reached its climax in an unmistakable statement of the death and resurrection of Jesus, centred on several Old Testament passages (Ps. 2:7, 16:10; Isa. 55:3; Hab. 1:5). Finally Paul announces the benefits of Jesus' work, namely forgiveness and justification for all who believe (13:38-40). Once again, by the reading and exposition of the biblical text, the minds of the hearers were engaged, leading to an openness for further discussion (13:42-3). The powerful work of God's Word spread rapidly through the city and drew greater crowds on the next Sabbath, as well as stimulating intense opposition from the Jews (13:45). In light of the sustained hostility of the Jews towards the Word of God, Paul then applies Isaiah 49:6 to his own calling to preach to the Gentiles (13:46-7).

It was by the preaching of God's Word that the Gentiles responded in faith, demonstrating thereby that they were the ones appointed for eternal life as they embraced that Word of life (13:48). As preachers of the Word, we need to take note that the spreading of the Word of the Lord triggered opposition and persecution, forcing Paul and Barnabas on to Iconium (13:49-51). In spite of that, however, the Holy Spirit who had so mightily come down upon the Word in Pisidian Antioch, continued to encourage and yield joy in the hard-pressed missionaries. The Word of God truly is irrepressible.

ACTS 15:7-9

Should Gentile converts to Christ be circumcised and required to keep the Law? This was the issue that generated so much discussion during the Jerusalem Council. Following the debate, Peter reminded those present that God himself had ordained that the Gentiles might hear the words of the gospel from Peter's mouth and that this explanation would yield the fruit of belief (15:7). Not only this, however, but the God who intimately knows the state of our minds, hearts and wills, actually demonstrates the power of this gospel exposition and his acceptance of Gentile response by granting them the Holy Spirit (15:8) and by purifying their hearts by faith (15:9). God appoints the preacher, the audience and the message and by his sovereign power and choice, he determines that the preaching and explanation of the gospel must bear fruit. Profound change is wrought by the Word.

PAUL

The apostle to the Gentiles wrote almost a third of the New Testament and is worthy of serious consideration as we continue to paint a picture of the many faceted diamond called biblical expository preaching.

ROMANS

Paul's treatment of the nature of the gospel in his letter to the Romans is the most detailed and extensive in the entire New Testament. In a nutshell he explains it in terms of its being a revelation of the righteousness of God by faith (1:17). He then argues that the gospel is needed precisely because of the reality of divine wrath towards human sin (1:18). Only the gospel of salvation by grace through faith can bring deliverance from that wrath of God. The section Romans 1:18-32 pivots on the issue of knowledge and truth, for both have been lost as sources of life-giving power. This loss can be traced through Paul's tightly-packed argument.

Knowledge of God has been rejected by fallen mankind and this has led to failure in every aspect of life: in philosophy, that is human thought processes (1:18-22); in religion, that is worship of various idols (1:25); in ethics, that is depraved minds and actions (1:28).

Mankind has rejected knowledge of God through its loss of *truth*. This tragic process is highlighted very clearly by the apostle Paul. Sinners, firstly, have 'suppressed' the truth (1:18) by living out their wicked ways, in opposition to the clearly revealed knowledge of God (1:18-20). This is a highly significant reference to general truth that is open to all people, rather than specifically revealed gospel truth. If truth can be hindered by mankind, then this implies that truth is an active force that is actually capable of performing something. Sinners are deliberately seeking to prevent the activity of this truth. Sinners, secondly, have refused the truth (1:21). They did this because their thinking had become futile and their hearts darkened. This reference to 'foolish hearts' refers to the centre of the inner life of a human being. In other words, sin has affected the entire orientation of a human life and that includes the thought-life. Boasting of its independence from God, mankind refuses to glorify God and erects idols. That is why, thirdly, Paul is able to say that sinners have 'exchanged the truth of God for a lie' (1:25). Instead of the truth God has revealed, mankind has opted for idolatry. The consequence has been horrendous, for as mankind deserted God, so God abandoned the people to a multitude of lusts. Sinners, fourthly, abandoned truth (1:28) with the result that God gave them over to a 'depraved mind', and of course, as we have seen repeatedly already, failure of the mind leads on to failure in moral action, demonstrated so tragically by the mountain of sins listed in 1:29-31. Predictably and finally, sinners have so totally ignored the truth (1:32) that they incur death for themselves, yet continue to encourage others to pursue the same disastrous course of thought and action. Their conduct was not even acceptable by the standards of pagan morality.

The process that underlies Paul's chain of argument is highly significant. Rejection of divine revelation leads to rejection, and therefore absence, of knowledge of God. The result is the depraved or unapproved mind which is incapable of making sound moral judgments. This guarantees a distorted conscience which inevitably leads to perverted and improper conduct, focused on idolatry and expressed through the immorality of self-centred attitudes and actions.

In view of such a total disaster, how can mankind possibly attain to a righteousness that is acceptable to God? Paul's mind-blowing answer is that God, in his overwhelming love, grace and mercy, has a plan to deal with mankind's overturning of knowledge and truth. The divine solution is staggeringly simple – righteousness can only possibly come by faith (1:17), but that faith comes 'from hearing the message, and the message is heard through the word of Christ'

(10:17). This is the most amazing claim. Only by hearing the Word of Christ, can the dreadful downward spiral be reversed. Only by hearing the Word of Christ can mankind be lifted from the depths of depravity to the heights of eternal glory with the God who alone grants righteousness by faith. 'Hearing the word' triggers the great reversal.

Paul's deep concern for the Israelites is that, though zealous for God, their zeal was not based on knowledge. They had tried to attain their own righteousness, failing to realize that true righteousness comes through faith because the 'word of faith' is near them, proclaiming and inviting faith. The verb 'proclaiming' here in Romans 10:8 is a present continuous tense indicating that preachers constantly proclaim the message that has been passed on. This message is for the whole world, both Jews and Gentiles (10:12), and Paul's promise to those who call on the Lord and put their trust in him is once more grounded in Old Testament Scripture – Isaiah 28:16; Joel 2:32. Indeed, if those Jews are ignorant of salvation by grace, it must have been because they had not heard God's voice in Scripture.

The apostle to the Gentiles begins another chain argument in Romans 10:14-15, claiming that before people can call on the Lord, they must believe in that Lord; before they can believe, they must hear of the Lord; before they can hear, someone must preach to them; before someone can preach, that person must be sent. Preachers are commissioned by the Lord himself and they proclaim and explain the Lord's words, the focus being on what God has given in his Word, not what the preacher has thought up in the mind. Paul then rounds his argument off by reasoning again from the Old Testament Scriptures – that the Jews had in fact been given opportunity to hear the Word of the Lord (10:18; cf. Ps. 19:4), that justification by faith was open to Gentiles as well as Jews (10:19; cf. Deut. 32:21), and that God was pleased to reveal himself to those not actually looking for him (10:20; cf. Isa. 65:1). Paul repeatedly quotes and explains Scripture in driving home his foundational message that righteousness by faith comes through that medium with which first century society was very familiar – 'hearing'. Saving faith and knowledge of divine truth come through the responsive hearing of God's Word.

I Corinthians

Paul's teaching in I Corinthians 1–2 is a veritable gold mine of encouragement on the basis of biblical expository preaching. Lessons abound in the biblical text and as we dig into the material, so the nuggets rise to the surface and become quickly visible as Paul expounds them for us.

(a) Power in the Word (I Cor. 1:17-31)

After an opening thanksgiving for the Corinthians – in itself an amazingly gracious act in light of the huge problems that this church presented to the apostle – Paul quickly calls for the believers to agree with one another (1:10). There has been severe splintering in the church because of an obsession with hoisting certain leaders onto pedestals – a common enough trend in modern day evangelicalism. Paul calls, not for total uniformity, but for agreement so that the believers will display no divisions, but rather will be 'perfectly united in mind and thought'. He wants them to agree in their minds that there should be no divisions among them. The starting point for change lies, it seems, in the mind and thoughts. This is again highly significant. Paul's calling, he asserts, was to preach the gospel (1:17) and in spite of the KJV's rendering 'the foolishness of preaching', Paul makes it clear that foolishness refers, not to the act of preaching, but to the content of what is preached: the message of the cross (1:18). The wisdom of this world evaluates the message of the cross as foolishness. The thinkers of this world have put forward various routes for understanding and directing life in this world – communism, secular humanism, capitalism, tolerant pluralism and postmodernism. The scholars or experts in religion, whether biblical scholars or church leaders, have exercised all the power of their minds. The philosophers have tried to debate and discuss, drawing on all the skills available to them.

The devastating truth, however, is that within God's plan and purpose, no human wisdom has the power to lead men and women to the knowledge of God (1:21). Why? Because it leaves the cross out of the reckoning. It takes no account of the power of the cross for those who are being saved (1:18). Paul makes the astounding claim that people come to salvation through belief and righteousness (1:21, 30) as they are brought to knowledge of, and relationship with, Christ.

This happens by God's specific ordaining 'through the foolishness of what was preached' (1:21). It is through the declaration and explanation of words that God carries out his redeeming and transforming work in people's lives. The power of God resides in the preached message.

(b) Principles for the preacher (1 Cor. 2:1-5)
Paul underscores here some crucial lessons rooted in his own pastoral and preaching ministry experience.

(i) Paul had an overwhelming concern to avoid the style of the orators in the Graeco-Roman world, for their focus was on form and appearance rather than content. Paul's goal was to proclaim 'the testimony about God', that is, the revelation of God (2:1).

(ii) In proclaiming God's self-revelation, Paul must focus on the climax of that revelation, namely, the words and works of Christ. Not only that, but his preaching ministry must be rooted and grounded in his own personal knowledge of that Christ (2:2). Some of the worst extremes in preaching are those through which we see more of a performance than a personal walk with Christ; more of shadows than of substance; more of pretence than of honesty.

(iii) It was through the weakness, fear and trembling of Paul that the power of God was manifested (2:3). We need to be aware that biblical exposition, in releasing the power of God, is also the cause of Satan's antagonism. Yet it is precisely through the struggles and buffetings of the preacher that God glorifies himself. Paul testifies personally to this in 2 Corinthians 12:1-10 and elsewhere in that glorious letter which is so worthy of the preacher's attention.

(iv) Paul's preaching ministry had two irreplaceable and inseparable components. He taught the Word of God (Acts 18:11) and in doing so, he reasoned, explained and proved (Acts 17:2-3). Yet in doing so, his focus was on the Word, not on his own 'wise and persuasive words' (1 Cor. 2:4). As he expounded Scripture so he leaned heavily on his hidden yet indispensable resource, the Spirit's power. Only by the exposition of the Word in the power of the Spirit would men and women be brought into a stable, secure and lasting state of biblical, saving faith (2:5).

(c) Power for exposition (1 Cor. 2:6-16)

Having noted the role of the Spirit in 1 Corinthians 2:5, Paul explains at greater length the pivotal function of the Holy Spirit. He has already shown up the sheer impotence of the wise men, the scholars and the philosophers in trying to bring people to the knowledge of God and he restates this in 2:8. Understanding of the message of the cross can only come by revelation through the Spirit (2:10). Throughout this section, Paul makes a stark contrast between those who receive God's wisdom and those who don't (2:6-10a); between the Spirit of God and the spirit of the world (2:10b-13); and between the natural person and the spiritual person (2:14-16). God's words, says Paul, will always be foreign in this world, unless the Spirit gives the needed light and understanding to those divine words. The role of the Holy Spirit is inextricably tied to the understanding of the message of the cross. The Spirit alone enables us to grasp the truth of the cross and to be transformed by it. The lesson is clear – the preacher cannot hope to impact his hearers' lives by self-reliance. He must lean totally on the Word and the Spirit, for the sake both of himself and of his hearers. Froth may entertain. Eloquence may impress. Lasting change comes only as the Word is proclaimed and explained, and as the Spirit powerfully applies that truth into the minds, hearts and wills of listeners. That is the only route to deep and meaningful change in human lives.

EPHESIANS

Paul's pleas to the believers in the church in Ephesus are of immense relevance for the preaching ministry of the church. This New Testament letter illustrates vividly the marriage of doctrine and life. The apostle clearly states his threefold longing for the believers at Ephesus: reaching unity in the faith and in knowledge of Christ (4:13a); reaching maturity in the fullness of Christ (4:13b); reaching into Christ himself (4:15). Paul is not slow to point out the twofold and interrelated danger facing the Ephesians – that of forgetting their huge privileges as believers and that of forgetting their calling to live distinctly within pagan society. Much of the former danger is dealt with in chapters 1–3 so that Paul can then show the consequences in chapters 4–6 of their new status for the nitty-gritty of living. The section 4:17-24 is thus crucial to the aim and intent of the entire letter and opens with a strong 'earbender' for the church, namely that new status in life demands new lifestyle.

As we probe the exhortation further, however, we discover a staggeringly similar diagnosis of the human dilemma to the one revealed in Romans 1. Having challenged the Ephesian believers to live differently from the Gentiles, Paul immediately draws their attention to the Gentiles' minds and inner life, or rather absence of life. A profound connection is recognized between living and thinking (4:17). The Gentiles are ignorant for two reasons. Firstly, their understanding has been darkened, that is to say, the core of their ability to perceive truth has been destroyed. Secondly, they have been separated from the life of God, that is their ability to relate to the living God has likewise been wrecked. The two tragedies are of course profoundly related. Paul puts the blame fairly and squarely on the Gentiles, who are culpably ignorant. Their loss of the knowledge of God means separation from the truth of God which means absence of the life of God. Ignorance in their minds thus means defective and deficient moral sensitivity, leading to overwhelming selfishness and uncontrollable immorality. The diagnosis unpacked in verses 17-19 points the finger at the underlying cause: absence of knowledge of the true God. Paul is fully aware that in pointing to changes in conduct, he must begin with the problem of the mind. Having identified the cause, he then moves swiftly to the remedy.

In a devastating crescendo of argument, Paul points the way forward by recalling what had already happened to the Ephesians. How had they come to know Christ? Through hearing and teaching. They had heard and been taught. In short, they had learned Christ (4:20). They had heard and responded to the proclamation of the gospel and had been changed by the teaching of the gospel tradition in the power of the Spirit of the living, risen and reigning Christ. The church matures by the hearing and teaching of God's Word. Such exposition is comprehensive in its effects – it means 'putting off the old self' (4:22), being renewed 'in the attitude of your minds' (4:23) and then and only then 'to put on the new self, created to be like God in true righteousness and holiness' (4:24). This is of paramount importance. Loss of truth opens up the field for deceit to yield desire and immoral living (4:22). On the other hand, the present tense of the infinitive construction 'to be made new' indicates continuous renewal and the passive voice tells us that this occurs as we allow ourselves to be renewed. The crux is that this renewal takes place in the inner person, in the mind. Paul elsewhere describes this process as 'being renewed in knowledge in the image of its Creator' (Col. 3:10). In short, believers are to manifest *now* that which God has already made them. Active involvement on the part of believers is of course demanded by the call to 'put off' (Eph. 4:22) and to 'put on' (4:24). The changes that this dynamic produces are then detailed in the section 4:25–6:9.

But how will these changes be effected? Just as Paul explained in Romans 12:1-2, so here, it is through the renewal of minds that the new conduct becomes both possible and visible. That renewal will take place as the church, and especially its leaders, address those minds by passing on the apostolic tradition. The presence of false teaching in the Ephesian church (4:14) served as a strong additional incentive for Paul's admonition in the following verse – 'speaking the truth in love' (4:15). Hearing words, speaking words and teaching words are the roads to maturity but it all starts in the mind, as the Word and the Spirit begin, continue and complete their powerful work of transformation. The process is awesome. Indescribably immense is the responsibility God lays on the shoulders of his preachers and teachers to proclaim and explain the words that lead to a changed and changing life. Exposition is the key to light and life for the church of Christ. The problem is loss of the truth and the solution is for people to have that truth ministered to them. That is the glorious privilege of expository preaching.

I Thessalonians

In the space of a few verses written to believers in this city north of Greece, Paul incorporates challenges to the church in a number of areas related to the ministry of God's Word.

(a) The application of the Word to the mind invariably led to the transformation of visible conduct. Indeed the fruit of the proclamation and explanation of God's Word in the lives of these people was so obvious that Paul realized they must have been chosen by God unto salvation (1:5-7; 2:13-14). Once again the changed conduct came about through the work of words in the mind (1:5). The Thessalonian believers had welcomed a message (1:6) and then sent forth a message themselves (1:8). Indeed they were convinced that what they were receiving – a body of gospel instruction – did have a divine origin (2:13).

(b) The attending power of the Holy Spirit meant that the explained Word wrought definite change in the hearers. Paul makes plain the truth that human words cannot produce spiritual life (2:13). Unless the Spirit's power is at work, the spoken Word will not produce faith (1:5). As it was, however, the gospel message came to the Thessalonians in spiritual power and conviction and was received in like manner. The effect was palpable in changed lives (1:3, 5, 6, 7, 8-10).

(c) Paul confirms that in order to witness the life-changing power of biblical exposition, God required three conditions to be fulfilled in the lives of his preachers:

(i) Those who preach the Word must also embody and live out that Word (1:5, 7). The apostles preached as those called and equipped by God and they knew that they had to demonstrate that gospel through the quality of their own lives if they wanted to see others transformed by that same gospel. The display of genuine godliness in the lives of the apostles is recounted in detail in 2:1-12. Two things that unbelievers can discern very quickly in the life of a preacher are inconsistency and hypocrisy. They can be detected very easily and will speedily neutralize the impact of the Word of God if they are seen in a preacher's conduct.

(ii) Paul is at pains to point out that the gospel is not his own message (2:13). It came to Paul by revelation from God himself (Gal. 1:11-12). He is grateful that the Thessalonians recognized it as divine truth (1 Thess. 2:13). The consequence of this is huge: Paul realized that, having been entrusted with the divine gospel, his task was to present the Word of God undiluted and unchanged in order to please God. The temptation to please men by tampering with God's Word was as real for Paul as it is for preachers today. Our task is the same as

Paul's – to preach the whole counsel of God, regardless of the whims and preferences of our congregations.

(iii) We cannot escape the fact that the proclamation and explanation of God's Word will involve us in varying degrees of pain and suffering. Herein lies a mystery and a paradox, for even in the midst of 'severe suffering' (1:6), the Thessalonians received the Word in the power and joy of the Holy Spirit. To embrace the Word and to live it out with joy in the midst of agony is one of the greatest challenges of the faith. Even the expounding of the gospel to the Thessalonians had been attended by strong opposition (2:2) and the apostles could rightly point out the toil and hardship that came because of their gospel ministry (2:9). Both the preachers of the Word and the recipients of the Word knew the ferocity of the spiritual battle. Satan had tried to prevent Paul's communication with the church at Thessalonica (2:18). That tactic had been aimed at silencing the apostles in their ministry of proclamation and explanation of the Word (2:16), and the opposition from Satan had inflicted pain on those persecuted believers (2:14-16). Nevertheless the apostles had been cast ever more heavily on the help and strength of the Lord (2:2b) and the church was being carried from strength to strength (1:3). Because it restores men and women to the true and life-changing knowledge of God, powerful biblical exposition will inevitably provoke the fury of the powers of darkness which oppose that Word. Yet it is that very Word which God, in his sovereign and incomparable power, has decreed to use in order to change my life, your life and the lives of men and women everywhere.

PETER

Peter wrote his first letter to scattered and oppressed believers who in various ways were being severely tested in their obedience of faith (I Pet. 1:6). His message is a remarkable blend of assurance and challenge. In reminding the believers that they had been chosen in Christ for salvation (1:2), Peter recalls their experience of new birth into an unfading hope (1:3-4). God's protecting power should be a source of great comfort and confidence for these believers as they pass through stressful circumstances which will test, stretch and strengthen their faith. Peter's encouragement of these believers in the first chapter of his first letter yields valuable insight into his view of Scripture and the relationship between Word and life.

(a) The gospel that came to the believers in Peter's day was the fulfilment of the Messianic prophecies given by God's prophets hundreds of years previously (1:12). The same Spirit who had inspired the Old Testament prophets has now inspired, authenticated and empowered the preached message of the gospel.

(b) Peter has a reason for referring to the believers' reception of the gospel. The consequence of that welcoming of the gospel message is that the believers are to 'gird up the loins of your mind' (1:13). Eastern workers hitched up their flowing robes so that they would not be impeded as they moved into action. Using language that recalled the Exodus events (Exod. 12:11), Peter urges a Christ-centred attitude of mind that will mould and control personal conduct. Such an attitude must be founded on disciplined self-control and should be characterized by balance, determination and single-mindedness. All of these qualities are to be evidenced in the lives of Christian believers, not least those who aspire to preach. The message of the gospel should yield the fruit of holiness.

(c) The holy living to which Peter has just referred (1:15-16) is made possible solely because the believers have been obedient to the gospel message. The truth of God's Word has opened up for them the path of holiness and the purification of their lives will be ongoing, as suggested by the perfect tense of the verb (1:22). Its major fruit will be love for the brethren, a product so vital among believers who are being persecuted for their faith. Lest they might feel inadequate for such a challenge, Peter quickly assures them that the love being asked of them does indeed require divine life and power. Such power is now theirs precisely because they have been born anew, the perfect participle implying continuous results (1:23). Through the powerfully preached message of the gospel, these believers have met the living Christ, exercised faith, received the Holy Spirit and are consequently energized and equipped to love their brethren (1:22).

(d) Peter rounds off his encouragement by underlining the abiding nature of this life-changing Word in 1:23b-25. Divine life will be planted in human beings by their obedient response to the preached words of divine revelation. Those words are both living and life-giving (1:23). Not only is that true, but Peter then recalls Isaiah 40:6-8 which in its own context referred to Isaiah's prophecy proclaiming the restoration of Israel. Peter uses the text to underline the glorious truths that not only does spiritual life come by responsive hearing of the Word of God, but also that very Word of God will always do this in people's lives. It will never fail or become ineffective (1:25). The living and enduring Word of God revealed the truth about Christ and at the same time implanted the power and reality of the living, eternal Christ into the lives of believing listeners. That work of God's Spirit will never end. Indeed the power of God's Word to convert and change men and women is so overwhelming that Peter then spends the rest of his letter outlining the expected practical results of the powerful working of God's Word. Indeed he tells the believers that they must not be satisfied with the initial impact of God's Word in their lives. Rather must they crave for more of the Scriptures and their power in their drive for maturity (2:2-3). Likewise, there should never be a state of unemployment for those called and equipped to proclaim, explain and apply the living and enduring Word of God. Until Christ returns, exposition will be of permanent importance. It is the means for change that God himself has appointed.

John

The apostle John's understanding of the place and power of Scripture is extensive, beyond the scope of a brief treatment, but even a glimpse of one small portion of his writings is sufficient to pull back the curtain and show us something of the majesty of God in relation to his revealed Word and will.

Through Revelation 4–9 John has watched visions unfold from his viewpoint in heaven. By contrast, Revelation 10 opens with the apostle witnessing the descent of an angel from heaven who declares the coming retribution of God which heralds the end-times as having been set in motion. What seems to emerge is a two-pronged emphasis: persecution and martyrdom are guaranteed for the church but so also is the final divine destruction of all evil. In the midst of this vision,

John is told by a voice from heaven to take the little book which lies open in the hand of the strong angel (Rev. 10:8). He is told furthermore to eat it, with the statement that it will be sweet as honey in his mouth but bitter in his stomach (10:9-10). Some equate the little scroll with the content of Revelation 11:1-13 where the church is told the extent of the Satanic anger that will be directed against it. Bitter will be the suffering that the church will experience yet sweet will be the assurance of God's final cosmic triumph. Others believe that the little scroll symbolizes even more, namely the entirety of God's revelation in his Word. What seems clear is that John is trying to encourage faithfulness and perseverance in the suffering and struggling church on earth. That encouragement profoundly involves the Word of God.

(a) In Revelation 10:7 the mystery of God is said to be certain of accomplishment. Usually this term refers in Scripture to the content of the gospel message. In a real sense God's victory in heaven has already occurred through Jesus' triumph on earth. Although the kingdom of God has thus begun, its final consummation awaits the future second coming of Christ. Revelation 10 shows how the Word of God concerns the church but it reveals also the cosmic dimension of God's purposes. John was called to prophesy 'about many peoples, nations, languages and kings' (10:11). Salvation involves the particular people of God, but at the same time that brings the church into an interacting relationship with the entire world order. John repeatedly brings assurance that the Word and will of God will be fulfilled in the unfolding of earthly, historical circumstances. The Word of God carries an awesome authority.

(b) Alongside the nature of God's Word as authoritative, Revelation 10 reveals the staggering fact that Almighty God has chosen to speak through the frailty and weakness of human beings. Again and again the prophets and apostles demonstrate that the one, true, holy and transcendent God has committed his Word to writing compiled through human agency. Not only that, but he has so ordained that his Word be proclaimed and explained through his servants on earth. God chooses human instruments through whom to reveal and communicate his Word. As John was commissioned to prophesy (10:7, 11), so Paul also was overwhelmed that the ministry of reconciliation had been placed in the hands of weak and inadequate people (2 Cor. 5:18-20). God's treasure is set in jars of clay (2 Cor. 4:7) so that God's power can be revealed.

(c) In between the sovereign authority of his Word and the delegation of its proclamation into human hands, God has set a crucial condition. Many interpreters believe that the angel and little scroll symbolize and announce the worldwide proclamation of God's Word throughout the whole gospel age by preachers and teachers of that Word. If so, then the condition is clear. As John was commanded to digest the Word of God (10:9), then so must we. Why? Because only by digesting the whole Word of God will we know *what* to proclaim and explain. Only by digesting the whole Word of God will we be able to avoid the temptation to preach a selective and shallow message. Only by digesting the whole Word of God will we be able to assimilate its contents into our own living before we dare preach it to others. Living in the Word and living out the Word are absolute prerequisites for our proclamation and explanation of the Word. Because life and ministry are inseparable, we dare not move on to the practicalities of biblical expository preaching until we have examined that intimate relationship even more closely. Preachers who ignore that link do so at their peril, risking the loss of the very ministry they seek to fulfil.

4

The Need for Holiness in the Expositor

*B*efore we consider the nature and practicalities of expository preaching ministry, we need to address an issue that we ignore to our peril. Most, if not all, evangelicals will have heard, if not come into contact with, at least one case of a preacher, teacher or leader who has seriously gone astray in the course of ministry. Whether the root problem be sex, power, finance, or a combination thereof, evangelical disasters are by no means uncommon. Churches are devastated and witness to unbelievers can be extensively, if not irreparably, damaged for years. In a real sense, this should not surprise us. Satan, the enemy of God's church, works unceasingly to discredit God and, if possible, to destroy the church of God. Being the father of lies, he will do anything to prevent men and women from receiving and responding to the true knowledge of God. In Satan's eyes, expository preaching will never be flavour of the month and he will oppose it, and those who minister it, with every weapon at his disposal. Because of the ferocity and seriousness of this opposition, God has wisely given ample warning throughout Scripture of his expectations for the Christian lifestyle and conduct of preachers. Perhaps nowhere in Scripture is this issue more pertinently addressed than in Paul's Pastoral Epistles.

DOCTRINE AND LIFE

Traditionally the Pastoral Epistles have been viewed as a manual for church order, valid for God's church at all times and in all places.

However, the more we dig into the biblical text and context of these letters, the more it becomes clear that, as in his other writings, Paul was seeking to address certain problems arising primarily in specific churches. As the apostle penned his letter to Titus in Crete and his first letter to Timothy in Ephesus, the background centred to varying degrees on the issue of false teaching. Seen against the context of heretical, deviant teaching, each letter yields profound challenge, as well as comfort, for those called to proclaim and explain divine truth.

I TIMOTHY

The situation in Ephesus was so urgent that Paul omits his customary opening thanksgiving and simply reasserts his apostolic authority (I Tim. I:I). Paul wanted the Ephesians to realize that Timothy also embodied apostolic authority and that, amidst all the conflicting voices they were hearing, their only final authority lay in the voice of God revealed in Scripture. That the central issue involved false teaching is clear from Paul's immediate command for Timothy to stay in Ephesus to deal with the deviant teachers and teaching (I:3). The origins of this Ephesian church can be traced in Acts 18:19-21, 18:24–20:1 and 20:17-35. A survey of Acts 19 indicates a mixed situation – some disciples there had not even heard of the Holy Spirit (Acts 19:2); others had at some stage been heavily involved in sorcery (Acts 19:19); many had been deeply committed to the worship and trade of the Artemis cult (Acts 19:23-41). In such a complex matrix, the existence of confusion about the newly emerging Christian faith would not have been surprising. Sure enough, even though the Word of the Lord was being widely heard and powerfully manifested (Acts 19:10, 20, 20:20, 21, 25, 27) – indeed because of that preaching – there was mounting opposition to scriptural exposition. Indeed, Paul knows that even from within the church at Ephesus, some will distort the truth and will deceive and distract many (Acts 20:28-31).

What is not clear is the nature of the heresy, though we do have certain pointers in the text that suggest a twofold deviation. According to I Timothy I:4-7 some were teaching 'myths and genealogies' which probably reflected Jewish, or Hellenistic Jewish, influence. These false teachers were probably insider elders who aspired to be teachers of the law (1:7), but the outcome of their communication was 'meaningless talk' (1:6, 6:20) and consequently 'controversies', 'quarrels', 'strife' and 'constant friction' (6:3-5). The concern over elders is widespread throughout the letter and the real and potential dangers are suggested at a number of points (1:7, 19-20; 3:1-7; 5:17, 19-25). In contrast to such false and wasteful teaching was the sort of teaching that promoted God's work by faith (1:4).

A second area of false teaching, and one which carried serious consequences, was the assertion that the end had come and the resurrection had already taken place (2 Tim. 2:18). The return of Christ was thus marginalized and the view was widely held that believers had already been raised in a spiritual sense. The proof of this, it was claimed, lay in their possession of the Holy Spirit, which was seen as evidence of a person's resurrection rather than as the first fruits that pointed to and guaranteed a future resurrection. This error has been described as 'over-realized eschatology'. Thus the emphasis, deriving from Greek philosophy, was on the spiritual rather than material existence. Such thinking could trigger either or both of two opposing lifestyles, already familiar to Paul from his struggles with the Corinthian Church. Some felt that physical life was irrelevant in view of the believer's already attained spiritual completion. Libertinism thus involved abuse of the body in an immoral lifestyle (1:9-10). At the other end of the spectrum stood the position that physical life needed to be controlled through ascetic practices so that the spiritual dimension retained its purity (1 Tim. 4:3). The problem seems to have been that the false teachers viewed the Holy Spirit as the power that brought completion to a believer's spiritual life and granted final victory already. Thus the physical pain of suffering and struggle was seen as being in conflict with the presence of the Spirit and was even counted as evidence for lack of true spirituality. It was into this maelstrom of confusion and error that young Timothy was thrust with instructions from Paul to sort out the mess. It is Paul's strategy for dealing with the serious errors in this church that is so instructive for the life and ministry of the preacher. To this strategy we now turn, briefly but necessarily.

The entire letter of I Timothy is like a tapestry woven together with two major threads that are impossible to separate from each other: the divine call to proclaim and explain the Word of God, alongside, and undergirded by, the divine command for visible holiness in the life of the preacher and teacher. A few brief examples will help to elucidate this twosome.

I. Paul's first task in his letter is to establish the link between Scripture and life. How does the dynamic operate? The apostle has instructed Timothy to silence the false teachers (1:3-4). Why? In order that love might be restored in the church. Such New Testament 'love' is neither sloppy nor sentimental but is highly practical and is a product, says Paul, of three things: 'a pure heart and a good conscience and a sincere faith' (I Tim. 1:5). But how does that work? The 'heart' and the 'conscience' are very closely related and constitute the joint 'faculty' that makes moral decisions. The nature of that 'faculty' is determined by whether it operates in relationship with Christ or Satan. Hence, 'sincere faith' involves a genuine personal relationship with Christ, in sharp contrast to the false pretensions of the deviant teachers. What is it that triggers this inner 'faculty' to make the correct behavioural decisions that will reinstate practical love within the church community? One scholar has recently expressed it in a nutshell:

> it is the acceptance or rejection of correct doctrine (the Word of God) that determines the condition and effectiveness of the 'conscience'. That is, the standard of behaviour accepted by the group (the community of faith or church) is the Word of God properly interpreted. It is necessary to operate with this standard for the 'conscience' to perform its function of encouraging correct behaviour (the behaviour deemed appropriate by the Christian community).[1]

The heretics were exercising strong influence as leaders, but their error, dogmatism and false authority combined in a deadly cocktail to prevent themselves and others from coming under the life-changing power of God's Word. This was a depressing situation and yet not

---

I. Philip H. Towner *I-2 Timothy and Titus*, (The IVP N.T. Commentary Series, IVP 1994), pp. 47-8.

totally so. Such was the power of the Word, if its hearers truly repented, that even the false teachers themselves were not beyond redemption and reformation (2 Tim. 2:25-6). For genuine believers, the Word by the Spirit would produce visible products rooted in faith and love, but such fruit was painfully absent in the lives of false teachers.

2. This crucial relationship between Word and holy living is confirmed again in I Timothy 2 as Paul continues his appeal to Timothy and the Ephesian church to 'hold on to faith and a good conscience' (I Tim. 1:19). In order to promote the latter, the church is urged to pray for all in authority (2:1), so that the church will be able to demonstrate godly and holy living (2:2). It is significant that Paul pleads prayer for all people, including preachers, and hints at a theme to be developed even more strongly in Titus, namely, the impact of the church's holiness on the unbelieving, but watching, world. The context is now the worldwide mission of the church and it is of overwhelming importance that Paul views salvation as inextricably linked to coming 'to a knowledge of the truth' (2:4). In the context of falsity, Paul insists that men and women must be engaged in their minds by the Word of God. This is God's appointed way of producing the fruit of godly behaviour in believers' lives.

3. Because biblical truth carries God's power to produce godliness and because the church is being undermined in this process by false teachers, Paul gives detailed guidance as to how people should live in the church (3:15). The phrase 'above reproach' (3:2-3) involves the realm of visible behaviour and although the apostle's guidelines apply to all believers, they are specifically addressed to the appointment of teaching elders (3:1-7). Of vast significance is the fact that the godliness expected of elders and deacons is centred on evidence of spiritual fruit and relatively less concerned with spiritual gifting. If a preacher appears to be exceptionally gifted in the pulpit, yet fails to offer evidence of personal holiness and godliness, this should ring immediate alarm bells in those to whom the preacher is, or should be, accountable. Forget the gifting; look for the fruit! Christian leaders are particularly singled out as being called to holiness.

4. Paul's challenge for believers, especially preachers, to back up their words with a godly life, is pressed again in I Timothy 4. Indeed the exhortation in 4:16 to 'watch your life and doctrine closely' is unpacked throughout that chapter. Time and time again, Paul sets the challenge of keeping ministry and life firmly in step with one another. Right from the start, Paul refuses to mince his words – the teaching and lifestyle of the false teachers shows that their conscience has been rendered impotent as a faculty for decision making. They have forsaken true knowledge of God, having been utterly deceived by Satan (4:1-3). The only known antidote for such cases of potentially fatal poisoning of the mind lies in the truth of Scripture (4:3, 4, 5, 6). Thus Timothy is appointed by Paul to administer this antidote. The challenge to preachers is clear: we must saturate ourselves in the 'good teaching' which means either the gospel or the right use of Scripture. Secondly, we are to proclaim and explain this Word. Thirdly, we are to pursue godliness (4:7-8). The call to training in godliness suggests that a struggle for holiness, through discipline and perseverance, is involved. All sincere preachers will agree! Expounding the Word, and living it out, is the preacher's greatest challenge. Yet it is also a glorious privilege for it is intimately tied to God's goal of worldwide mission (I Tim. 4:9-10).

5. The depth of Paul's anxiety over the damage being done by deviant elders comes across in I Timothy 5. It seems that younger women in the church have been a particular target and some have been completely deceived by Satan's emissaries within the church (5:15). Paul's plea to the true elders in the midst of this turmoil is to press on unswervingly with the task of preaching and teaching (5:17). Alongside that commission, their ministry in the Word must be accompanied by that purity of lifestyle which was so absent in the lives of the fakes (5:20-5).

6. All the main ingredients of Paul's argument appear yet again in the final chapter of his letter. False teaching is like a rotten apple whose core is to be found in the corrupted minds of its practitioners (6:5). As regards truth they are totally bankrupt and although they claim to be wise, they are seeking gain from their 'godliness'. I Timothy

6:3-10 contains a severe warning to those who lead and preach. Greed — whether for sex, power or in this case money — can utterly destroy a ministry. Paul offers the two indispensable weapons for fighting off this terrible danger. Timothy is called to pursue practical holiness (6:11-16) and to be faithful in guarding the priceless jewel entrusted to him (6:20); he is to protect the Word and faith of Christ by proclaiming and explaining it. Only then will men and women be able to hear and receive the true knowledge of God that transforms life and living (6:17-19). Exposition that changes people is the outcome of ministry by preachers who live in the Word and who live out the Word. Paul put it even more briefly: it is 'godly teaching' (6:3).

Such was the bottom line of Paul's message to Timothy. He was to resist the evil work of false teachers by keeping his own life pure and by faithfully proclaiming and explaining the truth of God. The apostle to the Gentiles offered the same fundamental challenge to his other son in the faith, Titus, and to that letter we now briefly turn, that we might hear the voice of God yet again concerning the required holiness of preachers.

TITUS

On the surface, Paul's letter to Titus bears great similarity to his first message to Timothy. Both share a background of false teaching that has arisen through church elders. Titus has been left on the Mediterranean island of Crete and is given authority by Paul to appoint elders (1:5). The false teaching seems to have been rooted in the errors of converts from Judaism who were replacing gospel truth with religious rules and regulations, thereby causing great damage (1:11, 14). Human ideas and commands were, it seems, being mixed with Scripture or were replacing Scripture; either way a perilous enterprise for preachers and teachers. Again material gain was the incentive and many were piling onto the bandwagon (1:10-11). The evidence of Titus 2:1-10 suggests that social relationships and church unity were being severely disrupted. Clearly these rebels were seeking to satisfy their own cravings while their hapless victims were left in blind confusion. The essence of the problem is clearly elaborated in 1:15-

16. These rebels were deceiving many because they claimed to know God (v. 15) but in reality were themselves deceived and had neither true knowledge of God nor changed life in Christ (v. 16). Why was this so? Because their minds and consciences had been corrupted (v. 15) to the point that God could not work through true faith and true knowledge to produce the fruit of godliness (v. 16). The rebels may have neither understood nor experienced the grace of God in Christ, yet Paul does not seem to be devoid of all hope for such people (v. 13). Whatever their spiritual standing before God, such false teachers are neither holding nor communicating true knowledge of God and as such must be stopped by Titus. Having already tackled a similar problem in Ephesus through Timothy, what will be Paul's Cretan strategy through Titus?

In the course of a single Greek sentence, Paul encapsulates the entire philosophy of his ministry (1:1-4). His heart's longing is to see men and women brought to faith and knowledge, and thereby to new life (1:2). This goal is attainable for it is not a mere possibility but on the contrary has been ordained by the eternal and trustworthy God. It is a guaranteed certainty for the people of God. The dynamic is crucially important here. True faith can only come as a product of, and response to, true knowledge of God. That truth is primarily in this context knowledge apprehended by the mind, but that very truth, says Paul, leads to godliness (1:1). It is not a matter of choosing between doctrine and godliness. For all God's people, and especially for preachers, the two are utterly inseparable. If we are to ask how the dynamic operates and whether it actually works, Paul is equally clear and firm. The Word of God incarnate has appeared in the historical birth, life and death of Jesus (1:3), but the consequent fruit of faith and knowledge was revealed and administered through Paul's preaching (1:3). This preaching was God's appointed means (1:3), and its fruit was visible in the lives of the Cretan believers. Conversion was the necessary starting point, mature godliness the goal. God's eternal purpose, valid for the entire gospel age, is to fulfil his promise of giving new life, through faith and truth. And his method? The preaching ministry of the church. It should come as no surprise therefore that the function of a true elder is precisely that: to treasure

God's Word and to minister it to others, so as to encourage the faithful but oppose the unfaithful (1:9).

In what manner is the Word to be preached? In order for an elder to fulfil this ministry, that servant of God must be blameless in the household of God, as well as blameless in himself and his own household (1:6-8). In a word, the preacher must pursue 'godliness', as well as showing it visibly in his own and his family's life. Right doctrine and right practical living are like the yolk and white of an egg – inseparable. Right living without right doctrine is a contradiction in terms and cannot, in and of itself, lead the preacher's listeners to true knowledge of God. Right doctrine without right living is at best hypocrisy, at worst dangerous and damaging.

Perhaps our greatest temptation at this stage is for our minds to be dulled by the consistency and predictability of Paul's directives. His letters are simply saturated with the link between truth and living. Unless we are willing to live out the Word of God that we preach, we ought not to step into a pulpit. God makes us responsible for holding our doctrine and life in balance. That is the undisputed message of Titus 2, as well as Titus 1. It is by grace that God saves sinners (2:11) but he does so in order that he can purify a people for his own possession (2:14). That people is called 'to do what is good' (2:14) not in the hope of finding salvation, but as a response to God's amazing grace (2:11-12). 'Ungodliness' and 'worldly passions' begin in the mind and reflect a worldly way of thinking. That pattern can only be reversed as and when people hear and receive the true knowledge of God through his Word. Grace, properly understood and received, has only one goal and fruit: holiness. Grace demands, and yet at the same time enables, redeemed men and women to make decisions of their will in favour of holiness (2:12).

Paul knows that if Titus and others in the church are to be effective agents of this salvation, then they must fulfil two conditions. Firstly, the words of God must be proclaimed and explained (2:1, 2, 3, 7, 9, 15). Yet even the content of that teaching and preaching is focused on the distinctive behaviour expected of different groups within the church. Older men, for example, are to be holy in their personal qualities but also understanding the faith with their minds and loving in their relations with others (2:2). Secondly, in his teaching – both content, style and attitude – Titus is called to set a strong example (2:7-8). Not only does God require this marriage of doctrine and life because he has destined us for holiness, but he requires it because it will affect the way outsiders evaluate the gospel and Word of God (2:5b, 8b, 10b). Proclamation, holiness and world mission form three sides of an unbreakable triangle. The world will only show interest in the Word when it witnesses its power to produce godly behaviour in human lives.

Paul's concern for witness in the world spills over into 3:1-2, but he is careful to give a timely reminder that such godly behaviour is possible only by the rebirth, renewal and continuing work of the Holy Spirit (3:5-7). Only by God's grace and power, and by a realisation of this fact can a believer practically reveal the fruit of goodness that God produces through the believer's mind, heart and will. Titus is to teach this (3:8), and all believers are to live it out, thereby proving their distinctiveness from the false teachers (3:9-11). Perhaps it is a sense of relief at having made his point so forcibly that causes Paul to conclude with a few personal remarks. Even here, however, he will not allow the issue of holiness to drop (3:14).

THE MAKING OF A PREACHER – 2 TIMOTHY

Paul's Second Letter to Timothy is a profoundly personal and moving plea. The problems that lay behind 1 Timothy have reappeared with a vengeance but Paul himself is in prison again with only a slim chance of release as he awaits trial. Paul desires Timothy's personal presence with him, therefore the traumatic impact of false teachers at Ephesus must be handled by others. To this end, Paul gives counsel on a number of issues so vital to the ministry of preaching and teaching, not only for the work in Ephesus but also for all preachers engaged in proclaiming and explaining God's Word.

The apostle begins his letter by pointing out the resources made available by God for the preaching ministry.

1. Called by God

Paul was very conscious of having been called as a herald, apostle and teacher (1:1a, 11). To the gospel and Word of God, the apostle was totally committed and he longed to see his preaching used of God to give life (1:1b). His role as herald centred on evangelistic proclamation whilst his teaching ministry involved instructing the church. In both functions, he had been endowed with God's own authority and calling to exercise a ministry in the Word. Paul reminds Timothy of their close relationship and of Timothy's receipt of a gift at some point previously (1:6). God gifts all those that he calls to the preaching ministry, but if that is the case, how, some will ask, do I know that I am called and gifted for this work? My answer would be as follows. To those called and gifted for preaching, God does give a basic longing and yearning to expound Scripture and a real assurance that such ministry is right. That conviction, however, needs to be tested on two levels. The individual concerned needs to test out the gifting. Having done that, however, the preacher ought then to expect some form of appraisal by the church as the body of Christ. Wise and discerning believers in the church can be a great help in sensitively evaluating our gifts and potential as preachers (Acts 13: 1-3). Timothy must not only treasure his calling and ministry by grace (1:9) but also seek consistently and continually to 'keep on being strengthened' by that very grace of Christ himself (2:1).

2. Equipped by God

Paul reminds Timothy right from the start that 'grace, mercy and peace' are all free gifts of God (1:2). Human beings, even redeemed ones, do not, in and of themselves, possess resources for ministry. We all need to be equipped for spiritual ministry. Never must we forget that it is first and foremost the Word of God which is our equipment for ministry. All Scripture is divinely inspired. It is our basis for teaching gospel truth in its widest and deepest sense, but it is needed as a tool for dealing with false teachers. It also functions for 'correction' in the area of ethical behaviour and produces righteousness in the form of visible Christian living (3:16-17). The Word of God contains God's revealed will, and only as we soak up and digest that Word will we be enabled to fulfil our twofold calling as preachers – to preach the whole counsel of God and to live it out in the nitty gritty of daily living. It is the taking in and giving out of Scripture which alone can equip believers to show forth good works.

3. COMMITTED TO PRAYER

Paul encouraged Timothy by assuring him of his regular prayer support (1:3). Every preacher of God's Word needs to know that there are those who are regularly and consistently praying, on the one hand for the preacher and on the other against the powers of darkness who seek constantly to damage the mighty work of preaching the divine Word. We as preachers must enlist and covet those who will support our work of preaching by their prayers. Not only that, we must do our part in praying for those to whom we minister.

4. DEPENDENT ON THE SPIRIT'S POWER

Our preaching must begin, continue and end in a state of absolute dependence on God's Holy Spirit. This is surely the great paradox. The Spirit is invisible but invisibility does not mean impotence. The very preservation of the gospel and Word of God requires the work of the Holy Spirit. Faithfulness in preaching it, and faithfulness in living it, are only obtainable as the Spirit is at work in the preacher (1:14). Timothy, and preachers in all ages, are to submit to the Holy Spirit, for he alone is the source of the three commodities most needed by the preacher (1:7). Firstly, we need power for holy living and for perseverance when our preaching meets or triggers opposition. Secondly, we need love in our approach and attitude to those who listen to us and that love must be real, visible and tangible. Thirdly, we need self-discipline especially over our thought processes as we prepare and present God's Word in pulpit ministry. All these come from the Spirit's work within us.

Having established the resources available to those who proclaim and explain the Scriptures in ministry, Paul then throws the spotlight on the central demands of that ministry.

5. PREACH THE WORD

There is no chapter in this second letter to Timothy that omits this central task of Christian ministry. Whilst preserving and maintaining the apostolic teaching, Timothy and the other preachers must model that faith in practical love, even in the midst of their conflict with the false teachers (1:13-14). Even more though is required. Just as Paul was desperately concerned that Timothy should reach his full potential (1:2ff.), so Timothy must be willing to pass on the apostolic teaching to other reliable ministers (2:2). Training others might even mean our own eclipse by more able workers.

Paul's challenge in 2 Timothy 2:14-15 is of profound significance. Timothy and the church are called to persevere in the true faith rather than quarrelling over words after the pattern of the false teachers. In contrast to the false teachers, godly preachers should work so as to 'cut straight' the Word of truth. Exposition of the Word involves accurate interpretation and responsible use of Scripture. Yet we are reminded again that the call for care and precision in our dealing with words must never blind us to our need to display godly living to a watching world (2:16).

The faithful testimony of Paul's life and lip should encourage Timothy to press on and continually exercise his own ministry (3:14). In the midst of the confusing and chaotic voices of the false teachers, Timothy must never forget what he has long known, namely, that only the Scriptures embody the power that brings men and women to life-changing salvation (3:15). Because of this awesome truth Paul is bold to make an equally awesome charge (4:1-2) to Timothy to proclaim and explain the Word on the basis of their responsibility to God, to Christ, to his second coming in judgment and to the hope of the eternal glory of God's kingdom. Expository preaching is a divine mandate.

6. SEEK TO MANIFEST HOLINESS

We have already seen Paul's return to the basis of the faith in 2 Timothy 1 where it is clear that the purpose of God's saving act in Christ is that his Church will demonstrate holiness of life (1:9). Thus the call to preserve and proclaim the apostolic teaching demands a practical proof of faith and love (1:13). This issue of the harmony between ministry and living is taken a step further in 2:20-26. The combination of sound teaching with godly lifestyle is a potent one. The word 'therefore' in the Greek text of 2:21 relates back to verses 19 and 20. The Word of God is his solid foundation for our lives. Therefore, Timothy must distance himself from false teaching in order to be a vessel useful to God (2:21). If he does this, he will be set apart from falsity and equipped by the Word for holiness and good works (2:21). As long as Timothy flees from evil and calls upon the Lord, he will be able to gain and show holiness of living (2:22-4). Indeed it is the very combination of sound teaching and gentle attitudes that is so powerful as to raise the possibility that even the perpetrators of false teaching might see the error of their wrong thinking and living (2:25-6; 4:2). Notice how the false teachers can still be redeemed. If that does happen, it will happen only as their minds are engaged by proclamation and explanation of the Word. The result will be a return to knowledge of the truth that will transform their living. The thrust of the Pastoral Letters in their entirety is that a sound and powerful expository ministry must be attended by visible godly living.

Having by now explained the resources, task and responsibility of the preacher, Paul considers some of the consequences of the preaching ministry.

7. Expect hard work and hardship

Hardship is part of the lot of all believers because of their relationship to Christ and his gospel. Such a relationship is guaranteed to draw the hostility of the world. However, the promised hardship is set here by Paul in the context of those involved in the teaching and training ministry (2:2). Life as a soldier means vigorous service that brings inevitable hardship (2:3). Paul uses the illustrations of athletics and farming to show how submission and hard work, including hardship, are necessary ingredients in the ministry of God's Word (2:4-6). It is vital that all God's workers reflect on this and count the cost of such ministry in God's truth (2:7). Lest Timothy should be tempted to wonder why he must accept hardship, Paul has the answer for that.

God's Word, unlike Paul, is not chained. It cannot be halted or deflected in its impact on human lives and therefore, says Paul, because the task of exposition is the instrument that brings salvation, we must be ready to 'endure everything for the sake of the elect' (2:10). Our own comfort must be set aside if it stands in the way of gathering in the church that God has bought for eternity.

The intensity of the hardship that stems from gospel ministry throughout the gospel age is vividly portrayed by Paul in 3:1-9. In his attempt to destroy the Church, Satan will use emissaries from inside and outside the church to deceive the believers. The weapon most feared by Satan is prayer-soaked, Spirit-empowered biblical exposition. That weapon alone can enable even depraved minds to grasp truth and be changed by it (2:25-6). No wonder Satan trembles at exposition. Even those whose lives are utterly founded on self and totally bankrupt in the currency of real godliness can be touched and transformed in their minds, emotions and wills through the proclamation and explanation of the Word of God. It is in such a ministry that we, like Timothy, are to persevere, regardless of the response and regardless of the hardship entailed (4:3-5).

8. READY TO SUFFER

A fascinating couplet is found in 2 Timothy 1:7-8. In verse 7 Paul assures Timothy of the availability of the Holy Spirit who works in us courage, power, love and self-discipline, the latter probably indicating the necessary degree of disciplined thinking for dealing adequately with false teachers. Because the Spirit is his sufficiency, Timothy can confidently press on with his preaching ministry, even though he knows that suffering will be his lot. His pursuance of gospel ministry will draw the ridicule and opposition of the world but Timothy can take courage because he will suffer as part of the wider body of Christ suffers and he will do so in and by the power of God's Spirit. Paul repeats this fact in 1:11-12. It is the apostle's ministry in the Word that brings him suffering but he is conscious that he can confidently entrust his life and his ministry to God, who will take care of both. That is a tremendous encouragement to all who are called to the ministry of preaching.

It must have been a massive boost for Paul who was suffering the humiliation of prison in spite of being not only a Roman citizen but also innocent of criminal charges. Even in such dire circumstances of suffering, Paul realizes that the Word of God is still performing its powerful work (Phil. 1:12-14).

Suffering, in the form of persecution, was a reality for Paul and yet he was able to testify that God rescued him in those trials, from those trials or through those trials (3:10-12). Even in the agony of impending death, Paul looks forward to receiving the crown of righteousness (4:6-8). Indeed he says almost the same thing in Philippians 2:16-17, adding the fact that he can rejoice in the midst of suffering, knowing that he, like the Philippians, has given himself faithfully to the ministry of 'holding out the word of life'. It is surely no coincidence that this reference to suffering is set in the context of Philippians 2 in which Paul calls the believers to seek unity through submissive humility. I am convinced that at times God allows pain into the lives of preachers in order to keep them low and weak and dependent. He trains us in humility, often through humiliation, precisely because its opposite, pride and arrogance, is the greatest danger that threatens the life and ministry of any preacher. Adversity stimulates humble dependence.

The believer's possession of the first fruits of the Holy Spirit does not guarantee freedom from suffering in life and ministry. Nevertheless in the midst of all the opportunity for ministry, and in the midst of all the opposition that will come because of it, God gives ample encouragement to persevere in proclaiming and explaining that divine Word. Ultimately God has a glorious purpose for Scripture – 'so that through me (Paul) the message might be fully proclaimed and all Gentiles might hear it' (2 Tim. 4:18).

5

The Nature of Biblical Expository Preaching

*T*hat the word of God, rightly proclaimed and explained, does powerfully change human lives is backed up extensively by the Scriptures themselves. What then are the ingredients of the expository method of preaching? Two illustrations lend help towards a definition.

Appearing regularly in the world's media are reports of forthcoming marriages and completed divorces of the rich and famous. Even a mildly cynical frame of mind quickly senses the low chance of success that many of these relationships had for any degree of survival and permanence. There is a sense in which the expository preacher is seeking to act as matchmaker for a seemingly impossible wedding. The preacher is trying to effect a powerful and meaningful relationship between two partners. One partner is a biblical text that is at least 2,000 years old, set in other places, times and cultures. The other partner consists of human beings living in far-flung corners of our third millennium global village. Somehow the preacher must bring the two partners together for a life-changing experience. Such a task would indeed be ludicrous were it not for two certainties: the word of God is living and eternal; the Godhead is in that word, behind that word and determined to bring that word powerfully to bear on people. However thrilled and excited we are about exposition, the Godhead is always and consistently more so!

The other image conjured up by exposition is that of the tightrope walker earnestly seeking not to lose his or her balance in either of two dangerous directions. Expository preaching begins with the past and probes two issues: what God was saying through the biblical writers to the original recipients of a biblical book and how the original contexts of that revelation help us to grasp the meaning of those words. This is basically the work of exegesis. On the opposite side of the tightrope walker lies the space that is occupied by the needs and circumstances of twenty-first century hearers of those ancient biblical texts. This is the work of exposition and application and it is inseparable from exegesis. Or at least that is how it ought to be. In other words, and mixing the metaphors, few tightrope walkers are successful in arranging marriages between ancient biblical texts and modern/postmodern readers. Some preachers tilt their balancing pole firmly towards the past and produce a sermon so densely laden with textual and contextual intricacies that the average twenty-first century hearer, if he or she has not died of boredom, will simply want to embalm the sermon and place it in the bowels of the nearest museum. Other preachers lean so strongly into the current world that they either start in the world and scarcely get into the biblical text or they dive straight into the text and quickly pull pieces of text out of their original context. The result can easily be a wrong interpretation and a misdirected application that lead to shallowness at best and misunderstanding at worst. The preacher who slips into either of these directions will tend to produce the sorts of sermon that we described in chapter one.

Exposition grows out of exegesis. Contrary to the way many would view it, there is a real sense in which we must live in the past. We must seek to discern what God said to the first readers and in what contexts. In doing that, we discover God's purpose in that text and we understand the application of the ancient text which we take into the current circumstances of our sermon listeners. Exegesis and exposition, in short, are inseparable. If we fail to expound Scripture, and fail to do the necessary prior work of exegesis, then our preaching will lack the authority of God himself. It will lack the power of God which alone can build life and faith in hearers of the word.

What then are the necessary ingredients of expository preaching? Those components, I firmly believe, derive from two sources:

1. The requirements and guidelines set out in Scripture itself, the dynamic of which we have begun to see already.

2. The very nature of Scripture itself.

With regard to the latter we need to explode a few widely held myths. The Bible did not magically fall from the skies sometime in the second century AD. Nor is it a book of highly structured and systematic rules and regulations or clinically arranged theology. Nor is it a promise box made available for the hand picking of one's favourite chocolate. Scripture is divine revelation delivered through the minds and pens of human beings, over a period covering in excess of 1,500 years and in widely scattered geographical locations and cultural situations. In a real sense, it is divine *and* human. The 'word of the prophets' to which Peter calls the attention of his hearers and readers in 2 Peter 1:19 is most probably a reference to the entire Old Testament Scriptures, and possibly even the New Testament as well. The context yet again involves the need to counteract false teaching. Peter is saying that the apostles' teaching on eschatology, or the future consummation of the gospel age in the return of Christ, is firmly based on Old Testament prophecy. His message is that until Christ comes, light and life are to be found for this present darkness in the written Scriptures. This is crucial. The false teachers had rejected the authority of Old Testament prophecy by denying its divine origin, claiming that Old Testament prophecy and the apostles' teaching were simply products of the human mind (2 Pet. 1:16a). Peter denies this and affirms that the Holy Spirit not only inspired dreams and visions, but also their interpretations (2 Pet. 1:20-1). This is very significant for it confirms that revelation, wholly true and fully divine, did actually come through the history, circumstances and personalities of the human beings whom the Spirit caused to write. This being the case, our proclamation and explanation of Scripture in the ministry of expository preaching must take account of, indeed it must include, all the following vital ingredients.

I. THE SERMON CENTRES ON BIBLICAL CONTENT

It is the word of God which the Spirit of God applies to the mind, heart and will of a human being. It is thus of paramount importance that a sermon, in its very heart and content, must reflect the thought of the biblical writer. In a real sense, this should be so obvious as not even to require mention. Yet it is precisely at this point that many sermons fail right from the start. Whatever our own thoughts and ideas might be, whatever doctrinal camp might hold our affection or allegiance, whatever well-known preachers or scholars might have spoken or written, none of these must be our starting point. All our thinking, living and speaking must be brought into line with the biblical revelation of God's word. To reverse this relationship, and to use the Bible to justify our own ideas and thoughts, is to court disaster. Our commitment to biblical content in preaching should be such that our hearers not only bring and open their Bibles when we preach, but that they follow and evaluate our message by the measuring stick of revealed Scripture.

2. THE SERMON PAYS SERIOUS ATTENTION TO CONTEXTS

All biblical texts – whether individual verses, passages or entire books – are set in particular historical circumstances and possess specific social, cultural, religious and literary contexts. Each book of the Bible is a unity of revelation, written for a particular reason or reasons and reflecting a matrix of historical, social, cultural, religious and literary contexts. Literary style, devices of rhetoric, grammar points, social customs and historical circumstances do actually affect our understanding and interpretation of biblical texts and we ignore them at our peril. It is one thing to say that the word of God in its entirety is fully true and completely divine, it is quite another thing to say that it does not therefore matter how we *use* that divinely-revealed truth. It matters greatly. We will shortly see just how badly astray we can wander if we choose to ignore the role of context in our understanding and exposition of biblical truth.

3. THE SERMON REFLECTS THE PURPOSE OF THE BIBLICAL WRITER

As we study the content and context in a biblical text, we will not be concerned primarily with the meaning and significance of individual words on the page. We shall be looking for signs, both explicit and implicit, of how the writer is using groups of words, sentences and whole sections to express intention and meaning. That is not to say that individual words are never significant. Far from it, but our concentration on words – the individual trees of the forest – must never obscure our view of the entire forest of meaning. In a world that increasingly rejects the notion of absolute truth, denies objective meaning to words, and doubts any effort to know the intentions of the authors of words, we need to stand firm on the biblical doctrines of inspiration and authority. Only by seeking to know the purpose of a biblical writer can we stay in the position and direction to be a channel for the Spirit of God to implement his ongoing purposes for the word. To deny purpose and meaning to a biblical text is to declare open season where any and all interpretations can be equally valid and where the revelatory voice of the Lord himself is liable to be eclipsed and excluded from the reckoning. It is the equivalent of drifting on the open sea in a rudderless boat during a tropical typhoon.

4. THE SERMON APPLIES THE THOUGHT OF THE TEXT

Content and contexts are our tools for discovering purpose and all three will help to shape the form and structure of our sermon, but all our efforts will be wasted if we fail to make appropriate application of a biblical text to the lives, needs and circumstances of our listeners. If as preachers we are really to communicate with our hearers, then we must possess knowledge not only of Scripture but of the lives, issues and circumstances of those to whom we preach. Exposition without application will produce head knowledge but will truncate the transfer of that knowledge through to the heart and will. It will leave our listeners feeling frustrated and asking two questions. Some will say at the end of an unapplied sermon – 'So what?' They will fail to see the relevance of the ancient text for their contemporary living. Others will join the serried ranks of hearers who complain that the sermon gave no guidance on the 'how to' of Christian life. It is sadly true that many sermons are strong on theory and principle but weak on practical implementation. That is sad because the biblical books themselves are profoundly practical in nature. Doctrine and duty embrace each other in application.

THE CHALLENGE

Recently I was teaching a group of students at Asian Theological Seminary in Manila, Philippines. The issue of expository preaching was raised and several students enquired why such preaching was still a rarity in their experience of Asian church life. A number of explanations were offered before I heard a small voice from the back row: 'Preachers don't expound Scripture 'cos it's hard work.' That student had got to the core of the issue. Expository preaching *is* hard intellectual and spiritual work that is costly in time and energy.

The preacher stands between the world of the biblical text and the world of contemporary life. The goal is that our hearers will understand what God is saying to them and be empowered by his Spirit to apply the word into the practical reality of daily living. The calling to expound Scripture is an awesome and glorious privilege. Yet that very privilege brings preachers the enormous responsibility of personal obedience to the Word of God they preach. Our own personality and the quality of our personal relationship with God will profoundly affect the validity and power of our preaching ministry. The message we preach must become a part of us before it can impact the lives of others. In order to achieve that, we must make ample provision for time spent vertically with God and horizontally with people.

Hard work. Awesome privilege. Huge responsibility. Great outcome and reward. All preachers and all listeners live alike under the authority of God's Word. We are learning obedience together and we all fall short of perfection. All preachers are still learning their task, not least myself. Some preachers shy away from exposition because it is indeed hard work. Others are simply ignorant of its nature and method – for many years I myself was in that group. Let us now learn together a practical method for biblical expository preaching.

6

Practical Steps for Sermon Preparation

THE AIM

$\mathcal{M}$y ultimate goal is to offer the reader a simple but thorough, hands-on, no frills, practical approach that will equip both Western and Eastern Christian preachers to produce faithful, relevant and powerful expository sermons. Central to achieving that goal is our need to equip ourselves to handle biblical passages in their historical, grammatical and literary contexts in order to seek to discover their intention, meaning and application, both in their ancient contexts and in the lives of twenty-first century hearers. I shall try to explain and illustrate skills of sermon preparation and presentation with the purpose that such sermons will not only inform the minds of our listeners, but will also powerfully move their hearts and stir their wills into action. That process of course must be visible first and foremost in the lives of those who preach expository sermons.

THE ASSUMPTIONS

As the skill of expository preaching is a lifelong process, the challenge facing me is how to condense such a training into the pages of a single volume for a potentially wide range of readers. Recognizing also therefore the humanly-speaking impossibility of that task, I have made the following basic assumptions in writing this book.

First, I don't want my readers to feel overwhelmed by detail, so that their view of the forest is obscured by the density of the trees. I also want to avoid conveying the impression that good expository sermons are possible only after three or four years' full-time study in a Bible College or Theological Seminary.

Second, this book will aim to help the preacher who has little or no skill in the biblical languages of Hebrew or Greek to deal faithfully with the text of Scripture and to translate that study into powerful, relevant and effective expository preaching ministry. I hope that those who do possess skills in the biblical languages will also find benefit in this suggested method of expository preaching. This book is aimed at pastors, preachers, teachers, students, elders and lay people. Sound exegesis must form the basis of every good sermon, but such exegesis – aiming to discover the purpose, meaning and application of a biblical text in its original ancient contexts – must also be carried out by those leading Bible studies, giving devotional talks, preparing evangelistic messages or teaching Scripture in any situation.

Thirdly, the availability of time, and our organization of that time, is a constant challenge to all of us. I want to give guidelines for the Christian preacher who is already overstretched and for whom even the reading of this book will demand disciplined effort. Other books, especially in the vital area of biblical interpretation, will be recommended for further reading, but this book, based as it is on a taught course, will require neither large quantities of reading nor huge doses of highly technical academic data. It is for those with limited time and resources who want to treat Scripture seriously and expound it faithfully, clearly and powerfully. Each step of preparation is necessary and this method will be treated as thoroughly as possible in the material I shall present. You will then have to decide for every sermon just how much time and energy you can spend in applying the method to the biblical passage. The general guideline is: the more the better!

THE METHOD

The focus of this method will be a hands-on, skill-based consideration of the actual stages of practical preparation and presentation of expository sermons. Each step of the process will be dealt with through a threefold matrix: explanation, practice exercise and example. We will gradually build two case-study sermons. Some writers and scholars claim that preachers and preaching cannot be taught, in the sense that they are born into it or gifted into it, and as such either cannot be helped or do not need help. I can see that argument but do not share those conclusions. The preaching gift needs to be recognized, developed and exercised. The basic ingredients required for expository preaching are in fact needed by anyone who seeks to handle, communicate and apply biblical truth.

Having stated that, we must be aware that in expository preaching we are dealing with necessary ingredients rather than fixed formulas. I do not want to give the impression that good expository sermons can be produced by applying a slick formula in a short space of time and with little investment of energy. There is a real sense in which an expository sermon is a creative work in the way that a symphony is a creative work. At the same time, however, the sermon is not the product of a freethinking, 'anything goes' mindset. It is the fruit of sustained work within certain parameters and boundaries. I shall suggest ten steps for the preparation of an expository sermon. The necessary ingredients will be set out in the form of ten steps, but that sequence must not be considered as set in concrete. There is room for flexibility, combination and backtracking in steps. The actual mix of those ingredients may vary for any one sermon, depending on such factors as the nature of the biblical passage itself, the expertise and experience of the preacher and the time available for preparation. I remain convinced, however, that whatever quantity of the ingredients enters the recipe, and whatever the relative mix might be, the basic ingredients must all somehow be represented in the final product that we will preach.

The challenge

The evidence of both Old and New Testament Scripture that we have so far considered leads to one inescapable conclusion: the work of proclaiming and explaining biblical truth demands the total commitment of the whole person. The work of expository preaching is holistic.

I. THE BODY

The writers of the books of Scripture have already shown us something of their perceived relationship between mind and body. All believers, and especially those involved in exposition of biblical truth, live under a divine compulsion to demonstrate harmony between what they preach and what they practise. Evidence of physical purity and holiness in leaders and preachers is demanded by the biblical authors. Self-discipline and self-control are crucial in the care which preachers take of their own bodies, for expository preaching is physically demanding. I recall being told by my teachers during my Bible College days, that an average twenty minute sermon requires at least eight hours of preparation. We shall discuss that one later! I was also assured that in preaching that twenty minute sermon, the expenditure of effort was equivalent to an eight hour working day! In the midst of a heavy schedule of preparation and preaching, we need to take sufficient doses of rest, diet, exercise and personal relationship interaction.

2. THE MIND

We have already seen repeatedly how it is through engaging the minds of our listeners by biblical exposition that God brings people to knowledge of himself and the righteousness which is by faith. That is the mechanism ordained by God for effecting radical change in human behaviour. Exposition is divinely ordained to that end. But what about the mind of the preacher? Our principal responsibility as preachers is to keep on feeding our own minds and visibly showing the power of God's Word to mould our lives. Yet there is more than this. As preachers we are called to use our minds extensively in the preparation of our sermons. In this book, I want to seek to help preachers to think, especially those who have not experienced an education system that encourages critical and analytical thinking or who have not gained the benefits (as well as the problems!) that come from formal and prolonged theological training.

3. THE SPIRIT

The testimony of the apostle Paul was that through persecution and suffering he gained the two most precious commodities needed by a preacher: humility and weakness. They are the diamonds and gold of expository ministry. Our sermons must become a part of us. Our exposition must live in us and through us, yet the very act of expository preaching makes us painfully aware of our own weakness, frailty and shortcomings. Always in my preparation and preaching of a message, I feel nervous, sometimes very nervous. Sometimes I feel like escaping and asking God to take me off the playing field and put on a substitute instead. Moses felt the same way! (Exod. 4:10-13). Always I feel a strong awareness of my own sheer inability to achieve any lasting results at all. Yet I rejoice that in these very infirmities, God delights to intervene and show his power to help both preacher and hearer alike. It is with that great assurance of God's awesome commitment to the exposition of his own Word that we begin the glorious task of assembling a sermon.

6. Practical Steps:
Step One
Reading and Thinking

Some years ago I recall finding a quiet room in our house and starting to prepare a sermon. Two hours later, my wife, who is always my greatest support and strongest sermon critic, entered the room to see if I had completed the task. I remember vividly the blend in her facial expression, bewilderment, amusement and irritation, when I told her that I had got nothing down on paper but had spent two profitable hours in reading and thinking! Though too gracious to say so, she clearly was wondering what game I was playing and why I was so slow in moving forward. Yet it is precisely by our thinking that we gain discernment, insight, sensitivity and understanding, for it is only through our own understanding of a passage (exegesis) that we can hope to bring its meaning into the minds, hearts and wills of our listeners (exposition). If parts of our own sermons are misty to us in terms of clarity and understanding, then they will probably escalate to form a dense fog of confusion in the minds of our hearers. Our greatest aspiration should be that people will say of our exposition that which even his critics said of Martin Luther: 'it is impossible to misunderstand him.' It is imperative that we exercise our thinking ability right from the start of our preparation in Step One. Much of that thinking process, as will later become clearer, revolves round:

1. What questions to ask of the biblical text.
2. How to ask those questions.
3. How to recognize the answers that come from the text.

At this point it will be useful to draw a distinction between content and context. The two terms are indeed closely related, nevertheless we must distinguish between them.

The *content* of a passage of Scripture refers simply to the actual material contained within the boundaries of that biblical passage.

So, for example, the content of Philippians 2: 1-11 means all the words contained within the verses of that passage, together with the ideas, thoughts, themes and purposes which those words reveal to the readers.

The *context* of a passage of Scripture refers to the elements that surround the passage and determine, or at least influence, the words that were written down by the original author. The contexts that affect the writing of a biblical passage and therefore that also affect our ability to understand that passage, are basically fourfold: the historical circumstances in which the biblical book was written; the social, cultural and religious backgrounds of the writer and readers; the literary setting of the passage and the significance of the location of the passage within a chapter, section, book and even the entire testament; the wider biblical and theological setting of our chosen passage. Contexts and contents are thus closely related, yet different.

Before we can even begin to read and think about a passage of Scripture, we shall need to choose the passage on which to preach. A number of factors will help to determine our choice.

(1) Often if we are preaching systematically through a biblical book, say Colossians, then Colossians 1:15-20 might simply be the next logical section to take. Consecutive preaching in a series does have the great advantage of allowing systematic and comprehensive Bible teaching. For example, a progressive series of studies in Genesis will eventually include Genesis 39 and the issue of Joseph's confrontation by Potiphar's wife. If, however, we were suddenly to choose that chapter out of the blue, the listeners to the sermon might be forgiven for wondering whether the preacher knew something about the congregation of which they themselves were unaware! Preachers cannot be accused of targeting individuals if they are preaching systematically through a biblical book.

(2) Sometimes, and especially if we are invited to preach 'away from home', we might be given a set passage on which to preach. This saves us the struggle of praying and discerning which particular passage is most suitable for that time, place and circumstance.

(3) If we do have to choose a passage, or break down a biblical book into units for a series of sermons, then we need to read the

whole book carefully and seek out the biblical writer's ideas and themes, rather than mechanically chopping up the book every ten verses. We need to look for changes and transitions in the thought of the author. Sometimes, but not always, the titles of sections in our English Bibles can guide us in our choice of a suitable passage. On occasion, however, such titles do not accurately represent the biblical text.

(4) Some passages of Scripture might be self-contained in the sense of having no preceding or succeeding context. For example in the book of Psalms, we will often treat a psalm in its entirety, unless it happens to be Psalm 119!

(5) Narrative passages, especially in the Old Testament, are often lengthy and account will need to be taken of this in our choice of expository method. Sometimes narratives, especially of biblical characters, will span more than a few verses and we will need to consider the length of our material in adapting our exposition. The life of Joseph could easily occupy a number of sermons (Gen. 37–50).

(6) Effective topical preaching deals with an issue across a spectrum of Scripture. Some examples are: the Trinity (in a series on Christian doctrines), Resurrection (an Easter theme), Incarnation (for the Christmas service), marriage, forgiveness, tithing and the biblical basis for world mission. In preaching topically, we need to be especially cautious of grasshopper sermons which jump backwards and forwards across Scripture or which name proof texts to justify or argue in favour of a particular point of view. The thought of the Scripture, as well as the context in which it is set, must be allowed to guide and determine our exposition. We must never impose our own ideas or agenda onto a passage of Scripture.

In treating our chosen biblical passage, we need to have some idea, as we begin preparation, of the approximate time available to us once in the pulpit. Time constraints will directly affect the amount of material that we can include in the sermon. Over recent years, different churches have given me the following sorts of guideline – 'Please do not exceed twenty minutes because the service includes a celebration of the Lord's Supper.' 'Please keep it to a maximum of fifteen minutes.' 'Twenty minutes is your maximum length and after fifteen minutes, a notice will be held up, saying "five minutes left".' 'Our members are used to sermons which are always thirty minutes long.' 'It's entirely up to you, as long as you don't preach for less than forty-five minutes.' If we prepare an expository sermon using the ten steps described in this book, we will usually end up with more material than can be included in the final version. It is painful to exclude good material but often we will need to do precisely that, so that our hearers are spared the information overload that easily produces indigestion. As preachers we do not want to kill our listeners with kindness, as we pack all manner of material into the sermon. Nor do we want to leave our hearers starving for lack of spiritual food. Experience will help us to select a diet that will maximize the learning of those who listen to us. We shall return again to this issue at a number of points in our preparation.

The other factor, of course, that will affect the outworking of our sermon preparation will be the time available in another sense, namely, the amount of notice given to us before sermon delivery takes place. This can vary from a few months to a few hours and our implementation of the ten steps will need to be adjusted in line with the available preparation time. As a general rule, I suggest that, for a Sunday sermon, preparation be under way on the previous Monday. If we leave it till the day before preaching, that could be the day when we feel unwell or a church member has a serious accident.

As soon as we know the passage or passages that we will eventually expound, we can begin our sermon preparation.

(1) The goal of Step One is to gain an initial and provisional idea of what is happening in our passage and in the wider setting of the book in which that passage is set. In order to do this, we must read the passage a number of times. Those with expertise in Hebrew and Greek should certainly read and browse the original text, attempting their own translation of the passage. Preachers working from an English translation can and do produce excellent and competent exposition of the biblical text. A number of Bible versions are widely available. Many will want to use The King James Authorised Version (KJV) or The New International Version (NIV) or New American Standard Bible (NASB). There are also other translations such as The Revised

Standard Version (RSV), The New Revised Standard Version (NRSV) and The New King James Version (NKJV). Read the passage several times in one translation and compare it to the version in one or two alternative translations. If you are preaching, for example, on the Feeding of the Five Thousand in Luke 9:10-17, then you should also read through the parallel and similar accounts in Matthew 14:13-21, 15:29-39; Mark 6:30-44, 8:1-13 and John 6:1-15.

Reading of the passage for exposition is necessary but not sufficient because every passage is set within a wider context. Anyone preaching a passage in a New Testament letter ought to read that letter in its entirety at least once in order to gain an initial overview of the whole letter before trying to analyse any of its constituent parts. Particular attention should be paid to the chapter in which the passage is located, to the preceding chapter and to the succeeding chapter. Hard and fast rules are difficult to set for this task but anyone preaching from Gospels, Revelation or the longer books of the Old Testament ought to read the relevant wider sections and major thought-units in which their exposition passage is found. Thus, for example, a sermon on I Corinthians 1:17-25 should involve at least one reading of the whole letter of I Corinthians if time allows, and should certainly involve a couple of readings of the thought-unit that spans chapters 1–4 concerning divisions in the church at Corinth.

(2) Depending on time available, repeated reading of the passage and its surrounding context, in an attitude of prayerful dependence on God, will begin to trigger initial seed thoughts in your mind. Go back to the passage again and again and turn it over and over in your mind. Pray, read and meditate and do it again so that God can begin to make the passage a part of your thinking and living. At this stage you do not want to get bogged down with large amounts of detail but as you read, you can begin to ask yourself questions such as:

a) Does the author explicitly or implicitly reveal his purpose?

b) Are we told anything about the circumstances of the passage?

c) Are there words or ideas that reveal the main theme?

If answers to these questions are not immediately obvious, do not be anxious. Understanding and light will appear as you move through the steps of preparation.

(3) The main goal at this stage is for reading, prayer and meditation on the chosen passage. You must seek to soak yourself in the passage until you begin to absorb its message and the passage comes alive in you. If ideas occur to you, write them down either on computer disc, in a notebook or on the sheets of rough paper that will contain your sermon preparation notes. Sometimes God can speak to you from that passage in the middle of the night or in the mental freshness of the early morning waking moments, so it is always worthwhile to keep pen and paper by your bedside! Organization and order in the things you write down are not important at this stage – just get your thoughts down on paper because failure to do so may mean permanent loss of those ideas! Continue to pray, read and meditate even over a period of days or weeks if your preaching schedule allows. Begin to seek, even at this early stage, the application that God might be revealing in and through the passage.

CASE STUDIES

My students have often asked me to show them the development of an actual sermon from its conception, through its gestation and into its final delivery. As case study passages I have deliberately chosen an example of a Gospel narrative. In this way we shall be able to witness the impact of each step on the growth of the sermon from its embryo to its final form. As well as following the life cycle of this case study sermon, I suggest you choose a biblical passage for your own sermon and begin now to apply the ten steps of preparation as you work your way through this preaching book.

CASE STUDY – GOSPEL NARRATIVE: LUKE 4:1-13

The following initial seed-thoughts emerged during the preliminary period of reading, meditation and prayer.

(1) After the childhood of Jesus, the ministry of John the Baptist and the baptism of Christ, Luke launches into his gospel through

Jesus' experience of temptation in the wilderness. The attacks come early in Jesus' ministry.

(2) Three temptations are recorded and Jesus responds to each challenge by using Old Testament Scripture (Luke 4:4, 8, 12).

(3) The temptations are preceded by a statement that Jesus was filled with the Spirit and led by the Spirit (Luke 4:1).

(4) Matthew, in his parallel account, reverses the order of the second and third temptations and also offers a slight difference in his quotation of Psalm 91:11-12 (Matt. 4:6), omitting the phrase 'to guard you carefully'. There is also a difference in Matthew's wording of the third temptation (Matt. 4:8-9), compared with Luke 4:5-6. Matthew adds a point about angelic help in 4:11 which is missing in Luke's account. Luke concludes simply by saying that the devil 'left him until an opportune time' (Luke 4:13).

(5) Mark's parallel account is very brief – a mere two verses (Mark 1:12-13). Mark underlines the immediacy of Jesus' being sent out into the desert for forty days, being tempted by Satan, being with the wild animals and being attended by angels.

(6) The main thrust of the incident clearly concerns Jesus' temptations by the devil who appears to be pushing the Lord to achieve legitimate ends by illegitimate means. That idea needs further investigation in subsequent preparation steps.

6. Practical Steps
Step Two
Themes of the Passage

THE GOAL

The basic aim of this step is to try to establish the biblical writer's, and thus the Holy Spirit's, purpose and intention in a particular biblical passage. Our goal is to identify the main theme or thought of a passage which will eventually become the main focus of our sermon. Related to this main theme will be one or more sub-themes that substantiate, develop or explain the main theme of the passage. The task of identifying the main theme or themes, along with the sub-theme or themes is not merely a matter of academic interest. It is of crucial significance. The theme and sub-themes must arise out of the biblical text itself. If we fail in this specific task, then there will be a real danger that we shall simply be putting forward our own views and ideas rather than expounding divine truth. Such a message will not – indeed it cannot – carry the authority of God himself.

THE METHOD

At this second step of our preparation, we are seeking to use the wide angle lens of a camera to scan the contents of the passage in order to identify the main theme or thought, followed by the sub-themes that tell us more about the main theme. Later on, in Steps Three and Four, we shall use the zoom camera lens to perform our detailed exegetical study of the text. For the moment, however, we are scanning the contents of the passage but bearing in mind its surrounding literary setting. We must never forget that the biblical books were written as continuous texts in Hebrew, Aramaic and Greek. Chapter and verse divisions came later.

The concept of a passage containing a main theme is not new. Miller put it like this:

> Any single sermon should have just one major idea. The points or sub-divisions should be parts of this one grand thought.... Every sermon

should have a theme, and that theme should be the theme of the portion of Scripture on which it is based.[1]

This view is echoed in a similar statement that the 'preacher must develop his expository treatment of the text in relation to a single dominant theme'.[2] A word of caution here. In our personal preparation for an expository sermon, it is important that we pay attention to the entire contents of a passage. That is necessary for our own understanding of a passage. However, if a passage contains more than one dominant theme, together with a multitude of sub-themes, we must later decide what to include in our sermon and what to leave out. The richness of God's Word is such that a passage may have two or three main themes and we must be very careful not to force our own theoretical grid of 'one theme only' onto every biblical passage. That might cause distortion or even twisting of the text and that is to be avoided at all costs. Now to the practicalities of tracing the main and sub-themes in a passage of Scripture.

MAIN THEME

Already we have seen that our identification of the main theme and sub-themes of a passage is the only guarantee we have that we are touching the revealed mind, word and will of God. Only in this way can we claim to be proclaiming and explaining God's Word. There is, however, another reason why Step Two is crucial. Unless our sermon relates to, is based on and is an exposition of, the main and sub-themes of the passage, it may easily lack cohesion and our hearers will find it hard to see where our message is going and even harder to remember it afterwards.

Locating the main and sub-themes is an exercise in which preachers use their minds, directed to the biblical passage, to try to discover the

1. Donald G. Miller, *The Way to Biblical Preaching*, (New York: Abingdon, 1957), pp.53-5.

2. Alan M. Stibbs, *Expounding God's Word: Some Principles and Methods*, (London: IVP, 1960), p.40.

3. One way of locating this main idea is that suggested by Haddon Robinson who employs the concepts of Subject and Complement in a helpful section on pp.31-48 of his book *Expository Preaching: Principles and Practice* (Leicester; IVP, 1986).

concepts that had formed in the mind of the biblical author. In short, we are trying to gain access to the thoughts of the biblical authors through the evidence before us on the printed page. The task of identifying the main and sub-themes is thus vital. It helps us to discern the author's intention and thereby the intended meaning and application of the biblical passage. In addition, the themes will form the structure and framework for the later development of the sermon. Indeed we shall constantly check, develop and, if necessary, revise the themes until they appear in our final outline (Step 6). Step Two constitutes our initial and provisional attempt to identify main and sub-themes. This choice can then be modified as our understanding of the passage widens and deepens.

Let us now see how to identify main theme and sub-themes in a selection of biblical texts.

EXERCISES

1. So do not fear, for I am with you; do not be dismayed, for I am your God. I will strengthen you and help you; I will uphold you with my righteous right hand (Isa. 41:10 NIV).

Faced with this verse, we shall try to get to the main theme by asking some basic questions about the form of the words. This verse is a classic example of the need to take account of context. The first word is 'So'. We therefore realize that the verse is a consequence of the teaching contained in previous verses. By examining, albeit briefly, verses 8 and 9, we see that their theme is that God has chosen and called his people Israel from the ends of the earth. We have established this simply by asking ourselves the question 'Are there any words in the text which link the passage to a previous or succeeding context?' The word 'so' in verse 10 is such a link word.

Turning now to Isaiah 41:10 itself, and bearing in mind God's reassurance to his rebellious people in verses 8-9, we ask the question 'What is the consequence of God's choosing of his servant Israel?' In deciding the answer to that question, look at the basic grammar of verse 10. We can identify a negative command, 'do not fear', followed by a reason which is also a promise, 'for I am with you'. Next we have a second negative command, 'do not be dismayed', followed by a reason which is also a promise, 'for I am your God'. Then we have three further reasons and promises why Israel should not fear: 'I will strengthen you'; 'I will help you' and 'I will uphold you with my righteous right hand'. Thus in the midst of Israel's fears that her disobedience guarantees abandonment by God, the Lord steps in and promises active intervention to help exiled Israel, the right hand being symbolic of God's saving power.

Drawing together our two negative commands, each followed by a reason, and the whole followed by three further promises, we can now suggest the following breakdown of content:

Main Theme: Why the people of God have no cause for fear or confusion.
Sub-themes:
    i). God is present – he will not desert us.
    ii). God is personal – he owns his people.
    iii). God is powerful – he will strengthen, help and uphold us.

In building this framework, we have used no tools or resources or books other than the Bible itself. We have simply read the text carefully, checked the context, thought about the text and directed specific questions towards the text. We have located the main and sub-themes.

2. Let us reinforce our practice of the method with a simple verse:

A generous man will himself be blessed, for he shares his food with the poor (Prov. 22:9).

In this lengthy recital of the proverbs of Solomon, we have a promise, founded on a reason.

Main theme: Our guarantee of sufficient provision.
Sub-theme: Our own willingness to share with the needy.

3. Now for a slightly longer passage, this time in Hebrews 12:7-11. A reading of this short section underlines for us the fact that no passage

of Scripture can be treated in total isolation from its surrounding contexts. The theme of discipline does not suddenly start in verse 7. It is already present in 12:5-6 but in order to be safe, we need to backtrack at least to verse 1 and check out the flow of the author's argument prior to verses 7-11.

The section Hebrews 12:1-6 makes three main points:

(a) Believers are called to reject sin and pursue holiness (12:1).

(b) Their encouragement and incentive in obeying that calling comes by looking to their example, Jesus, who suffered so appallingly in order that believers might be sanctified (12:2-4).

(c) In this process of sanctification believers are disciplined because God treats them with compassion as his own sons (12:5-6).

The main theme of Hebrews 12:7-11 becomes clear in two ways. Firstly, the issues of discipline and sonship are very clear as we leave Hebrews 12:5-6 and enter 12:7ff. The text simply continues this twin theme. Secondly, if we are to ask what key words are present in the passage, it is immediately clear that words related to 'discipline' occur eight times, words related to 'son' occur three times, and words related to 'father' occur four times in the course of a mere five verses! The main issue is unmistakable – it concerns discipline. That being the case, we need to 'ask' the passage what it is telling us about discipline. A number of points are made in the passage regarding discipline, but by reading Hebrews 12:7-10 it becomes clear that the dominant thought centres on relationship, in which the idea of fathers and sons controls the whole argument. Indeed, four out of five verses revolve round the way God disciplines those who are his sons. We shall therefore fix our main theme on the latter point and then gather the remaining information about 'discipline' as a list of sub-themes, each of which is related in the passage to the dominant main theme. Thus, the following framework of thoughts emerges as we take account of the broad spectrum of the passage:

Main Theme: God disciplines us as his sons (12:7).
Sub-themes:
    i). God calls us to submit to hardship as discipline (12:8-9).
    ii). God calls us to holiness through discipline (12:10).

iii). God calls us to produce a harvest of righteousness through our submission to discipline (12:11).

Notice how all the above statements have their solid basis, not in the thoughts, ideas or speculations of a preacher, but rather in the text of the biblical passage itself. This is our vital starting point for expository preaching. Without that basis, our preaching will not – indeed cannot – be rightly called expository.

4. Determining the main theme and sub-themes of a passage is not always easy. In fact sometimes it can be frustrating, even irritating, but nevertheless necessary. As preachers, we must be ready and willing to think, as we seek to discern the basic structure of the main theme and then identify the way in which that main theme is developed through its related sub-themes. In some passages it may be possible to decide more than one way to express the main and sub-themes, but context will help us to determine the author's purpose. One thing is sure. Those who listen to our sermons will not understand them unless we can pinpoint the main and sub-themes of the biblical passage and deal with them appropriately through the remaining steps of preparation. Let us return to the Old Testament and draw out the themes of a narrative – Genesis 45:1-15.

We begin by checking the literary setting of the passage and we note that Genesis 44 concerns the discovery of the silver cup in Benjamin's sack, followed by Judah's pleading to stay in Egypt in place of Benjamin, rather than have the appalling scenario of the brothers returning to their father Jacob without Benjamin. Genesis 45:1-15 then deals with Joseph's emotional revealing of his true identity. Those fifteen verses form a narrative in which Joseph reveals himself (vv.1-3), recounts the past two years of famine (vv. 4-8), and explains his plan to settle his family in the Goshen region so that they will be preserved during the continuing famine (vv. 9-15). If the main theme and sub-themes are not immediately apparent to us, we need to pray, read and think again. One way to identify the themes would be along the lines of the breakdown just stated.

Main theme: Joseph's revelation of his true identity.
Sub-themes:

    i). Joseph reveals himself in the present (45:1-3).

    ii). Joseph recalls the past (45:4-7).

    iii). Joseph explains his future plan (45:8-15).

This is a possible division, but in reading the text even more closely, another possibility begins to emerge as we study Joseph's conversation with his brothers. Here we can detect an emphasis on the role of God in the central section of Joseph's address (vv. 4-11). In particular there emerges the recurring theme of God's sovereign intervention in human affairs (vv. 5, 7, 8, 9). This then can be chosen as our main theme and we will need therefore to gather evidence in the passage for sub-themes that are related to that main theme.

Main theme: Joseph reveals his true identity and reaffirms the sovereignty of God.
Sub-themes:

    i). God in his sovereignty deals with our fears (45:4-5).

    ii). God in his sovereignty overrules circumstances (45:6-7).

    iii). God in his sovereignty provides for the needs of all his people (45:8-11).

5. This task of identifying main and sub-themes is so vital that we will study two further passages, this time from the New Testament, as practice exercises. One of the best known passages in the New Testament is Christ's commission to his disciples for the task of world mission, recorded in Matthew 28:16-20. Let us begin to unpack the text and identify its themes. Initial inspection of the passage indicates two verses of narrative (vv. 16-17) and three verses of direct speech (vv.18-20). Is there a main theme? Frequently in Scripture, when God issues a challenge to his people, he attends that challenge by promising the resources needed to meet it. Let us direct that concept of command and promise to this particular biblical passage. The central command lies in verses 19 and 20, though in the Greek text, the only direct

command is 'make disciples', whilst the 'going', 'baptizing' and 'teaching' are participles. Having pinpointed the central command to engage in world mission, we can then seek out in the text the promises of resources to fulfil that task. Thus we have now located themes which encompass the majority of the content of our passage.

Main theme: God's Commission to make disciples for his Church (28:19-20a).
   Sub-themes:
      i). God's promise of his personal care of workers, even those who doubted (28:16-18a).
      ii). God's promise of his power and authority (28:18b).
      iii). God's promise of his continual presence (28:20b).

6. Our final exercise comes from Paul's letter to the Philippians 2:1-11. Here is yet another example of the pivotal role played by context, as we try to establish themes. If we were to read solely the biblical passage, without reference to preceding and succeeding text, then we might well feel that the main theme would have to be 'imitating Jesus' or 'humility'. In reality I suggest that those issues are more likely to be sub-themes rather than main themes. Let us read the whole letter again and see what emerges. In 1:1-11 Paul praises God for the Philippians and prays for a deepening of their love. Paul then testifies to the progress of the gospel even through his own imprisonment (1:12-26). Paul then shifts his emphasis in 1:27-30 by challenging the believers to holy living and to unity in the midst of opposition. So here is a discordant note – there is evidence that strife and disunity are threatening this church. Then, in the section which begins after our chosen passage, Paul continues his call for holy living (2:12-14) in the midst of severe opposition (2:15-18). The danger of disunity caused by troublemakers is apparently a continuing threat (3:2, 18-19; 4: 2). Now that we see the wider context of 2:1-11, it seems that church unity may well be the central theme of the letter and verses 1-2 appears to confirm that view. Thus I suggest the following breakdown of the themes of 2:1-11.

Main theme: A call for the Church to show unity, through the practice of love and the attitude of humility (2:1-2).

Sub-themes:

i). Love and humility involve a right view of ourselves in relation to others (2:3).

ii). Love and humility involve looking beyond our own selfish interests (2:4).

iii). Love and humility involve imitation of, and indwelling by, our supreme example, the Lord Jesus Christ himself (2:5-11).

Review of Procedure

In order to determine the main and sub-themes of a passage, we need to address three basic questions to the text.

(1) Are there any words in the passage which link our sermon text to a previous or succeeding context? Step Two does require some initial work on the biblical material that surrounds our passage but this study of context will become our major concentration as we move into Step Three.

(2) What is the overall main issue being dealt with in our passage? The main goal of Steps One and Two is to give us a basic grounding in content, structure and the flow of the author's thinking.

(3) What elements in the passage offer us consequences, results, developments or explanations of that main issue? These are the sub-themes and they are related to the main theme of the passage. It is crucial that all themes must arise, not from our own ideas, imagination or blessed thoughts, but from the text of the passage itself.

Let us review our preparation thus far. The fundamental aim in identifying the main theme and sub-themes is to establish the biblical author's and thus the Holy Spirit's intention and purpose in any particular passage of Scripture. Only in this way can we expect to be effective agents in expounding the Word of God with authority and with life-changing power. It needs to be emphasized, however, that the finding of themes in Step Two is provisional. It will be reviewed in Steps Five and Six, following the refining and testing work of context and content analysis. The locating of themes is our first vital door into the process of exegesis that will become the bedrock of expository sermon construction. The work that we do in Steps One to Five involves biblical exegesis and it is this work which will set the parameters for interpreting our passage.

Preparation of an expository sermon, in line with the method presented in this book, falls into two parts. From Step One to Step Five, as you seek to prepare materials for an expository sermon, all your notes will need to be placed on a computer or on sheets of rough paper or on index cards. Steps Six to Ten then involve using your notes to write up the full and final version of the sermon. Whilst Step One is primarily occupied with prayer, reading and thinking, as you turn the biblical passage over and over in your mind, nevertheless you should be using paper or computer, for preparation of the raw material that you will accumulate from Steps One to Five.

Let us now work together on Step Two of our case study passage, observing the embryo stage of what will become a sermon.

CASE STUDY – LUKE 4:1-13

Having begun with the initial and provisional work of praying, reading and thinking, we now come to the text of the passage once again, to try to establish its main theme and sub-themes. First impressions of this passage on Jesus' temptations indicate a mixed bag of narrative and dialogue that seems to fall into several clearly defined units: introductory narrative (vv. 1-2), first temptation (vv. 3-4), second temptation (vv. 5-8), third temptation (vv. 9-12), closing narrative (v. 13). If we stick fairly and squarely to the strict parameters of the passage itself, a very basic but reasonable analysis would be this:

Main theme: The devil's temptations of Jesus in the desert.
  Sub-themes:
  (i) The temptation to turn stone into bread (vv. 3-4).
  (ii) The temptation to worship the devil for material gain (vv. 5-8).
  (iii) The temptation to jump from the temple and trust the angels to save him (vv. 9-12).

When I recently preached this sermon, those were the themes I initially set down on paper, yet somehow I was left feeling dissatisfied. That prompted me to read the wider context of Luke 1–4 in the hope of enriching my understanding of 4:1-13. Luke 4, in the wider context of that gospel, certainly marks the start of Jesus' earthly ministry, following the descent of the Holy Spirit upon the Lord at his baptism (3:22). In the same verse, the divine voice declares the Sonship of the Saviour and the love that exists between Father and Son. Sonship, moreover, is the key element of the genealogy in 3:23-38 and occurs again even in the devil's temptations of Jesus in 4:3 and 9. Could it have been the case that the Father's affirmation of his love for his Son in Luke 3:22 triggered the attempt of the devil to deflect Jesus right at the start from fulfilling the life and ministry that would lead him finally to the cross and ultimately to the devil's own destruction? Thus the words 'Son' and 'Spirit' function as links into the surrounding context. I began to dig deeper into other Scripture like Job 1–2 and ask myself the questions 'Why did the devil seek to tempt Jesus? What was his agenda? What drove and motivated the Devil?' I then made a second, but still provisional, attempt to identify the basic themes:

Main Theme: The devil's attempt to discredit God and destroy the mission of God's Son.

   Sub-themes:

   (a) The devil's attempt to doubt the Father's power to provide (vv. 3-4).

   (b) The devil's attempt to steal the sovereignty that belongs to God alone (vv. 5-8).

   (3). The devil's attempt to destroy trusting submission to God's will (vv. 9-12).

These themes will need to be checked again as our understanding deepens through Steps 3–5.

6. Practical Steps:
Step Three
The Contexts of the Passage

So far, we have prayed, read and thought about the passage and have provisionally identified its main and sub-themes. In the course of those first two steps, one thing has become clear – context and content, though essentially different – are nevertheless inseparable. Content means all the written material contained within the biblical text of our passage. Contexts are those factors that have helped to shape that material and that are therefore necessary aids to our current understanding of that material. Contexts exist outside the biblical passage but are related to that passage. Contexts and contents are like two sides of one coin. Contexts and contents are complementary, not contradictory. For the sake of clarity, comprehension and organization, contexts and contents form two steps but they must never be completely separated in our thinking and preparation. These two steps are the heaviest ones of all, yet through our perspiration will come inspiration, along with purpose and application. It is our preparation of Steps Three and Four that will make or break our expository sermon. Indeed, unless we take contexts and contents seriously, we will never produce a sermon that can be called expository.

If we try to use a biblical text with little or no regard for its various contexts, then there is a real danger that we may misunderstand, misinterpret and misapply that text. The degree to which the various contexts will affect our grasp of a text's meaning, interpretation and application varies from text to text but we must be ready, for any given passage, to investigate the relevance of the three major contextual influences. We shall now deal with those contexts, one by one, following a pattern of explanation, brief examples and reference to the main tools through which we can study biblical contexts. Finally we shall apply the method of Step Three to our case-study passages. When you apply this step to your own sermon passage, write down your notes on computer, rough paper or index cards, continuing your work from Steps One and Two. You will need at least one sheet of paper for each step of preparation. This is your vital raw material. After establishing the main and sub-themes of your chosen passage, you will need to read the passage again in order to identify and note down those issues of historical, social, cultural and religious background on which you and your hearers may need clarification.

One important word — at a few points in our sermon preparation it may be helpful to refer to the reference books and commentaries. This can pose a danger — we must complete our own work on Steps One to Five, with minimum use of other tools. We must master the text and make it our own. The biblical text is our primary and constant point of reference.

(A) HISTORICAL CONTEXT

Why should the preacher be concerned with history? I suggest that at least three reasons compel our interest in the historical framework of our text.

First, all the biblical books were composed, under divine inspiration, by human authors who lived in a period spanning about 1500 years which came to an end in the latter part of the first century AD. The biblical documents were all written in contexts of language, society, culture and religion that were in many ways radically different from those of the twenty-first century readers of the Bible. This distance in time and space needs to be considered if we are to reach an adequate understanding of the text.

Second, we, as twenty-first century readers, undoubtedly bring to our texts a considerable amount of our own linguistic, social, cultural and religious baggage which can colour our reading and interpretation. The search for historical context helps to neutralize the subtle influence of bias on our interpretation.

Third, more will be said later on the issue of biblical interpretation but for the moment, we need to be aware that in recent years there has been a revolution in thought, originating in Western society, that has expressed itself in at least two forms.

i) The New Hermeneutic: this is a vast subject which really would require a separate book for adequate treatment but we dare not avoid at least a cursory consideration here. Until recent decades, the interpreter was considered to be the subject, the text was the object and the goal for the subject was to use various techniques to interpret the text objectively and correctly. Now it is true that there is a danger here, namely, that the interpreter does carry the baggage we have just mentioned and there is thus a risk of bias in interpretation. Some supporters of the 'new hermeneutic' however argue that a text has many meanings, none of which is objectively true, and all of which can be called valid or invalid depending on their effect on the interpreter. Thus the author's intent in a biblical book becomes difficult or impossible to know. The frustrating, indeed irritating thing about such a position is that the adherents of such views fully expect us to understand their intention and argument! Certainly we need to take serious note of the matter of historical distance, but the real peril is to take on board the 'new hermeneutic' to the extent that it relativizes all opinion about what Scripture is saying. The danger is that, taken to its logical conclusion, the 'new hermeneutic' takes the line that knowledge of objective truth is impossible. Such a view forces history and theology out of the picture or at least far into the background. It threatens indeed to undermine the whole ethos, methodology and power of expository preaching.

ii) Radical Hermeneutics: this more recent position is best known through its development of the idea of deconstruction, one of the hallmarks of postmodernist thinking. This contends that there are no safe methods or foundations for interpretation, because all methods are theoretical. The result is that there is no such thing as the authoritative meaning in the text itself. Different individuals and communities thus construct and control meaning as they relate to the biblical text. If there is thus no objective meaning in a text, then the argument could be extended that there cannot be absolute truth or authority. In order to deal with this challenge from postmodernism, preachers must pay serious attention to biblical history.

A couple of examples from I Corinthians will serve to illustrate what can happen when preachers fail to consider historical context or when they misuse or misunderstand that context.

One of the most misused verses of the New Testament lies in I Corinthians 9:22 where Paul claims 'I have become all things to all people so that by all possible means I might save some'. Some have gone to extremes on this one, arguing that adoption of the ways of sinners is acceptable in order to win them to Christ. Others say that we can justifiably use worldly methods in our evangelistic endeavours. Others interpret the text to mean that Paul was willing to compromise his own lifestyle and message in order to win converts. All such interpretations fail to take account of the historical and literary context of I Corinthians 9:22b which is the struggle between conflicting viewpoints over Christian participation in sacrificial meals in Corinth in the middle of the first century AD. Paul wrestles with this issue in I Corinthians 8–10 and in 8:13 affirms that he will readily change his diet rather than cause anyone to stumble. Thus in I Corinthians 9:22b he will be flexible in social situations and thereby free to place himself, without compromise, alongside those to whom he preaches in the hope of saving some. Far from being selfish, compromising, and morally weak, the true historical context shows that Paul is the very opposite in his overwhelming concern for gospel life and ministry.

A similar case of tearing a biblical text out of its literary and historical context is that of I Corinthians 10:13: 'No temptation has seized you except what is common to man. And God is faithful; he will not let you be tempted beyond what you can bear. But when you are tempted, he will also provide a way out so that you can stand up under it.' This text is frequently quoted, and sometimes preached, as a kind of blanket promise for believers who get into various states of temptation, suffering or dilemma. The promise is offered that because God is faithful, he will set limits to the temptation and provide either help to endure it or an escape route to avoid it. The actual context in history was the involvement of Christians in the cultic sacrificial acts of pagan religion, addressed by Paul in the section I Corinthians 8-10. I Corinthians 10:13 is actually sandwiched between a warning of the danger of falling in 10:12 and a command to flee idolatry in 10:14. It was not a question of God testing the believers but on the contrary of believers pushing God to the limit of his tolerance by their involvement in pagan sacrificial cult (I Cor. 10:9)! Paul is thus saying that, yes, God can be trusted in the trials of life but in the case of this specific historical and literary context, God's escape route is to flee the temptation (1 Cor. 10:14). Far from being a universal crutch and comfort for believers who suffer for whatever reason, 1 Corinthians 10:13 is actually both a promise for those living in the tensions of pagan society and at the same time a profound challenge to avoid any path that might damage our Christian life and witness.

A further example involves misuse of historical context, by which assumptions are sometimes made without any firm basis. Some, for example, have argued that Paul, during his Mars Hill address in Acts 17:22-31, used a philosophical rather than biblical approach. The result they say was that he failed to impress many hearers (Acts 17:32-4) and that when he reached his next city, Corinth, he regretted his Athenian tactic and decided instead to 'know nothing while I was with you except Jesus Christ and him crucified' (1 Cor. 2:2). Such an interpretation, amidst other weaknesses, tries to make an unsubstantiated causal connection between sections of two documents separated in time, place and circumstance. It would be a false conclusion to argue from this that preachers must never allow any philosophy whatsoever to creep into their sermons.

THE ROLES OF HISTORICAL CONTEXT

If these then are the results of mishandling historical context, what then are the areas that we should aim for in our investigation of historical context?

Firstly, we should seek knowledge of the general situation of the writers and recipients of biblical books.

Secondly, a grasp of historical chronology and sequence helps enormously. Errors are commonly made because of historical inaccuracy. Historical sequence is not only important for New Testament exegesis. The significance of large tracts of prophecy in the Old Testament only becomes clear when those passages are studied against their corresponding historical backgrounds.

Thirdly, letters written by the New Testament apostles to churches or groups of believers invite study of the nature and composition of those communities. Some of this material appears in the biblical text itself but other useful historical context can be filled in by turning to the various reference books that will shortly be listed.

Fourthly, letters in the New Testament were generally responses to particular historical circumstances and cannot be adequately expounded without an examination of the specific historical factors that triggered those biblical texts. Reference to historical context not only helps our own understanding and exegesis of texts. It also gives credibility to our interpretation when our hearers can see the text as a response to concrete situations.

QUESTIONS TO ASK REGARDING HISTORICAL CONTEXT

Although it is true that every biblical book was written at a particular point in time and in specific historical circumstances, it is also true that historical significance varies from passage to passage. As you study the biblical text and check details in one or more of the reference tools that follow this section, you should be checking the following sort of issues, as you seek to build up your own understanding of the historical context.

First, look for information and clues in the biblical text that shed light on the historical background of the passage and indeed of the whole book that includes that passage. Try to establish the author's year or period of writing and place of writing. This may not be clear. Indeed it may be difficult or impossible to ascertain. If there are degrees of uncertainty, we must beware of making dogmatic statements that cannot be verified by hard, concrete evidence whether in text or background. In situations where genuine doubt exists, we should not fear losing the respect of our listeners by being open and honest with them concerning the options. Limited use of 'Introduction Books' (see Study Tools) can help us to determine dates, authors, locations, circumstances and chronology. This can be useful, particularly if we plan to preach a series of sermons, but beware of 'information overload'. The biblical text itself is always our primary tool and source of information in sermon preparation.

Secondly, try to extract from the biblical passage information which might indicate the factor(s) that caused the author to put pen to paper. Clues can sometimes be found in the evidence of wars, royal reigns, festivals, crises, doctrinal issues, heresies, people, places, events and circumstances. For example, I Corinthians 7:1 indicates that Paul is responding to a letter from Corinthian believers. We are asking such questions as: Who wrote this biblical book?, What caused the author to write?, Can we detect the author's purpose in writing?, How does the author seek to deal with the situation addressed?

Thirdly, try to locate information in the biblical text and/or in reference books that will shed light on the recipients of the biblical book. For example, we need to ask such questions as:

To whom was the book addressed?

What was the relationship between the author and the readers?

What do we know about the recipients of the author's writing?

Does a weakness in Christian behaviour underlie the letter?

Does a doctrinal misunderstanding underlie the letter?

How does this passage relate to the overall theme of the biblical book that contains it?

Fourthly, try to express the nature of the historical context by writing one or two tentative paragraphs. At this stage, our work on contexts is designed to aid our own understanding of the biblical passage and in the final sermon, it may well be that only a fraction of our work on historical context will actually appear. Nevertheless, historical context needs to be investigated, written out on rough paper and reviewed in subsequent stages of our exegesis and exposition. Historical context, after all, is one of the key parameters by which we reduce the chances of misunderstanding, misinterpretation and misapplication of a biblical text. We need to take great care in handling historical data, lest we become guilty of using misleading, inaccurate or exaggerated information. Remember the motto: 'Honest with the text; honest with the people'. We can now add: 'Honest with the context'!

STUDY TOOLS FOR HISTORICAL CONTEXT

Material that helps us grasp the historical context of our expository passage is to be found not only in the biblical text itself, but also in various sections of such reference books as:

R. B. Dillard, and T. Longman III, *An Introduction to the Old Testament* (Grand Rapids: Zondervan, 1995)

R. K. Harrison, *Introduction to the Old Testament* (London, The Tyndale Press, 1970)

E. J. Young, *An Introduction to the Old Testament* 3rd ed. rev. (London: The Tyndale Press, 1964)

W. S. Lasor, D. A. Hubbard, F. W. Bush, *Old Testament Survey – the Message, Form, and Background of the Old Testament* (Grand Rapids: Eerdmans, 1982)

E. H. Merrill, *A Historical Survey of the Old Testament* (NJ : Presbyterian and Reformed, 1979)

D. Guthrie, *New Testament Introduction* (London: IVP, 1970)

D. A. Carson, D. J. Moo and L. Morris, *An Introduction to the New Testament* (Leicester: Apollos, 1992)

W. G. Kummel, *Introduction to the New Testament* (Nashville: Abingdon Press, 1966)

L. T. Johnson, *The Writings of the New Testament – an interpretation* (London: SCM Press, 1986)

Various Old Testament Commentaries recommended in Tremper Longman, *Old Testament Commentary Survey*, 2nd ed. (Grand Rapids: Baker Book House, 1995)

Various New Testament Commentaries recommended in D. A. Carson, *New Testament Commentary Survey*, 4th ed. (Leicester: IVP, 1993)

CASE STUDY – HISTORICAL CONTEXT: LUKE 4:1-13

Bearing in mind historical datings in the book of Acts, together with the destruction of the Jerusalem temple in AD 70, scholars have tended to date Luke's Gospel between the late sixties and late seventies of the first century AD. The place of composition of his gospel is uncertain, though there are strong arguments that he was a native of Philippi and also that he originated in Syrian Antioch.

Of greater significance for the purpose of exegesis and exposition is the immediate historical context of our specific passage. The temptations of Jesus are firmly linked with the baptism account in Luke 3:21-3, sharing the common themes of 'Holy Spirit', 'Jordan River' and 'Son of God'. Luke sees the temptations of Jesus as part of the divine preparation of Jesus for his ministry. Historical sequence is important here.

Two issues regarding historicity will require at least our consideration, as they may well arise in the minds of our listeners.

(a) Clearly there were no witnesses to these temptations and therefore some scholars have doubted the reality of these temptations in Jesus' life. This is only really a problem for those adhering to a narrow literalism. Jesus himself connected temptation with the work of Satan (Mark 8:33) and Jesus may well have presented his temptation experience as teaching material for his disciples.

(b) Some of our sermon listeners may question how Jesus could have seen in an instant all the kingdoms of the world (Luke 4:5). This raises the issue of whether Jesus' experience was literal or visionary. A number of scholars concur that the three temptations were possibly experienced in a vision, but that does not stop the vision being real and true.

(B) SOCIOCULTURAL AND RELIGIOUS CONTEXT

It is to the sociocultural and religious background that we now turn our attention. Study of these matters can greatly enhance biblical exposition but we must be careful to select material in relation to three overriding concerns.

(a) Will this background information enrich and deepen the preacher's and hearers' understanding of the main and sub-themes of the biblical passage?

(b) Will this material aid the process of clear communication of the biblical text?

(c) Will this material actually make a difference to the meaning of the text?

If our study of sociocultural and religious contexts produces a positive answer to any or all of these three questions, then we must pay serious attention to it.

The sort of issues that will stimulate our study include: the sociocultural environment, the customs and practices, and the thought-worlds of the biblical author and readers. This is an enormous challenge. Indeed these three contexts present a lifelong project for study and research. At least three warnings need to be heeded as we embark on such a venture.

First, in the ancient world, it is impossible to separate the social, cultural and religious elements of background issues. They are intricately related and overlapped because of the people's holistic world view and communal, rather than individualistic, ways of thinking. The study of religion cannot therefore be attempted in isolation from study of its associated societies and cultures. This makes study of cultural backgrounds fascinating, but at the same time complex.

Secondly, common cultural assumptions were not normally explained by the biblical writers. That means that part of our task as expository preachers is to check out and consider those elements of a biblical passage whose meaning and significance may not be obvious to the twenty-first century reader and listener.

Thirdly, in studying sociocultural and religious background, we need to try to find out the date and actual location of material. Some practices in the ancient world were universal but others were restricted to certain localities only. Of course we must also realize that most of the material that existed in ancient times has been lost to us, so we are working with limited, yet important, resources. Thus we must often draw cautious and tentative conclusions, not becoming despondent over the paucity of direct parallel evidence, but rejoicing that background study can and does produce helpful insight and therefore deeper understanding. Certainly we must avoid making dogmatic claims unless there is solid, concrete evidence for such claims in our biblical texts or backgrounds.

WHY THESE CONTEXTS MATTER

Just as we have argued that social, cultural and religious contexts are inextricably linked, so also there exists great overlap between historical context, sociocultural and religious context and literary context. These three contexts of a biblical passage constantly touch each other and although we are here treating them separately for the sake of clarity and organization, nevertheless we cannot think of any one facet without taking account of the other members of the trio. Social, cultural and religious backgrounds sometimes do exercise major bearing on the meaning and interpretation of a biblical passage and we ignore them at our peril. Two brief examples will serve as evidence.

First, sometimes evangelical preachers have treated the book of Proverbs as a treasure chest of promises ripe for the claiming, like grapes pleading to be plucked from the vine. Such an approach is in danger of ignoring both the religious mindset of the ancients and the literary contexts of the proverbs themselves. The religious context of the Old Testament Wisdom Literature as a whole includes an underlying realization that all human activity is surrounded by a real element of mystery that includes the mysterious role of God. Many sayings indeed point out the ambiguities and uncertainties of life. The proverbs do give direction on how to live under the fear of God but the contexts in which they were written and compiled in ancient times did not treat the proverbs as simple promises or as case law. If we fail to take account of this background, we will fall into the trap of preaching individual proverbs as guaranteed promises which must work in all situations and circumstances.

Second, Paul wrote a letter to Philemon concerning the latter's slave, Onesimus, who for some reason had run away from Philemon and taken refuge with Paul. The apostle is writing to Philemon to make a request, without explicitly stating the nature of that request, though strongly hinting at the possibility of Onesimus' being released by Philemon for ministry to Paul in the stressful days of his imprisonment. The letter throws up a number of questions in the mind of an expositor. Why does Paul praise God for the evidence of Philemon's love and faith (Philem. 4-7), only to follow it by a veiled threat to command Philemon to take action (vv. 8-10)? Why does Paul wait until verse 21 before making a veiled demand for Philemon's granting of the request? The answers may well lie in the subtleties and indirectness of interpersonal social obligation and communication in the ancient world, closely paralleled today in some societies of the developing world. Why does Paul say he is sending Onesimus back to Philemon (Philem. 12)? Why does Paul offer to make financial restitution for Onesimus' absence from Philemon (vv. 18-20)? The answers lie in the requirements of the Graeco-Roman legal system which compelled fleeing slaves to be returned to their masters and required compensation to be paid to the masters for loss of income due to the slaves' absence from work. Such background study truly will enrich our understanding of the text and greatly enhance our exposition of that divine Word. Once again, however, beware of excessive detail which can so easily produce information overload and indigestion for our hearers.

Study tools for sociocultural and religious contexts

D. R. W. Wood, *New Bible Dictionary,* rev. 3rd ed. (Leicester: IVP, 1996)

E. H. Merrill, *Kingdom of Priests: A History of Old Testament Israel* (Michigan: Baker Book House, 1987)

E. M. Yamauchi, *Persia and the Bible* (Grand Rapids: Baker Book House, 1990)

Walter Kaiser, *The Messiah in the Old Testament* (Carlisle: Paternoster Press, 1995)

Eduard Lohse, *The New Testament Environment* (London: SCM Press, 1976)

H. C. Kee, *Understanding the New Testament* 4th ed. (London: Prentice Hall, 1983)

N. G. L. Hammond, and H. H. Scullard, *The Oxford Classical Dictionary* 2nd ed. (Oxford: Clarendon, 1970)

E. Ferguson, *Backgrounds of Early Christianity* 2nd ed. (Grand Rapids: Eerdmans, 1993)

G. A. Butterick, et al, *The Interpreter's Dictionary of the Bible,* 4 vols. (Nashville: Abingdon Press, 1962)

G. W. Bromiley, et al, *The International Standard Bible Encyclopedia,* rev. ed. 4 vols. (Grand Rapids: Eerdmans, 1979-88)

Case study – sociocultural and religious contexts: Luke 4:1-13

When we come to the Lucan text, we need to bear in mind both the world to which it gives witness, namely Palestine in the first decades AD and the world into which the gospel was written, namely the Graeco-Roman world of the later decades of the first century AD.

We know that in the ancient world there existed 'holy men', such as Honi the Circle-Drawer and Hanina ben Dosa, who called on Yahweh to work supernatural miracles. In Luke's Gospel, by contrast,

Jesus is portrayed as directly manifesting the saving power of God because he possessed divine authority to do so. The Christian apologist Justin, in his *Dialogue* 69.7, noted that some Jews taught that Jesus' supernatural powers of healing, for example, demonstrated deceitful magic arts. Within the Jewish tradition, Jesus was often portrayed as a sorcerer and deceiver of people, and it is this sort of background material that helps to explain why Jesus was charged with corrupting and deceiving the people (Luke 23:1-5). It helps also to explain why Luke's Gospel itself admits that there were those who saw Jesus' supernatural power and yet attributed it to Jesus' role as an agent of Beelzebub (Luke 11:14-15). We need to be mindful that in the ancient Near East, in contrast to much current Western religious thinking, the 'supernatural' was a perfectly 'natural' phenomenon. Familiarity with the spirit world was normal.

Such background material helps us to understand the worlds in which Jesus lived and Luke wrote, but at the same time, we must bear in mind that Luke's overriding concern was theological. He sought to provide meaning and significance for the events he described, rather than trying to argue or prove their veracity. Thus he shows how God is at work through the events he recounts. Salvation is Luke's overriding concern, and he sets the ministry of Jesus very firmly in the context of Spirit anointing in Luke 1–4. Though not uninterested in historicity, Luke offers no witnesses for example who might verify or corroborate the testing of Jesus in the wilderness.

(c) LITERARY CONTEXT

We have tried to establish the historical setting in which author and readers lived and the particular historical circumstances that triggered the writing of each biblical book. We have then sought to identify the sociocultural and religious background material that impinges on our text and might shed light on that text. Our next context – and one of great importance – is literary context. In other words, our preaching passage needs to be viewed in relation not only to its immediate literary setting in the biblical book but also within the wider context of the whole book. Thus, although we do not need to include detailed exegesis from outside our sermon passage, we definitely do need to decide how the preceding and succeeding verses shed light on our exposition of the preaching passage itself. In order to understand and explain the contents of our passage, we must be able to see how the passage develops out of what precedes it and how it relates to what follows it. It is thus in the area of literary context that we make the transition into the study of content. Literary context is the bridge that links contexts with contents. Generally speaking study of the surrounding literary context of a passage is seariously neglected in sermon preperation. Literary context no only yields vital clues to the meaning of a passage but it also helps us disern the purpose and application of the text. In my view it is failure to consider literary context that accounts for most weaknesses and errors in our interpration. Literary context is not an optional extra: to ignore it is to invite disaster. Thus for example, I Corinthians 9 has been considered a digression by Paul but in reality, that chapter is an integral part of Paul's arguement in chapters 8 and 10 regarding Christian particaption in pagan sacrificial meals. Paul reminds his readers in I Corinthians 9 of his apostolic authority in readieness for his attack on idolitary in chapter 10. He also expresses in chapter 9 his readieness to foresake rights for the sake of the gospel. This connects directly to his previous teaching in I Corinthians 8:13. He gives a warning to his readers not to insist on there rights to eat sacrificial food. Similarly, whilst it is true I Corinthians 13 appears regulary in the Order of Service at weddings, its real context lies in I Corinthians 12–14, for I Corinthians 13 is basically a corective for abuse in the exercise of spiritual gifts, notebly tongues. Context and contents are two sides of the same coin. Ignore literary context and we really do risk failure to locate the exegetical key to our sermon passage. It has to be said that preachers who dive straight into the content of their passage, without paying serious attention to its literary context, have potential for deficant, defective and deviant sermons. Literary context is that important.

The handling of literary context

The most vital tool we possess for the elucidation of the literary context of a passage is the actual biblical text itself. With the text open before us, a number of stages will help us to examine and evaluate the literary context of any passage of Scripture.

1. Content. In considering the role of our particular sermon passage within its wider literary context, we must begin with a brief examination of the sermon passage itself. There is great value in writing a paragraph about our selected biblical passage, in answer to the following questions:

Who is writing and who is being addressed?

What is the key central issue or theme?

What are the related sub-issues or themes?

What is being said about these themes?

This stage consists basically of the main and sub-themes identification from Step Two but with a little more detail..

2. Wider context. If we are dealing with a biblical book consisting of half a dozen chapters or less, then we ought to write out a basic summary of the main teaching of the book, with brief notes on the content of each section. Some of Paul's epistles lend themselves to this method. If, however, we are preaching a passage from the middle of Genesis, Isaiah or Revelation, we certainly ought to apply this procedure to several chapters before and after our passage. Our main guideline for the delimiting of wider context will be the thoughts, purposes, themes and organizational sections of the biblical writer. We must feel free to use our own discretion in deciding the extent of biblical text to be considered, for this will vary according to the passage being preached.

3. Immediate context. Special attention must be given to the chapter preceding and the chapter following our passage remembering of course that chapter and verse divisions were not a part of the original biblical text. Certainly we must focus especially on the six to ten verses immediately before and after our passage, asking the same basic questions that we asked in Section One 'Content' in this present analysis. Write a paragraph or series of notes.

4. Content in context. We must now give careful thought to the ways in which the 'Content' of Section One relates to the wider and immediate contexts. In order to make this comparison, we need to write a short explanation of how the content of our passage relates and contributes to the overall literary context and, vice versa, how the surrounding literary context affects our understanding of the passage itself. We must ask several questions of our content:

What is the point of each sentence?

What is the point of each paragraph?

How does our content relate to what comes before?

How does our content relate to what follows?

How does our content fit into the overall argument, encouragement or challenge of the biblical author?

What is the literary form of our passage, e.g. opening greeting, prayer, thanksgiving, main body, conclusion?

How does the surrounding literary context mould our understanding of the sermon passage itself?

These paragraphs of raw material on literary context do not need to be polished sculptures. Nor should we feel compelled to follow every detail of every step in the order presented in this plan – be flexible in your gathering of material, according to the needs of your own particular passage. Sometimes for example it may be more helpful to consider Immediate Context before, rather than after, Wider Context or to study both simultaneously. Nor should we expect to include in the final sermon lengthy quantities of material from passages before and after our specific sermon passage. Some of that material may well be included, but the main issue in studying literary context is to gain insight into, and understanding of, the content, contexts and purposes of the biblical authors. If, as preachers, we fail in that task, then we will have nothing of value to offer our sermon listeners. God has revealed his Word and his will through the verses of Scripture, but individual verses or passages must never be regarded or treated as islands. Verses and passages only gain meaning and significance as they are viewed in relation to their wider literary context. It is that process which helps us discern the point and purpose of the biblical author's words in any given context. That is the basis of sound exposition. As we identify purpose, so we can expound the intention, meaning and application intended by the Holy Spirit for that passage. That is what makes expository preaching so powerful and life-changing.

CASE STUDY – LITERARY CONTEXT: LUKE 4:1-13

Working from the English text of the NIV, let us now apply this framework of stages to our case study passage in order to gather raw material on its literary contexts. This will add to our collection of rough paper material that will be used eventually but selectively for the construction of the complete sermon. One of the benefits of studying literary context is that it forces us to read, reread, study and apply our minds to the biblical text in which God's power resides.

Stage One: Content. Luke's Gospel is an account compiled from eye-witness accounts and presented to Theophilus for the purpose of strengthening faith and assurance concerning the things he had been taught (1:2-4). The passage for preaching (4:1-13) falls into three major units, each of which deals with one of Satan's temptations of Jesus – vv. 3-4, 5-8 and 9-12. Short narrative sections both open (vv. 1-2) and close (v. 13) our chosen passage. The key theme certainly revolves round the devil's attempts to tempt Jesus and in response to each of the three temptations, Jesus quotes Old Testament Scripture from the book of Deuteronomy. The three temptations challenge Jesus:

a) to change stone into bread to satisfy his physical needs;

b) to worship Satan in order to receive from him earthly power and glory;

c) to throw himself off the temple in order to demonstrate the power of the angels to save him.

Stage Two: Wider context. The preceding context of our sermon passage deals with the foretelling and fulfilment of the births of John the Baptist and Jesus (Luke 1:1–2:20). The remainder of Luke 2 records the appearance of Jesus in the Jerusalem temple, both at his presentation (2:21-40) and at a later celebration of the Passover (2:41-52). The ministry of John the Baptist is described by Luke in 3:1-20, followed by the baptism of Jesus (3:21-2) and a record of his genealogy (3:23-38).

In the literary context that follows Luke 4:1-13, Luke picks up the inauguration of Jesus' public ministry (3:23) and develops this by relating Jesus' rejection at Nazareth (4:14-30). Subsequent chapters give account of Jesus' ministry of exorcism (4:31-7), healing (4:38-44, 5:12-26, 6:6-11), miracles (5:1-11) and teaching (5:27-39, 6:1-5,12-49).

Stage Three: Iimmediate context. The immediately preceding context of 4:1-13 seems to lie in the text of 3:21-38. In addition to the event of Jesus' baptism and the descent of the Holy Spirit, the main focus is on the Sonship of Christ and his approval by the Father (3:22b-38). Indeed, the Sonship of Christ had been referred to previously by Luke in his opening chapters (1:32, 35, 2:49).

The immediately following context of Luke 4:1-13 can be read in 4:14-30 in which a number of crucial themes are developed: Jesus' Spirit-anointed teaching ministry (4:14-15), his personal fulfilment of Old Testament prophecy (4:16-21), his rejection by the people of his home town, Nazareth and God's care for those outside Israel (4:22-30).

Stage Four: Content in context. When we review the content of our sermon passage in light of its contexts, a number of patterns begin to emerge.

a) The opening of Jesus' public ministry at the age of thirty was attended by severe testing in the wilderness. Thus Luke 3:23 links with 4:1.

b) The anointing of Jesus with the Holy Spirit (3:22) links with the fullness of the Spirit in 4:1a, his being led by the Spirit in the desert (4:1b) and his return to Galilee in the power of the Spirit (4:14) following his wilderness testing.

c) The reference to Jesus' Sonship in 3:22, 23-38 is picked up again in 4:3, 9 and 41 in the challenges thrown down by Satan. This is a 'seed-thought' to which we must return.

d) The power, authority and victory attributed to Jesus and manifested through his temptations (4:1, 4, 8, 12 and 14) appear again and again as marks of his early ministry (4:18-19, 21, 30, 32, 35-6, 39, 40-1).

Thus several patterns have already emerged from the text, indicating the existence of a network of links between content and literary context. It will become apparent in later steps just how vital this study has been — none of it will be wasted on the journey towards powerful and effective exposition of our preaching passage.

6. Practical Steps
Step Four
Contents Analysis

In Steps One and Two we sought to establish the Main and Sub-themes of our passage by opening the wide angle lens of our camera across the whole passage. The purpose of Step Three (Context Analysis) and Step Four (Contents Analysis) is to use our zoom lens to focus on the detail of our biblical passage. Steps Three and Four are the heavy, detailed and time-consuming stages of exegetical work on the biblical text, but without them our sermon will be seriously flawed. Eventually the detail of these two steps will enable us to reconsider the Main and Sub-themes of Steps One and Two, confirming, modifying or rejecting those themes, according to our discoveries. It needs to be said that Steps Three and Four can bring discouragement and a temporary sense of loss of direction in the preparation. The greatest temptation to take shortcuts in preparation will be experienced during Steps Three and Four. Do not yield to temptation or discouragement – the fruits of faithfulness in study of contexts and contents will soon become wonderfully clear and abundant. Steps Three and Four must be treated with great patience and perseverance, not to mention prayerfulness. The final reward for diligence in Steps Three and Four will far outweigh the struggle and sweat of preparation.

GOALS OF CONTENT STUDY

Step Four involves study of a number of angles from which we want to approach the actual written material contained within our chosen biblical passage/theme. Our primary concern at this stage is still to discern what the biblical writer was trying to communicate to the original readers. Whilst the overall emphasis of Step Four focuses on the actual content and make-up of the sermon passage itself, this work will be rendered inaccurate and inadequate if we ignore all our previous work on contexts in Step Three. These two steps are like the two sides of a single coin. In a real sense, Step Four is the most vital of all and for a number of reasons.

First, it is our God-given call and responsibility faithfully to proclaim the Word of God. In handling God's Word, our personal goals must be true understanding leading to clear explanation. Even if some of our hearers might be less than energetic or committed to their own study of Scripture, we ourselves must never be open to that charge. Exposition involves understanding, proclaiming and explaining the Word of God as clearly as we can.

Second, although Scripture is divinely inspired and fully authoritative, it was nevertheless written down by human beings and is now being prepared for exposition by human beings. Precisely because of these human elements, we must seek a way to avoid the potential and real pitfalls of personal viewpoints, speculative opinions, haphazard interpretations and appeals to various human authorities. It is by serious study of context and content that we give sound and sufficient justification for our interpretation of biblical texts.

Third, there is the peril of assuming that all our theological views are biblical and thus true. Failure to take context and content seriously in our preparation could and does reinforce errors and weaknesses. That is the danger posed by uncritical preparation and uncritical acceptance of inherited traditions and traditional interpretations. It is by being critical in the right and positive sense that we treat Scripture most honestly, effectively and powerfully.

Fourth, we, as twenty-first century preachers, suffer the consequences of distance — our separation in time, space, thought and culture from the original biblical authors and readers. In seeking to understand a biblical text, we must allow our own thoughts to be controlled by the thought of the biblical text in its various contexts. We must beware of imposing our own thoughts on the text. Failure to face the challenge of distance often produces preachers who think they know what the text means but actually don't!

METHOD

The purpose, meaning and application of any biblical passage will become clear to us only through our detailed attention to the words of that Scripture. Every passage, however, has many words, built into phrases, sentences, verses, paragraphs and finally the complete passage. So where do we begin if we are not to lose sight of the overall wood because of all the trees in that wood? In order to avoid that very danger, let us reverse the order of those constituent parts, so that we do not get bogged down in the tiny details of many words. This suggested order of treatment is not to be thought of as set in concrete, for we can alter the sequence freely and move frequently backwards and forwards within this method. In short, every passage content that we prepare for exposition – paragraphs, verses, sentences, phrases and words – ought to be considered from at least four angles, as we continue to gather raw material on index cards or rough paper or on computer. Our work on the content of the passage must incorporate, to some degree, each of the following considerations, though the precise mix of these ingredients will vary with each passage. Our goal at this step is not the production of perfect, polished notes, but rather the steady accumulation of all the raw material information that we shall use in the eventual writing up of the sermon.

STAGE ONE – COLUMN ANALYSIS

Our first task within content study is to examine and evaluate our passage in its entirety. Let us begin by assessing the structure of the passage. This will require not only the wide angle lens to discern the broad structure and big picture but also the zoom lens to allow us to focus on the finer points of the detail. So we begin with the whole passage in its structure and work towards those multiple component parts, the words. That should reduce any tendency toward frustration, discouragement or despondency in the preacher!

One of the best methods for seeking an overview of the structure and content of a biblical passage is that proposed by Denis Lane[1] in which he suggests that the content of the passage can be handwritten or typed down the left-hand side of a sheet of paper. This can be done verse by verse with a space between each verse. Each verse needs to be divided into its constituent thoughts. It can be helpful to locate

---

1. Denis Lane, *Preach the Word* (Welwyn: Evangelical Press, 1979), p.37ff.

the main verbs along with subject and object. All the other phrases in a verse can then be listed down the left-hand half of the page, allowing a space between phrases. Following a time of prayer, thought and meditation, you can then use the right-hand side of the sheet, corresponding to each phrase of each verse on the left-hand side, to express briefly, and in your own words, the main points being made on the left-hand side. If thoughts occur to you from your study of main theme, sub-themes, background and contexts, then a brief note could be added on the right-hand side but keep the right-hand half as simple and uncluttered as possible. An alternative method might be to divide the sheet into three vertical columns – left for biblical text, centre for your own brief version of what the writer is saying, and right for short exegetical comments that might occur to you as you think about the passage.

The vital thing in this column analysis is that the thoughts that you express briefly on the right-hand side of the sheet must arise from what is stated in the passage. These thoughts should not be speculation or invention or development: they must be absolutely rooted in the text of the biblical passage. We are not at this stage looking for a highly polished, literary masterpiece on the right-hand side of your sheet. Once you have finished all the right-hand side comments, you can begin to look for patterns, reasons, results, causes, statements, commands, questions and doctrines. If there are a number of distinct themes, similar ideas, connected thoughts or contrasting units, or combinations thereof, it is helpful to employ a system of numbering and/or lettering in order to highlight such patterns on the right-hand side of your sheet. This material will form the basis of the Outline for our expository sermon (Step Six).

This type of column analysis could actually be attempted between Steps One and Two or Steps Two and Three, for one of its values lies in its help in establishing the main theme and sub-themes of the passage. Its second major contribution is in identifying the specific issues of grammar and exegesis that need to be addressed during our preparation of Step Four. Of significance also is the usefulness of column analysis in helping us to see patterns of thought in a passage. Thus column analysis leads us to grasp the overall thinking, intention and purpose of the biblical writer and this in turn sheds light on a possible outline that will act as a framework for our move from exegesis to expository sermon through Steps 5-7.

CASE STUDY – COLUMN ANALYSIS
LUKE 4:1-13

v. 1 Jesus,	Son of God the Father (see Luke 3:21-38)
full of the Holy Spirit,	empowered by the Spirit, the third person of the Trinity
returned from the Jordan	place of baptism – recognition by the Father and anointing by Spirit
And was led by the Spirit in the desert	under the Spirit's leading and control even in remote places between Jerusalem and Dead Sea
v. 2 where for forty days	Prolonged testing
he was tempted	Trial/ temptation came to Jesus
by the devil.	The devil as agent of temptation
He ate nothing	Total fast
during those days,	Continuous fast
and at the end of them	Completed fast
he was hungry.	A). Result: State of weakness
	Real and direct communication
v. 3 The devil said to him,	
'If you are the Son of God,	B). Goals:
	1. To doubt Jesus' Sonship
	2. To doubt divine provision
tell this stone to become bread'.	3. To misuse miraculous power.
	4. To act outside God's will.
v. 4 Jesus answered,	C). Response: Real and direct communication
'It is written: "Man does not live on bread alone".'	D). Biblical Authority – the needs of mankind are not merely physical (Deut. 8:3)
v. 5 The devil led him up to a high place and	Jesus transported by the devil

showed him in an instant all the kingdoms of the world.

offer of material/political power

v. 6 And he said to him, 'I will give you all their authority and splendour,
for it has been given to me, and I can give it to
anyone I want to.

B). Goal: Offer of worldly power and glory

v. 7 So if you worship me, it will all be yours.'

Basis: A deluded devil:
1. the world's glory did not belong to him
2. He was not free to dispense it
Condition for worldly gain:
devil worship

v. 8 Jesus answered,

'It is written:
"Worship the Lord your God and serve him only."'

C). Response: Real and direct communication
D). Biblical Authority – God alone is Sovereign and He alone merits our exclusive loyalty (Deut. 6:13).

v. 9 The devil led him to Jerusalem and had him stand on the highest point of the temple. 'If you are the Son of God,' he said, 'throw yourself down from here.'

Jesus transported by the devil to Another high place

B). Goal:
1. to doubt Jesus' Sonship
2. to put God to the test
3. to misuse miraculous power
4. to push Jesus outside God's will.

v. 10 For it is written 'He will command his angels concerning you
to guard you carefully;

The devil also uses Scripture from Psalm 91:11-12

The devil omits 'to guard you in all your ways'.

they will lift you up in their hands,
so that you will not strike your foot against a stone.'

The devil promotes false trust.

The devil misapplies Scripture.

v. 12 Jesus answered,

'It says: "Do not put the Lord your God to the test."'

C). Response: Real and direct communication
D). Biblical Authority – we must not put God to the proof
(Deut. 6:16).

v. 13 When the devil had finished

The devil works to a permitted plan

all this tempting,	
he left him	There are limits to testing by the devil
until an opportune time.	The devil waits for our vulnerable moments

STAGE 2 – GRAMMATICAL ANALYSIS

Grammatical issues constitute one element of sermon preparation that is liable to leave the preacher feeling inadequate, insecure and even threatened. At this point we all need to face the profound challenge issued by Haddon Robinson:

> Accuracy, not to speak of integrity, demands that we develop every possible skill to keep us from declaring in the name of God what the Holy Spirit never intended to convey.[2]

This is a very solemn warning; one to be taken with the utmost seriousness and one which we shall seek to address in this section. The danger of course is to slide to one extreme or the other. To ignore grammatical issues totally is to court disaster. Indeed any serious attempt to do biblical exegesis must of necessity involve us in grammatical issues, even if only at the most basic level of seeking the subject, verb and object of a sentence. At the other extreme, it will not help the cause of expository preaching if we become terrified in attempting exegesis, obsessed by the fear that we miss the one fine point of grammar without which our entire exegesis and consequent exposition will be utterly wrecked! Let us be realistic, realizing that God knows our limitations and in any case is more committed to effective and powerful expository preaching than we ourselves are. He helps and guides us constantly throughout our preparation, even with grammatical analysis, for such work will shed further necessary light on the purpose, meaning and application of a biblical passage.

2. Haddon Robinson, *Expository Preaching – Principles and Practice*, (Grand Rapids: Baker Book House, 1980), p.59.

METHOD OF TREATMENT

Again there is no fixed and set-in-concrete methodology, but grammatical issues can be broadly encompassed at four levels, beginning again with the broad picture and moving on to the smaller and finer details. The goal is not only to discern the meaning and significance of individual words but also, and ultimately more importantly, to reach a larger perspective on the relationships between the various words and word groups in the sentences that make up our biblical passage.

(a) The whole text

In seeking to analyse the details of content, a preacher who has competence in Hebrew and/or Greek can carry out a translation from those original languages. This process can certainly help to pinpoint the location of grammatical issues that may require further attention. Whether working from the text in its original language or using a good English translation, we may discover for certain verses in our passage that there may be one or more possible translations, for textual, grammatical or stylistic reasons. As a general rule, such textual variants ought to be checked by the preacher in his preparation but only sparingly mentioned in the actual sermon itself.

If, however, a textual variant might affect the actual meaning of the passage and therefore our understanding, interpretation and application of the text, then we must pay serious attention to the arguments for and against alternative renderings. Even where there is no textual variant, we may nevertheless encounter genuine differences of opinion over interpretation. In such situations, context will be our major arbiter for interpretation. If there are any difficult or inconclusive issues in the text of the passage, we need to be honest with our sermon listeners. We must avoid sweeping difficulties underneath the carpet or pretending they do not exist – that will lose us the respect of our more discerning listeners. If we know of a major textual variant that will be reflected in the English versions being used by our listeners, then, if appropriate, we ought to deal with the issue carefully, briefly and sensitively. At the same time we will be careful not to undermine the reliability and credibility of Scripture and translations.

(b) The individual sentence

Analysis of sentence structure enables us to identify key grammatical issues, the development of an argument, the relationships between words and word groups and the basic thought and purpose of the passage as a whole. The 'Column Analysis' method will help greatly in locating points of grammar. Any single sentence should be written onto rough paper or index card or typed into our computer to help our analysis of its structure. It will be best to start with the subject, verb and object of the first main clause and write this against the upper left margin. The rest of the sentence can then be spread out towards the right by indenting and downwards by subordinating the remaining and modifying elements of the sentence. A whole variety of useful information can be clarified by this process, as the following examples indicate.

Main subject, verb and object. Let us take a fairly complex sentence like I Corinthians 2:6: 'We do, however, speak a message of wisdom among the mature, but not the wisdom of this age or of the rulers of this age, who are coming to nothing.' Whenever we analyse a sentence in Scripture, whatever the genre or type of literature, we should look for the main verb, followed closely by a search for the main controlling subject and object of that main verb. Thus, in I Corinthians 2:6 the main verb is 'speak', with the subject 'we' and object 'a message of wisdom'. Subject, main verb and object provide us with the basic framework of the whole sentence and their discovery, particularly in a long sentence, can be vital for our grasp of meaning. 'Diagramming' is simply a tool that helps to break up a sentence so that we can identify its key ingredients.

Subordinate Clauses. Once we have established the subject, main verb and object, we can then consider additional phrases that complement the main clause and complete the meaning of the whole sentence. Thus, in the case of I Corinthians 2:6, several pieces of information now emerge:

'among the mature' – prepositional phrase.

'not the wisdom of this age, nor of the rulers of this age' – genitive constructions.

'who are coming to nothing' – adjectival participle.

Such a breakdown into parts of speech enables us to gain a picture of their form, function and meaning within the sentence. When we use this method to line up contrasting or similar words or phrases directly underneath one another, according to their form and function, we begin to get a clearer picture of patterns and relationships within and between biblical texts.

Thus, if we add I Corinthians 2:7-8,[3] the following breakdown of grammar emerges:

However
we speak   wisdom
   among the mature
      but
         not the wisdom   of this age
         not of the rulers
              of this age
        who are coming to nothing
but
we speak   wisdom
   a secret   wisdom   of God
        that   has been hidden
        that   God predestined
              for our glory
              before time began
        that none   understood
      of the rulers
      of this age
for
if they had (understood)
   they would not have crucified   the Lord
        of Glory

Having broken down the sentence, paragraph or passage in this way, we can now see the various relationships between the parts of speech by which the words and phrases operate. Such analysis helps

---

3. A fuller version of this diagramming, with Greek and English texts, can be seen, along with further helpful examples, in G. D. Fee, *New Testament Exegesis, Rev. Ed. – A Handbook for Students and Pastors*, (Westminster: John Knox Press, 1993), pp. 69-80.

us to identify contrasts, similarities, reasons, results, implications, all of which indicate the overall thoughts and themes of the passage. These could be further clarified if we give them numbers, letters or even colour-coding! Amidst the phrases, and often connecting the phrases, we can identify certain small, single words that can act as significant markers in a text. To these signals we must now turn, for their role can be of paramount importance in the task of expository preaching.

(c) The structural indicators

Despite their small size, such words can be immensely important in conveying the meaning of texts. Often these markers will take one of the following forms.

Conjunctions. Words that join related things together, such as 'but', 'and', 'nor', 'if', 'although', 'because', 'that', 'lest', 'since' or 'until'. Sometimes a conjunction can also function as an adverb, as in the case of 'therefore', 'so', 'however' and 'since'. The phrase 'in order that' expresses a purpose, 'because' offers a reason, and 'therefore' draws a conclusion or inference. The word 'but' can indicate mere continuation but it can also show a contrast with what preceded it.

Relative Pronouns. Words that play the part of a noun in a sentence and have reference to an antecedent, e.g. The boy read the book *that* he had just bought. Others are 'who', 'which', 'what', 'whose', 'such as', and 'as'.

Demonstrative Pronouns. Words that indicate which specific noun is intended by the writer/speaker, e.g's. *this* book, *that* pen, *those* bananas, *these* apples.

Returning briefly to our example of 1 Corinthians 2:6-8, we can observe the function of these structural indicators. In 1 Corinthians 1:1–2:5 the apostle Paul attacks human wisdom as a way of coming to know God (1:21) and in 2:4-5 he denies having spoken in words of persuasive human wisdom. Then, suddenly, in 2:6 we see Paul setting up a great contrast by using the conjunction 'but' and repeating it in the second half of that verse. A further contrast is triggered in 2:8 by the word 'but' as Paul reveals the nature of true wisdom. He then continues his argument by the use of further structural indicators –

'for if' (2:8), 'however' (2:9), 'but' (2:10). These short marker words function as structural hinges on which meaning and interpretation hang: their significance far exceeds their small size.

(d) Key word analysis

We have now arrived at the smallest unit of our passage: the individual word. As in the case of grammatical issues, so also the investigation of specific words will vary in importance from passage to passage but will be significant for the preacher's own preparation and understanding of the biblical passage. Words are vital but we must not let the final sermon become a 'patchwork quilt' of highly detailed word studies that will dominate and probably destroy the sermon. We must be very carefully selective of what we allow into our final product. With that in mind, here is a suggested procedure for the analysis of key words that might appear in our biblical passage. Bear in mind, however, that not every text will contain key words that require detailed study.

1. Select significant words. Not every word in a passage of Scripture will require our attention in terms of special study. A useful first step, however, is to list words of likely significance in our sermon passage. Thus, if we plan to preach from 1 Peter 2:18-25, our list might be as follows: slaves, submit, harsh, commendable, suffer, called, example, tree, wounds, healed, Shepherd and Overseer. To varying degrees, of course, the preacher will take account of all these words but as far as public explanation is concerned, confinement to just one or two key terms will normally be sufficient. Thus, for example, some background information on the wide variation in the nature of Graeco-Roman slavery would be very helpful. Some slaves lived in considerable comfort and could even gain Roman citizenship and rights. Others in the fields, docks and mines led a subhuman existence in appalling conditions. For the latter slaves, the 'stripes' suffered by Christ (1 Pet. 2:20, 21, 24) in order to secure their salvation would have evoked bitter memories of the black-and-blue welts they bore through repeated whippings. Some key words in a passage thus lend themselves to the study of historical, social, cultural and religious context that we have already considered. Here are some guidelines that will help us to choose the sort of words that might become a focus for special study:

Select a word or words whose meanings are not obvious. In the West, in particular, increasingly secular, post-Christian and postmodern tendencies mean that more and more biblical terms are becoming unfamiliar, even to the educated person in the street. A word like 'grace' is by and large meaningless to many people. Not only does 'grace' need to be explained and defined for the average unbeliever but in the context, for example of a Roman Catholic land, 'grace' means different things to different people. Not only that, but even within the Bible itself, there is variation in the use made of the word 'grace'. Thus in I Peter 2:19-20, Peter uses the Greek word *charis* in a way which is variously translated as 'approved' (RSV), 'commendable' (NIV) and 'God will bless you' (GNB).

Select a word or words that are known to be of theological significance, such as 'God', 'hope', 'justification', 'sanctification', 'sin'. In multifaith, multiethnic, pluralistic and postmodern societies, the intended meanings of these terms can no longer be assumed to be understood in any agreed sense. In lands where moral relativism is rampant, the only thing people can do wrong is for them to declare anything to be wrong. In many places, the preacher must now assume virtual or total ignorance in the realms of religious knowledge and terminology.

Select a word or words that may be culturally ambiguous for a twenty-first century reader or listener. I Corinthians 7:1 is translated in several versions as '... it is good/well for a man not to touch a woman' (KJV, NRSV, NASB). The NIV offers '...it is good for a man not to marry' but in a footnote manages to identify the real significance of this euphemistic term: '... it is good for a man not to have sexual relations with a woman'. Clearly in some cases, word translations can radically affect biblical meaning and interpretation.

Select a word or words that are frequently repeated or that function as the central motif of a passage. A key word in I Corinthians 1:26-31 is 'boast', while I Corinthians 14 revolves round 'edify'. An obvious example is the word 'love' which occurs nine times in the NIV translation of I Corinthians 13. Here there is need to offer a word of caution for it has to be said that the study of the root of a word – etymology – rarely helps us to discover and understand its current meaning. Thus, for example, preachers often try to make a sharp distinction between two New Testament verbs for 'love' – *agapao* and *phileo*, arguing that *agapao* refers to a special quality of love over and above all other loves. In reality there is considerable overlap in the range of usages of these two words. Thus, for example, in 2 Timothy 4:10 *agapao* is used with reference to Demas who deserted Paul because he loved this present evil world. The main point for us is to beware of using the root studies of etymology as an absolute and predictable guarantee for meaning at all times, in all places and for all authors. This is erroneous. Meaning derives from usage, not etymology. Indeed those who are equipped with skills in New Testament Greek need to take on board the scholarly realization that the strict rules, regulations and categories of classical Greek tended to relax over time, so that in the New Testament period we encounter a greater amount of flexibility of language, as well as a larger number of grammatical exceptions and irregularities. Caution needs to be exercised but this should not deter us from serious study of key words and phrases.

2. Establish their range of meanings. Sometimes a word exhibits a range of meanings across Scripture and there may be a need, therefore, to trace the historical changes in the meaning of a word. The Greek word *daimonion* in classical times indicated a 'divine being' but in the Hellenistic era it came to mean a being less than divine. In the New Testament the word gained a definitely evil slant for a fallen yet supernatural being. Likewise the Greek term *suneidesis*, used by Paul in I Corinthians 8:7, 10, 12, has a range of meaning from 'awareness', 'knowledge', 'consciousness' to one which approximates to 'moral conscience' and the ability to distinguish right from wrong. If we are dealing with words that do display a range of meanings, we may need to check how the word is used in other writings by the same biblical author and whether or not that author uses an alternative word as a substitute for that word. We may then need to see how the word is used by other biblical authors.

3. Determine meaning in the present context. The flow of an author's writing and our study of the various contexts in which the word is set, should help us to decide the best option for the current use that we are examining. There may even be similar or contrasting words within the same or nearby passages, or in parallel accounts located elsewhere in Scripture, that will act as clues to meaning in our sermon passage context. For example, the 'weak' and the 'strong' appear in Romans 14–15 and the 'weak' are considered in 1 Corinthians 8–10.

Study of these key words should not become an obsession that deflects our thinking about the passage. Ultimately we must remember that meaning is much more than the meaning of individual words, however vital those words might be. Meaning derives from the overall picture – phrases, sentences, genre or type of literature, style, rhetoric, contexts. Even in the writing of this book, I am constantly looking for a variety of ways to express the same word, idea or concept. Likewise biblical authors often selected words for the purpose of variety or alliteration. In the midst of our study of words, we must never ignore the contribution of logic, simplicity and common sense as we seek meaning and understanding. Our public explanations of individual words must neither confuse our hearers nor dominate the content of our expository sermons. Word studies should shed light on a text, not dazzle the hearers or blind them to the overall thrust and intention of the biblical passage. On a practical level, our investigation of key words can be recorded on rough paper, index cards or computer as another stage in the gathering of raw material. During Step Four it will be helpful to take an index card or sheet of paper and use it to deal with one or more verses of our sermon passage. During Steps One to Six, several sheets of paper might be used in this way and we shall then sort out, sift through a 'sieve' and select for inclusion, only the material that will become a part of our final sermon body (Step 7). The following list of tools is intended for selective use, as the biblical passage requires, as your own expertise permits and as available preparation time allows. The list is intended to be neither exhaustive nor exhausting. The very last thing intended is to force you to embark on a trip that leads to frustration, guilt or depression over your key word analysis.

TOOLS FOR KEY WORD ANALYSIS

CONCORDANCES: to search word occurrences and frequencies in the Bible, to see words in their sentence contexts and to identify different shades of meaning across Scripture.

J. R. Kohlenberger III, and E. W. Goodrick, *The NIV Complete Concordance* (London: Hodder and Stoughton, 1983)

Old Testament Hebrew-based: S. Mandelkern, *Concordance on the Bible* ed. C. M. Brecher. 2 vols. (New York: Shulsinger Brothers, 1955)

Old Testament English-based: G. V. Wigram, *The Englishman's Hebrew and Chaldee Concordance of the Old Testament,* 5th ed. (London: Bagster 1890. Reprinted 1980)

Old Testament in Greek: E. Hatch and H. A. Redpath, *A Concordance to the Septuagint and the other versions of the Old Testament,* 2 vols. (New York: International, 1954)

New Testament Greek-based: W. F. Moulton and A. S. Geden, *A Concordance to the Greek Testament,* rev. by H. K. Moulton. 5th ed. (Edinburgh: T & T Clark, 1978)

New Testament English-based: G. V. Wigram, ed., *The Englishman's Greek Concordance of the New Testament,* 9th ed. (Bagster, 1903. Reprinted 1981)

In English: J. Strong, *The Exhaustive Concordance of the Bible* (New York: Hunt and Eden, 1890. Reproduced New York: Abingdon. 1981)

In English: R. Young, *Analytical Concordance to the Bible* 22nd ed. (Guildford: Lutterworth Press, 1979)

LEXICONS: to locate word usages, root meanings and grammatical forms.

Word usages from the classical era to AD 600 can be consulted in H. G. Liddell and R. Scott *A Greek-English Lexicon,* ed. H. S. Jones, (Oxford: Clarendon, 1940)

W. Gesenius, F. Brown, S. R. Driver and C. A. Briggs, *A Hebrew and English Lexicon of the Old Testament,* Corrected ed. (Oxford: Clarendon, 1952). Also *Index* ed. B. Einspahr, (Chicago: Moody, 1976), listing words by book, chapter and verse.

W. Bauer, W. F. Arndt, F. W. Gingrich and F. W. Danker, *A Greek-English Lexicon of the New Testament and other Early Christian*

Literature, 2nd ed. (Chicago: Univ. of Chicago, 1979). Also *Index* ed. J. R. Alsop, (Grand Rapids: Zondervan, 1968)

J. M. Moulton and G. Milligan, *The Vocabulary of the Greek Testament Illustrated from the Papyri and other Non-Literary Sources.* (London: Hodder and Stoughton, 1930. Reprinted – Grand Rapids: Eerdmans, 1976)

WORD STUDIES: to analyse words in their English form.

W. E. Vine, *An Expository Dictionary of Old Testament Words* (New Jersey: Fleming Revell Co., 1971)

W. E. Vine, *An Expository Dictionary of New Testament Words* (London: Oliphants, 1979)

THE GRAMMATICAL ISSUES

Whilst it is a source of great comfort that most words in a sentence, paragraph or passage will be basically straightforward in meaning, there will nevertheless be occasions on which a grammatical point does become an issue that will affect exegesis and understanding of the text. Three brief examples will serve as illustration of this reality.

a) The Greek imperative of I Corinthians 12:31 gives two possible renderings – 'But eagerly desire the greater gifts ...' (NIV) or 'But you are eagerly desiring the greater gifts...' (NIV footnote). Both translations are grammatically valid. The overall context of a text will often help us to reach a right decision and the presence of the same verb in the form of a command in 14:1 and 39 suggests that 12:31 is probably also a command.

b) In I Timothy 3:6 (NIV) Paul deals with the required quality of elders – 'He must not be a recent convert, or he may become conceited and fall under the same judgment as the devil.' What does the genitive phrase 'condemnation of the devil' mean? This could mean the condemnation reserved for the devil because of his sin of pride or the condemnation produced by the devil as he does his work in those he has captivated. The former seems likely in the context of pride being a real danger among young converts who are promoted too quickly.

c) I Peter 2:24-5 is translated in the NIV as 'He himself bore our sins in his body on the tree, so that we might die to sins and live for righteousness; by his wounds you have been healed. For you were like sheep going astray, but now you have returned to the Shepherd and Overseer of your souls.' At the start of verse 25, the conjunction 'for' has an explanatory function such that the healing must be a metaphor for salvation. At least in this context, therefore, healing cannot be viewed as a reference to physical, bodily healing. This verse should not therefore be used to try to argue that Jesus' wounds guarantee physical healing for all of God's sick and suffering people. Careful reading and evaluation of the conjunction 'for' thus has major impact in yielding sound interpretation.

Our main task in all of this is to isolate any features of the grammar that might have some bearing on the interpretation of the biblical text. We need tackle only those grammatical issues that actually make a difference to our understanding of the text. The only issues of grammar that require attention are therefore those that affect the meaning of the passage, that affect our grasp of the biblical author's intention and that affect our interpretation and application of the text.

Most of the work on grammatical issues will contribute towards the preacher's own understanding of the passage but will not always feature in the public presentation of the final sermon itself. In dealing with issues of grammar, we must consciously remember the needs, capacities and limitations of our sermon listeners, as well as our own! We are after all preparing applied expository sermons, not scholarly, academic exegetical papers for a seminary or college grading. Nevertheless, let it be said again that disciplined use of the mind and sound exegetical methods are vital ingredients of powerful and relevant expository preaching. The hours we spend in careful study and preparation will be apparent and palpable during our actual preaching.

TOOLS FOR GRAMMATICAL ANALYSIS

P. Joüon, *A Grammar of Biblical Hebrew,* Trans. and rev. by T. Muraoka, (Rome: Pontifical Biblical Institute, 1991)

E. Kautzsch, ed. *Genesius' Hebrew Grammar,* 2nd English Ed. (Oxford: Clarendon, 1910)

T. O. Lambdin, *Introduction to Biblical Hebrew,* (New York:

Scribner, 1971)

Bruce K. Waltke, and M. O'Connor, *An Introduction to Biblical Hebrew Syntax*, (Indiana: Eisenbrauns, 1990)

D. A. Black, *Using New Testament Greek in Ministry*, (Grand Rapids: Baker Book House, 1993)

D. A. Black, *Linguistics for Students of New Testament Greek*, (Grand Rapids: Baker Book House, 1995)

F. W. Blass, A. Debrunner, and R. W. Funk, *A Greek Grammar of the New Testament*, (Chicago: Univ. of Chicago, 1961)

M. E. Dana, and J. R. Mantey, *A Manual Grammar of the Greek New Testament*, (New York: Macmillan, 1927)

J. H. Moulton, W. F. Howard and N. Turner, *Grammar of New Testament Greek*, 4 vols. (Edinburgh: T & T Clark, 1906-76)

W. J. Clark, *How to use New Testament Greek Study Aids*, (N.J.: Loizeaux Brothers, 1983)

CASE STUDY – GRAMMATICAL ANALYSIS: LUKE 4:1-13

(A) THE WHOLE TEXT

The only textual variant in this passage of Scripture is found in verse 4, where Jesus is recorded as quoting from Deuteronomy 8:3. The Greek text of the United Bible Societies (4th Revised Edition) can be translated as follows: 'And Jesus answered him, "It is written that man shall not live on bread alone".' Some Greek manuscripts omit the definite article 'the' which normally precedes such a general collective usage of a term like 'man'. Other manuscripts variously expand the quotation, rendering it closer to its Deuteronomy 8:3 original. Thus '... but on/by every word of God' and other manuscripts have '...but on every word which comes out through the mouth of God.' Matthew 4:4 quotes the full version of Deuteronomy 8:3.

The Greek text of the parallel passage in Matthew 4:1-11 has only one slight textual variation. Some manuscripts have the simple command 'Depart, Satan' in verse 10, but others carry a text which is best translated 'Depart from me'.

Jesus' response in Luke 4:4 clearly aims to counter Satan's suggestion that the Son of God should turn stone into bread. Hence Jesus' use of the word 'bread'. The alternative texts, however, provide the fuller context of Deuteronomy 8:3 with its emphasis on the words of God as the source and centre of all life.

(B) THE INDIVIDUAL SENTENCE

The sentences of this passage form a narrative structure that incorporates three episodes of dialogue between Jesus and Satan. The following is a possible diagramming breakdown of just one example of each type:

Narrative: vv. 1-2

    Jesus   returned

             full of the Holy Spirit   from the Jordan

    and   was led

             by the Spirit   in the desert

    where

             for forty days

    he was tempted

             by the devil.

    He ate   nothing

             during those days

    and

    he was   hungry

             at the end of them

Dialogue: vv. 3-4

    The Devil

             said

                       to him,

    'If

    you are   the Son of God,

    tell

             this stone

    to become

             bread.'

    Jesus

             answered,

    'It is written:

    "Man

    does not live

             on bread

                     alone".'

This grammatical breakdown of sentences helps us to see the subject, main verb and object of a sentence and then to identify the subordinate clauses that depend upon the main clause. Broadly speaking, it is helpful to try to arrange subjects, verbs and objects under their respective categories during this diagramming procedure.

(C) THE STRUCTURAL INDICATORS

Moving from individual sentence analysis, we can now trace the presence, location and function of those small but powerful clues to meaning: conjunctions and pronouns, to mention just two. This stage of grammatical analysis reveals a number of significant structural indicators in our passage.

Narrative:
i). The opening verse uses the adjective 'full' to show the complete indwelling of Jesus by the Holy Spirit and then employs the preposition 'by' to indicate that the Spirit was the agent who took Jesus through his wilderness experience.

ii). Verse 2 makes a huge comparison by using the same preposition 'by' to record that the devil was the agent of Jesus' temptation in that desert. The 'Spirit' of verse 1 and the 'devil' of verse 2 stand in stark contrast as far as their roles are concerned. Another preposition then appears at the close of the passage – 'until' (v. 13) – to affirm that the devil constantly and persistently seeks for strategic opportunities to attack.

Dialogue:
i). The three units – verses 3-4, 5-8 and 9-12 – each contain a clause introduced by the conjunction 'if'. In two cases – 'if you are the Son of God' (vv. 3 and 9) – the sense is more that of 'since' rather than the conditional sense of the challenge in verse 7 – 'if you worship me...'

ii). Likewise we observe another trio in the dialogue section: 'It is written' (vv. 4, 8, 10). This term can be literally translated as 'it has been written', which is to say that it was written in the past but still stands valid.

iii). Individual words assume significance in the midst of a sentence. For example, in verse 6, the devil claims to possess and disperse the authority and glory of all kingdoms: 'for (conjunction) it has been given to me'. The devil's logic is then expressed by another conjunction in verse 7: 'therefore/so, if you worship me...'

iv). The devil challenges Jesus to throw himself from the temple pinnacle and justifies his challenge by another conjunction: 'for it is written: He will command his angels...' (v. 10).

v). Verse 11 then uses a purpose clause to indicate the goal of angelic intervention: 'so that you will not strike your foot against a stone.'

(D) THE KEY WORDS

A further reading of this passage indicates two key terms that constitute motifs for the author: 'the devil' and 'tempted'. An examination of relevant biblical texts, in conjunction with Vine's *Expository Dictionary of New Testament Words*, reveals the following information:

Devil: The word used throughout Luke 4:1-13 is the Greek term *diabolos* meaning an 'accuser' or 'slanderer'. This term applies to Satan himself and is different from the word 'demon' for which a different Greek word is employed, namely, *daimonion*. This is a significant distinction for it establishes that there is one Devil but multiple demons. The devil is shown in Scripture as the accuser (see Job 1:6-11, 2:1-5; Rev. 12:9-10). He is also the instigator of sin (Gen. 3) and tempter of human beings (Eph. 4:27, 6:11; 1 Tim. 3:6; 1 Pet. 5:8). Significantly, the devil is viewed in Scripture as being doomed for final destruction (Matt. 25:41; Rev. 20:10). Before then, however, it is possible for human beings to be ensnared by the devil. Judas was even described by Jesus as 'the devil' (John 6:70). The Scripture does however give cause for confidence and assurance, for if believers resist the devil, then he will flee from them (Jas. 4:7).

Tempt: This Greek verb *peirazo* has a range of meanings: try, attempt, test, put to the test, prove. The Scriptures portray the act of tempting in both positive and negative contexts. In Hebrews 2:18 the writer refers to believers 'who are being tempted' in the context of Christ's own temptation and suffering. Christ is thus equipped to help believers. In Hebrews 11:17 we are told that God tested Abraham.

The results of such temptation are presented as positive outcomes in which the faith and obedience of humans are tested and demonstrated. On the other hand, there are negative contexts for this term. For example, some tried to ensnare Jesus in his speech (Matt. 16:1) and some are ensnared by responding to the call of their own evil nature (Jas. 1:13-14). Such tempting is not from God. Some are even viewed as trying to test God (Acts 15:10) and the Holy Spirit of God (Acts 5:9). These temptings of God by humans often occur in the Old Testament in situations where people doubt God's power and goodness. Finally, some temptation is specifically referred to as coming from the devil himself (Luke 4:1-13 and Matt. 4:1-11), designed with evil intentions and for sinful results.

Similarly the noun *peirasmos* – 'temptation'– has a number of positive contexts for trials intended to have beneficial results. Thus, James 1:2 uses the term in the context of the positive effects of divinely sent or allowed temptations. Some temptations could lead to negative results but God makes provision for escape or sufficient grace to cope. For example we are to pray not to be led into temptation (Matt. 6:13; Luke 11:4). Sometimes human beings are said to be tempting or trying God (Heb. 3:9). Lastly there are trials designed by the devil to cause deliberate damage and harmful effects (Luke 4:13).

Grammatical issues

It will be helpful to check out the quotation, based on Psalm 91:11-12, which occurs in Luke 4:10-11. The latter contains the phrase 'to guard you carefully' (NIV) which is somewhat differently rendered in its original occurrence in Psalm 91. The NIV translation of this portion in Psalm 91:11 states 'to guard you in all your ways'. This difference needs briefly to be investigated as a grammatical issue in case it is significant for meaning. The devil quotes Psalm 91:11 in Luke 4:10-11 but his promise is portrayed in Luke 4:10-11 as a promise to protect, guard and take care of Jesus, the key verb being the Greek word *diaphulassw*. In the original text of Psalm 91:11, however, an examination of the Greek text of the Old Testament (Septuagint) reveals the additional phrase best translated 'to keep you in all your ways'. At first sight this might not seem to be especially significant, but when we read Psalm 91 as a whole, then literary context does indeed shed light on this expression. Psalm 91 is all about taking refuge in God and being found in constant dependence on him. Those who know, hope and trust in God will receive God's protection, God's listening ear, God's presence and God's deliverance. These great promises and assurances are for those who walk in obedience and trust within the will of God. They need not fear even the evil spirit (v. 6). The devil carefully avoids quoting that promise to Jesus in the wilderness! Indeed, the protection of God is set clearly in the context of trusting and walking in God's will. The devil ignores the true context of Psalm 91 and seeks to push Jesus outside the will of God by suggesting that he throws himself off the temple. Tragically it is true that the devil will seek constantly to keep people away from God's Word. If he fails to accomplish that, then he will seek to detach Scripture from its proper contexts in an effort to distort and pervert truth. Without a shadow of a doubt, the devil knows the awesome power of expository preaching — and fears it!

STAGE 3 – EXEGETICAL ANALYSIS

We have come a long way and the heavy, detailed but necessary work on contexts and content is almost complete. The study of Contexts (Step Three) and Content (Step Four) is demanding and time-consuming but will yield the raw material that can then be analysed, sifted and selected for inclusion in the final sermon. Within the spectrum of content analysis, we have examined the overall structure of the passage, the form of individual sentences, the key structural indicators, the prominent word or words that need to be addressed and the relevant grammatical issues. A record of our findings should have been noted and having dealt with structure, grammar and words, we now concentrate our attention on the meaning of the passage. For this we shall attempt a verse-by-verse study of the biblical passage or a consideration of each verse that relates to each sub-theme.

If the passage consists of a few verses only, one index card or piece of rough paper should be sufficient for our notes on each verse of the text. Some preachers may find that a sheet of paper or index card can accommodate notes on several verses of the passage. Others may prefer to deal with the grammatical and exegetical analysis as a single united stage, carried out simultaneously. Flexibility and experimentation are good. All of these exegetical notes are written well before we start even to put together the final written version of the sermon during Step Seven of our preparation. With practice and experience the preacher will learn how much time and energy needs to be allocated to each step, how much flexibility is required in the sequence of the steps, and how much of this study needs to be committed to paper or hard drive. Our primary and overriding concern still, at this stage, is to discern what the biblical writers were trying to communicate to the original readers. Bearing in mind our threefold work of historical context, sociocultural and religious context and literary context, together with our threefold work of structure, grammar and words, we are now in a position to complete our study of content by carrying out exegetical analysis. This simply means that we examine our passage verse by verse and make brief notes that will serve to complete our work on content. Eventually our sermon preparation through ten steps — the suggested method of this book will become almost automatic and second nature.

For the moment, however, we need to study each verse of our sermon passage by using three brief sub-stages that will enable us to interpret the text and establish its meaning. Those four sub-stages are examination, evaluation, explanation and extraction.

1. Examination

At this point it will be helpful to refresh our memories by reading through the raw material we have thus far accumulated through Steps One to Four. We must read and examine each verse of our passage, not only in the strict sequence of the text, but also as each verse relates to the main and sub-themes. We need to take a long hard look at the content and ask the text what its author is trying to say in it. As we examine the text in light of its contexts we pose a series of questions: why, when, how, for whom, and what is the author actually saying to his original readers?

2. Evaluation

Thinking through the essence of what is happening and being taught in each verse we ask ourselves in particular how each verse helps to fulfill the overall purpose of the biblical writer in the passage as a whole.

3. Explanation

Using knowledge gained from our work in Steps One to Four, we should now try to write down the meaning of each verse in one to three sentences. Look for a basically valid and legitimate meaning. Avoid excessive technical detail – we are aiming for a sermon, not an exegetical thesis. Thus we seek to explain to ourselves as preachers, for our own personal understanding, what message the verse actually contains.

Unless we can adequately explain a biblical text to ourselves and grasp its intention and meaning, we will never be effective in the fourth sub-stage of our exegetical analysis of content. This fourth sub-stage actually constitutes Step Five 'Application' but it is so intimately related to exegesis that we shall introduce it here. Indeed though it is true that not all our exegetical work will appear in the final sermon, nevertheless expository preaching is basically applied exegesis.

4. Extraction

Having ourselves understood the intention and meaning of the passage for original readers, we now face the challenge of expounding that verse and passage for our twenty-first century listeners. Our exegetical notes revolve round the meaning of the verse for its original readers. Our expository notes indicate the ways in which the text applies in the lives of our contemporary sermon hearers. Exegesis of the meaning for the original readers is the foundation for our exposition to contemporary hearers. The profound unity of these two procedures lies in the applicatory principles which we must identify and extract from the unchanging biblical text itself. We must beware of getting bogged down in excessive exegetical material on each verse. We are simply seeking a valid, sensible and workable exegesis of the passage. Exposition forces us to think through and note down the relevance of all this textual detail to the needs of our listeners.

Using one side of paper or index card for each verse, we need to put down exegetical and expository notes on every verse or theme of our biblical text. Even at this stage we are not aiming for a polished literary product, we are simply making notes. Finally, as and when the need arises, this work can then be checked and supplemented by reference to commentaries. Additional points, useful clarifications or significant comments can sometimes be gleaned from commentaries but we need to pause here to offer a few cautions.

The use of Bible commentaries

It may be the case that during the preparation of Steps Three and Four, you have made reference to grammar books, reference works, Bible dictionaries or commentaries. Such tools should be used sparingly, but can be helpful as a means of checking your preparation with reference to difficult points, controversial interpretations or verses where specific background material might shed light on meaning. Reference to commentaries should be left as late as possible for even the best of commentaries have their limitations.

If we become over-dependent on a commentary, we may be strongly influenced or moulded by the thought of the commentator. Our own work of exegesis may be crowded out as a result and our sermon will be adversely affected.

We cannot be sure that the writings of commentators are always correct. Sometimes a commentator will borrow material from other commentators, so that errors are not detected but rather are passed on to the next generation.

If we spend too much time in commentaries, we can easily end up with far too much detail, which leaves us with the danger of overloading our sermon. Sometimes commentators are so preoccupied with technical detail that they ignore crucial issues like overall purpose, intention and application. We must seek to trace the reason behind the writing of a passage. The text will then be seen as a response to a particular situation and this will strengthen the credibility of our interpretation and application. The commentators can moreover, of course, be so focused on detail that they fail to see the main and sub-themes of the passage as a whole.

Having taken on board the problems of excessive use of commentaries, there are certain ways in which their limited use can benefit our sermon preparation.

Sometimes a commentator may mention a point of exegesis that we ourselves have failed to see. However, as with the biblical text itself, we must be ready to examine and evaluate a viewpoint, ensuring that we ourselves understand what is being claimed by the commentator. If we decide to use such material, we should acknowledge its source.

If a commentator differs widely from our own perspective on any issue, then we ought to think it through again. Sometimes, however, the commentator may not have done the level of research on contexts that we ourselves have done, and we as preachers may be better qualified to evaluate a text than the commentator is.

It may happen from time to time that a commentator has said something or other which is expressed in a more precise, lively or challenging way than we ourselves could say it. If the commentator has grasped a complex problem in a nutshell, then we may want to quote that material in our sermon. Such quotations should be short, to the point, decisive and supportive of the points we ourselves are making. They should, of course, acknowledge the person who said or wrote them in the first place.

Commentaries can be helpful tools in shedding light on unclear or difficult points in the biblical text. They can aid our search for a possible consensus of viewpoint among scholars on a particular issue or point of interpretation.

In all this, the key point is that a sermon should demonstrate *your* interaction with the biblical text. It must not be a patchwork quilt of ideas and quotations from commentaries. If you are spending more time in commentaries than in the biblical text itself, that is a reversal of right priorities.

Tools for exegesis and exposition
Exegesis

F. W. Danker, *Multipurpose Tools for Bible Study,* 3rd ed. (St. Louis: Concordia, 1970)

B. S. Childs, *Old Testament Books for Pastor and Teacher,* (Philadelphia: Westminster, 1977)

D. M. Scholer, *Basic Bibliographic Guide for New Testament Exegesis,* 2nd ed. (Grand Rapids: Eerdmans, 1973)

O. Kaiser and W. G. Kummel, *Exegetical Method: A Student's Handbook* rev. ed. (New York: Eisenbrauns, 1981)

J. H. Hayes and C. R. Holladay, *Biblical Exegesis: A Beginner's Handbook,* (Atlanta: Eisenbrauns, 1982)

D. A. Carson, *Exegetical Fallacies,* 2nd ed. (Grand Rapids: Baker Books, 1996)

D. Stuart, *Old Testament Exegesis: A Primer for Students and Pastors,* (Philadelphia: Westminster Press, 1980)

G. D. Fee, *New Testament Exegesis: A Handbook for Students and Pastors* rev. ed. (Louisville: John Knox, 1993)

J. A. Fitzmyer, *An Introductory Bibliography for the Study of Scripture,* (Subsidia Biblica, Rome: Biblical Institute Press, 1981)

EXPOSITORY PREACHING

J. W. Cox, *A Guide to Biblical Preaching,* (Nashville: Abingdon Press, 1976)

Jay E. Adams, *Preaching with Purpose,* (Grand Rapids: Zondervan, 1982)

Jay E. Adams, *Truth Applied: Application in Preaching,* (London: The Wakeman Trust, 1990)

Denis Lane, *Preach the Word,* (Welwyn: Evangelical Press, 1979)

H. W. Robinson, *Expository Preaching: Principles and Practice,* (Leicester: IVP, 1986)

J. MacArthur Jr., *Rediscovering Expository Preaching,* (Dallas: Word Publishing, 1992)

CASE STUDY – EXEGETICAL ANALYSIS: LUKE 4:1-13

We shall now work through the four E's – examination, evaluation, explanation and extraction – and make exegetical notes on each verse or group of verses. At this stage we can also check issues, as the need arises, from one or two basic commentaries. Again we are not aiming for a perfectly polished presentation, but rather for a series of rough notes which seek to highlight the purpose, meaning and application of the biblical text itself. Order, sequence and organization of material are less important at this point than the content of our notes. The matter of organization can be sorted out finally once we have established the outline in Step Six.

GENERAL POINTS

The account of Jesus' temptations by the devil seems to be strongly related to the baptism account of Luke 3 and both accounts relate to the divine preparation of Jesus for his ministry. Clear similarities exist between Matthew and Luke but the order of Luke's second and third temptations is reversed by Matthew. Only Jesus of course was the source of this story for the event had no other human witnesses. A key thought of the passage is that, although the devil is continually opposed to the purposes of God, it is God himself who sets limits to those demonic assaults (Luke 4:1-2). Thus although the devil attempts to deflect Jesus from obedience to God and from Jesus' divinely-appointed messianic task, nevertheless the sovereign and powerful Spirit overrules circumstances to guide and sustain Jesus. In the power of the Spirit, Jesus employs Scripture to oppose temptations inflicted by the devil. These quotations are taken from the context of Israel in the wilderness, in which the people of God tempted God and were tested by him. Jesus' calling was being questioned by the devil who wanted Jesus to prove his calling by signs. From the start, therefore, Jesus was compelled to think much about his divine calling – a calling that demanded perseverance and determination. Ultimately the temptations were designed to challenge the Father-Son relationship in the Godhead.

VERSES 1-2
- Mark 1:12-13 speaks about the Spirit sending Jesus into the desert and mentions the ministry of angels to Jesus.
- Matthew 4:1-2 states that Jesus was led by the Spirit into the desert.
- Luke 4:1-2 also mentions that Jesus was led by the Spirit but adds that he was full of the Holy Spirit.

— Notice the testing of Jesus at the outset of his ministry. A new work for God will often be opposed in its early stages.

— The temptations lasted for the forty-day period and it seems that the three specified temptations may have been inflicted on Jesus at the end of that period.

— These first two verses, in and of themselves, do not tell the reader exactly why Jesus was tempted.

— These opening verses link the section to the preceding accounts of Jesus' baptism (Luke 3:21-2) and Jesus' genealogy (Luke 3:23-38), the common theme being 'Sonship'.

— The power of God's Spirit (Luke 4:1) enables Jesus to overcome the tempter. Application here for contemporary followers of Jesus. God equips believers for triumph over Satan.

— Part of the devil's plan during the forty days would have been designed to destroy communion and fellowship between Father and Son.

Verses 3-4

— Verse 3 is a direct challenge to Jesus' Sonship.

— There are more important needs in this world than the purely physical.

— Adam fell over a 'food temptation'. The devil now seeks to bring down the second Adam in a similar way.

— Jesus reminds the devil that it is God his Father who has power to sustain, as he once had given manna in the wilderness when there was no bread.

— The devil thus seems to be challenging the Father's trustworthiness and to push Jesus to use miraculous powers to make provision for his needs.

— Christ thus reaffirms his trust in his Father's power, provision and care. The Father will supply our needs in his time and in his way. Application here.

— 'If you are the Son of God…' really means 'since you are the Son of God…' The devil knows the reality of Jesus' Sonship but pushes Jesus to act independently of his Father and seeks to misdirect the mission of Jesus.

– The devil is pressing Jesus to seek first his own interests rather than those of the kingdom of God. At an even deeper level, however, the devil is trying to undermine the obedience of Jesus towards his Father's will and word.

VERSES 5-8

– The devil claims to possess the authority and glory of all the kingdoms of the world and to have the right to dispense this power to whomsoever he might choose. Both are profoundly false claims.

– The purpose of the devil seems to be to offer a worldly, material route for Jesus' mission: to suggest the way of a kingly crown rather than a criminal's cross.

– Jesus' quotation from Deuteronomy 6:13 indicates that he was seeking to do precisely what his Father wanted him to do. Again the issue seems to be that of filial obedience.

– Probably this is a vision for it would be hard for anyone to see all the kingdoms of the world in an instant. Nevertheless, even though a vision, it was true and very real.

– The issue concerns sovereignty. It is God, not Satan, who exercises total sovereignty and against the background context of idolatry in Deuteronomy 6:10-15, Jesus reaffirms his absolute commitment to his Father's will and way.

– The devil tries to gain Jesus' allegiance and to cause Jesus thereby to deny his Sonship and abandon his dependence on the heavenly Father.

– The devil does have a real, though limited, influence (v. 5). The commentator John Nolland expresses this well: 'His influence is co-extensive with the influence of evil in the fabric of human affairs.'[4] The devil wants Jesus to seek worldly honour and glory, rather than that which accrues from his obedience as Son.

– In verse 8, Jesus is resisting the temptation to steal anything that belongs rightly to God alone and give it to the devil. Thus

---

4. John Nolland, *Luke 1:9-20*, Word Biblical Commentary, Vol. 35A, (Dallas: Word Books, 1989), p.180.

worship and service for Christ and his followers belong solely to
God the Father (Deut. 6:13).

VERSES 9-12

— Perhaps Luke makes this third temptation the climax of the
passage because it is located in Jerusalem to show how victory in
Jerusalem foreshadows Jesus' final triumph there through his death,
resurrection, ascension and glorification.

— No one else is mentioned as being present to witness the spectacle
of Jesus jumping off the temple. Thus we cannot presume that
the temptation is designed to produce an amazed audience.

— Jesus' response in verse 12, in which he quotes from Deuteronomy
6:16, suggests that he is making the point that he, and all
believers, are called to trust God and not to presume on God.

— The devil in verses 9-11 makes use of Psalm 91:11f. but omits
the phrase 'to guard you in all your ways'. The devil seems to be
trying to make God's offer of protection into a universal and
unconditional promise and guarantee, regardless of how Jesus or
believers think and behave in this world.

— The devil, in misquoting Psalm 91:11f., also fails to include
verses of Scripture which condemn rashness, sheer stupidity and
the danger of interfering with divine providence.

— Jesus is not willing to experiment in acts or decisions for which
he had no leading from his Father.

— Verse 9 again challenges Jesus' Sonship.

— Verse 9 also seems to teach that in urging Jesus 'throw yourself
down from here', the devil was not actually able to compel Jesus'
compliance. He was actually able to make a suggestion. The final
decision lay with Jesus himself.

— In the wilderness experience of Israel, the people of God did
put God to the test at Massah and Meribah by urging him to
provide water (Deut. 6:16; Exod. 17:1-7). Jesus in his wilderness
temptation refuses to test God by forcing him to give protection
on Jesus' own terms.

— The devil fails to realize — or conveniently omits — the crucial
context of Psalm 91, namely that faithfulness to God requires

living in his presence and walking in his ways. Ultimately Jesus would not be guarded from death but rather would be glorified through death.

— Application: God demands our obedience to his way, his plan, his will and his timing. Ultimately the devil wanted Jesus to abuse his privileged position as Son and to set aside his trusting submission to his Father's will.

— The devil, having been twice rebuked by Jesus' use of Scripture, now tries to use Scripture in his own effort to deceive the Saviour.

— In verse 12 Jesus asserts that he will never seek to test his Father's purposes. Instead of testing, Jesus will continue trusting his Father. Neither Jesus nor his followers, can dictate terms to God or make deals with him.

— Jesus' temptations are in a real sense unique to his own experience in the wilderness. Yet in a real sense, the root motive of the devil is the same in all of our own temptations: to persuade us that God cannot be trusted to bring about his perfect will and provision for the lives of his people through their submissive obedience to his love.

— Examples of presuming on God's protection might include the folly of expecting good health, whilst breaking all the basic rules for healthy living, or expecting God to take care of our children whilst we ourselves fail to give adequate input into their lives and upbringing.

VERSE 13

— Jesus' encounter with the devil continued throughout his ministry.

— This life offers no complete freedom from temptation for the followers of Christ.

— The devil seeks times and opportunities that seem most strategic for his destructive purposes.

— The devil failed to deflect Jesus from his Messianic goal, though he again attempts to do so during the climactic passion period (Luke 22:3, 31, 53) and especially the agonizing struggle of Jesus during the Gethsemane ordeal (Luke 22:39-46).

Conclusions

– Jesus' filial obedience as Son of God seems to have been the trigger for the Satanic attacks recorded in our sermon passage.

– The devil's goals for Jesus in the three temptations seem to be:
   1. To abuse his privilege from the Father by using his own powers.
   2. To abuse his status with the Father by seeking personal prestige.
   3. To abuse his trust in the Father by forcing divine protection.

– The constant pressure on Jesus is to take things into his own hands by acting independently of his Father.

– Jesus was anointed by the Spirit so he could withstand these temptations. The devil sought to oppose the will of God but the very temptations served to further the purposes of God and to equip Jesus for his ongoing life and ministry (Luke 4:14ff.).

– Jesus remained faithful to God and his Word.

STAGE 4 – BIBLICAL/THEOLOGICAL REFLECTION

We began our study of content by employing column analysis to help us identify the various issues that need further treatment. We then began to do detailed work on grammatical, and exegetical analysis. Finally, we must return to our widest possible camera lens in order to check and test the meaning and significance of our passage content against its wider biblical and theological contexts.

In a real sense this work does not constitute a separate step, for we should be thinking about our passage in its widest context right from the start of our preparation. Every biblical passage finally has as its literary context the entire spectrum of written Scripture. Every biblical passage ultimately has theological consequences, implications or connections that arise because of its relationship to biblical theology as a whole. A few brief examples will serve as illustration of this truth.

Some passages of narrative include material that is theologically significant, in the sense that we are given information about God, human beings and the relationships between God and people. Thus for example, the narrative account of Mark 10:13-16 records the disciples' efforts to stop little children coming to Jesus. The Saviour takes this ordinary event of life and makes it extraordinary by infusing it with a theological lesson – that entry into God's Kingdom is impossible without an obedient, trusting and humble heart.

Some passages of Scripture include a theological evaluation or judgment by the writer. The whole of 2 Samuel 11 records David's adultery with Bathsheba, followed in great detail by an account of the king's plot to remove Bathsheba's husband, Uriah, from the scene. Then, almost as a postscript, the text contains a statement that is theological in nature: 'But the thing David had done displeased the Lord' (2 Sam. 11:27).

Some passages describe the experiences of human beings that lead those people to declare truths of theological significance which enhance our understanding of God's nature and purposes for people. Thus in the midst of Joseph's revealing of his true identity to his brothers, he retells the circumstances that brought him to Egypt. Joseph is aware of the sovereign purposes of God even in trials and tribulations (Gen. 45: 5, 7, 8, 9).

METHOD

If we are preparing a passage for expository preaching, then Stage Four of Step Four is not so much a time for specific study, but more a time to check and evaluate our understanding of a passage against its much wider context of biblical revelation and theology. This will help us to safeguard the accuracy and honesty of our exposition, as we measure our interpretation of any single passage in terms of the total revelation of God's Word. Whether we are dealing with a passage or a topic, we need to allow time to consider the two widest contexts of our biblical text.

1. BIBLICAL CONTEXT

It almost goes without saying that in order to view our sermon passage or topic in light of its overall biblical setting, we face the enormous challenge of knowing the biblical revelation in its entirety and at least something of the theology built upon it. At the close of Step Four we have completed the basic work of data collection for the sermon, but before we move on, we should ponder three issues with regard to the wider biblical context of our passage.

a) What is the relationship between the message of our passage on the one hand and the section, book, similar group of books, testament and Bible of which it is a part? What are the main and sub-themes of this passage and how does that teaching fit into the wider portions of the Bible just listed? What sort of loss, if any, would be sustained if our passage did not exist? In short, does our passage offer explicit or implicit reasons for its inclusion and inspiration by the Holy Spirit?

b) Thematic or topical preaching in some ways is more difficult and challenging than treating a neatly defined preaching passage. If we are seeking to present the biblical view of marriage, tithing or forgiveness, we will usually need to spread our attention to a number of relevant passages, which means multiple backgrounds and contexts may be involved. Such preaching preparation will of course carry the benefit of forcing us to delve more widely into Scripture but topical preaching does demand very careful work on a range of contexts. In short, we must pay adequate attention to the contexts of every biblical text touched by our exposition.

c) Topical preaching clearly involves comparison and contrast of different portions of Scripture, yet sometimes it will be necessary in passage preaching to relate our sermon passage to other sections of Scripture. For example, a sermon from one of Paul's epistles may well require reference to narrative portions of Acts. In short, we must be ready to ask how the topic of one passage compares with other passages on the same topic, not only those written by the same author but also those written by other authors.

The overall goal of taking account of total biblical context is not only to enrich the understanding and exposition of our sermon passage or topic, but also to identify traps that we may have fallen into during our work on contexts and content. If there is a gross discrepancy between our conclusions on our own passage and the total revelation of Scripture, then we must review our work, especially on contexts and interpretation.

2. THEOLOGICAL CONTEXT

Every passage of Scripture is unique. Every passage of Scripture has its main and sub-themes. Every passage of Scripture has its own contribution to the totality of biblical theology. Thus, for example, in John 15:1-8 we can identify several theological points that touch on the nature of God, the nature of humankind and the relationships between the two:

— the sovereign activity of God the Father (vv. 1-2)
— Jesus as source of divine life (vv. 1, 5)
— abiding in Christ and indwelling by Christ (vv. 2, 4-7)
— fruit bearing by believers (vv. 2, 4-8)
— evidence of discipleship (v. 8)
— painful pruning process (v. 2)
— the power of the word (vv. 3, 7)
— God's ability to cleanse (v. 3)
— human inability in the spiritual realm (vv. 4, 5, 6)
— the conditions for effective prayer (v. 7)
— the glory of God (v. 8)

Even in this short passage of eight verses, we have readily identified eleven theological issues. In trying to assess the place of this, or any other, passage of Scripture in relation to its wider theological context, we ought to address three further questions.

a) How does the biblical passage treat theological problems, issues or misunderstandings? Much biblical theology is revealed in Scripture as a writer's response to particular problems or concerns among the people of God. The vast array of theological issues embedded in John 15:1-8 arose in the process of Jesus' preparation of the disciples for His imminent departure from this world. The Corinthian believers' misunderstandings of spirit, body and eschatology, mean that in I Corinthians 15 we now have a theology of the resurrection bodies of believers. It is a strange irony that much biblical teaching has come to us in the form of response to theological problems.

b) How does the biblical passage connect with specific doctrines? In John 15:1-8 we can trace necessary, but not sufficient, elements of certain biblical doctrines. No single passage embodies the totality of biblical doctrine but each passage makes a contribution to it. Every one of the eleven theological issues in John 15:1-8 recurs many times in other portions of Scripture. At the same time, however, we can say that every biblical statement about God is true in its own context. Thus we need to ask how our passage seeks to strengthen or challenge certain doctrines and to deal with tendencies toward deviation.

c) How does the biblical passage fit into the overall revelation of Christian theology? This is a crucial issue. There is value in checking the theological issues of John 15:1-8 to confirm that they are in line with the big picture of theological issues across the whole of Scripture. However it would be wrong to say that biblical passages should be checked for authenticity or consistency against the grand and final picture of biblical theology. The Bible is not a manual of systematic theology. Biblical theologies have been constructed by scholars out of the biblical material. If we treat our own personal and individual theology or theological presuppositions or doctrinal positions – albeit biblically based – as the measuring stick and grand blueprint against which the biblical content of passages must be evaluated, then there is a real danger that we will force or bend the pieces of our passage to try to fit them into the 'final theological picture' according to which we are assembling the jigsaw puzzle. This is a real danger. Our final authority does not lie in our humanly constructed theologies. It lies in the biblical text of the sixty-six books that constitute the revealed Word of God. That text is final and supreme. As far as biblical exegesis is concerned, theology is thus valuable as guideline but potentially dangerous as foundation. All our 'theologies' must be continually tested by the Word of God, regardless of whether that sometimes leaves us with loose ends, dilemmas or uncertainties.

All our sermon preparation thus far has involved us in this crucial task of interpretation, but we have now reached the point at which it will be useful to gather together some specific and concrete thoughts on the general principles and practice of biblical interpretation. We must consider now some guidelines for interpreting the material we have assembled during our labours through Steps One to Four sermon preparation. Prior to that consideration, however, here are a few suggestions for helpful theological resources, depending on our available study time and on the nature of our passage.

TOOLS FOR BIBLICAL/THEOLOGICAL REFLECTION

W. J. Dumbrell, *The Faith of Israel: Its expression in the books of the Old Testament,* (Leicester: Apollos, 1989)

W. C. Kaiser, *Toward an Old Testament Theology,* (Grand Rapids: Eerdmans, 1978)

D. Guthrie, *New Testament Theology,* (Leicester: IVP, 1981)

W. G. Kummel, *The Theology of the New Testament,* (Nashville: Abingdon Press, 1973)

G. E. Ladd, *A Theology of the New Testament,* (Grand Rapids: Eerdmans, 1974)

L. Berkhof, *Systematic Theology,* (Edinburgh: Banner of Truth, 1976)

J. L. Garrett, *Systematic Theology,* 2 vols., (Grand Rapids: Eerdmans, 1990)

W. A. Elwell, *Evangelical Dictionary of Biblical Theology,* (Carlisle: Paternoster, 1996)

English-based study of New Testament theological words and concepts is available in G. Kittel and G. Friedrich (eds.) *Theological Dictionary of the New Testament,* 10 vols., trans. and ed. G. W. Bromiley (Grand Rapids: Eerdmans, 1964-76). Greek words are arranged alphabetically for those with minimal Greek skills.

Good, clear English articles are available in Colin Brown (ed.) *The New International Dictionary of New Testament Theology,* 3 vols. (Exeter: Paternoster Press, 1982)

CASE STUDY – BIBLICAL/THEOLOGICAL REFLECTION: LUKE 4:1-13

The Gospel writers seem to make links between temptation, spiritual darkness and sin on the one hand, and the work of the devil on the other. This is seen, for example, in Jesus' rebuke to Peter (Mark 8:33), the parable of the sower (Luke 8:12), the betrayal of Jesus by Judas Iscariot (Luke 22:3), the sifting of Simon by Satan (Luke 22:31), and the deceiving of Ananias by Satan (Acts 5:5). The reality of Satan was not a matter for debate or discussion for Jesus. It is assumed by him.

Clearly the strategies of Satan emerge at a number of points in Scripture and in order to understand our sermon passage, it will be helpful to cast our net more widely across the Bible in an endeavour to sift and assess the motives and goals of the devil. Evidence can be traced beyond the Gospels and Acts quoted above. Biblical material for the devil's tactics can be identified, for example, in at least three areas.

1. HIS CHIEF FEATURES

In the New Testament, John informs us that 'the devil has been sinning from the beginning' (I John 3:8) and describes Satan as 'that ancient serpent'. Scripture traces the lying and deceiving function of the devil right back to Genesis 3. Here the Evil One took the form of a serpent and raised doubts in Eve's mind concerning the truth of God's word (Gen. 3:1-5). Satan sought to alienate humankind from God as he led Adam and Eve to fall into sin. In Genesis 3:3 we note Eve's addition to God's prohibition: 'and you must not touch it'. Deceit spread rapidly. Satan sought from the outset to suggest that God had unworthy motives. He contradicts God's word and claims that humankind can become as God Himself (Gen. 3:4-5).

2. HIS WORK IN INDIVIDUAL LIVES

The devil's work in deceiving Adam and Eve is echoed later in the life of Job. As Satan worked to alienate humankind from God in Genesis 3, so he tried to alienate God from a man in Job 1-2. How does he do this? Having accused God of having unworthy motives in Genesis 3:5, he now accuses Job, in the presence of God, of having wrong reasons for trusting in God (Job 1:9-11, 2:4-5). Satan accuses Job of trusting God only for what he can gain out of the relationship. God thus allows severe testing in order to vindicate Job's faith and discredit Satan. God sets definite limits to the suffering that Job will face (Job 1:12, 2:6). Satan is portrayed as being constantly hostile to God and working to destroy the purposes of God. Several individuals are shown in the New Testament as being under the influence of Satan's assaults: Ananias (Acts 5:3), Elymas (Acts 13:10) and Judas (Luke 22:3).

3. HIS HATRED FOR THE CHURCH

The New Testament shows Satan's varied forms of attack upon the church and its task of worldwide mission:

- the devil functions like a roaring lion seeking to devour men and women (1 Pet. 5:8);
- the devil functions craftily as an angel of light (2 Cor. 11:14);
- the devil sets traps for people (1 Tim. 3:7; 2 Tim. 2:26). The church must employ God's armour to withstand him (Eph. 6:10-20);
- the devil seeks a foothold in the church so he can promote immoral living and false teaching (Eph. 4:26);
- the devil seeks to hold humankind in a state of sin, ignorance and unbelief so that people are kept out of the church and the kingdom of light (Mark 4:15; Matt. 13:38f.).

Throughout Scripture, the biblical writers present Satan as being continually opposed to God's plans and purposes. The Old Testament contains relatively few references to the activities of the devil, but the New Testament portrays a very real and enormous conflict between the forces of God and of good, on the one hand, and those of evil directed by Satan, on the other. In this conflict, however, John gives assurance in 1 John 3:8 that Jesus appeared to destroy the works of the devil. Indeed many passages speak not only of Satan's divinely appointed limitations (1 Cor. 10:13; Rev. 20:2, 7) but also of his final destruction (Luke 10:18; John 12:31; Rom. 16:20; Rev. 20:10). Satan is unable to conceive of the love of God and cannot see that God is trustworthy. He is therefore unable to accept that believers can genuinely trust in God. His goal therefore, if possible, is to discredit God and destroy God's church. He works by making the church doubt the love, word, will and trustworthiness of the Godhead.

6. Practical Steps: Guidelines for Interpretation

Before considering Step Five, I want to give some guidelines on biblical interpretation. Biblical interpretation is not a magical or abstract procedure that we suddenly apply to the passage of Scripture we are preparing to preach. Indeed, biblical interpretation does not occur at a particular point or place in the biblical text, but rather it emerges as the result of a systematic process of study and preparation by the expositor. All the work of Steps One to Four involves us actively in the process of interpretation. Everything we have done so far amounts to a consideration of all the parameters which set limits for our interpretation. The work of exegesis, finding out what the text originally meant, is a necessary basis for the work that we shall do in Step Five on application. Interpretation is in a real sense the bridge between exegesis and application and exposition. Through interpretation we seek to hear the original meaning in the context of our own day. The greatest factor, I believe, in ensuring sound interpretation is our thorough examination of the various contexts of the passage, as laid out in Step Three. Failure to take account of some aspect of context probably explains the vast majority of errors and weaknesses in biblical interpretation. As we now reflect on the raw material we have gathered through Steps One to Four, we shall need to bear in mind a number of guidelines, both general and specific, that we must follow as we interpret the biblical text.

As we examine the following ten guidelines we must constantly hold fast to five fundamental truths:

a) the whole of Scripture is divinely inspired and carries divine authority (2 Tim. 3:16; 2 Pet. 1:21) being revealed by the work of the Holy Spirit;

b) the true meaning of any biblical text for us is that meaning which God originally intended to convey through his human authors of Scripture;

c) biblical interpretation now must therefore be grounded in the solid work of biblical exegesis, work to which the Spirit of God is absolutely committed;

d) the only proper and reliable control for biblical interpretation lies in the original intention of the biblical text;

e) only by continual dependence on the Holy Spirit can we do that work of exegesis, interpretation, application and exposition of the revealed truth that he himself inspired.

1. TAKE ACCOUNT OF HISTORICAL TIME

God has revealed eternal truth into the time framework of human history. Therein lies our joy and our challenge! It is our challenge because Scripture was given by God to people who possessed different vocabularies, historical circumstances, cultural backgrounds and thought patterns from our own. It is precisely because we ourselves are distanced in time, space and thought that the need for interpretation arises. Scripture is both divine words possessing eternal authority and at the same time human words possessing historical particularity. Interpretation attempts to deal with the tensions that arise from the interplay of those two worlds of the biblical text. First and foremost, therefore we need to hear God's Word as it was in the 'then and there' before we can safely hear that same Word in the 'here and now'. If there is no historical dimension in our handling of texts, we can all too easily read our own ideas into the biblical text and end up with interpretations that were never actually intended by God.

2. TAKE ACCOUNT OF PROGRESSIVE REVELATION

Progressive revelation does not mean that certain parts of Scripture have lost their significance or relevance. Neither is it to say that some parts of Scripture embody primitive, as opposed to advanced, religion. What we are saying is that we must not expect people in certain times and places to have the same understanding that we now have of certain passages of revealed Scripture. Thus for example, Hosea 11:1 'Out of Egypt I called my son' actually refers to the Exodus event through which Israel was delivered. Matthew 2:15, however, refers this event to Jesus' deliverance from Egypt. Matthew thus employs Hosea 11:1 as a 'type' of Jesus' own experience in a later historical setting.

3. TAKE ACCOUNT OF TOTAL REVELATION

Jesus recognized the authority of the Old Testament writings. Since the whole of Scripture is divine revelation, it is imperative that any one passage or topic must take full account of the totality of Scripture. Failure to do this will open the way to heresy, for errors can creep in so easily if we adopt an exaggerated interpretation of one side of truth.

In our biblical interpretation, we must hold together the various parts of Scripture as they complement one another. We must make sure that we permit one Scripture to check the interpretation of another and that we interpret obscure passages in the light of clear passages. The challenge of course is that we must commit ourselves to consecutive study of the whole counsel of God so that we can see how each book of the Bible fits into the overall picture of a single coherent unity.

4. TAKE ACCOUNT OF GENERALITY AND PARTICULARITY

We have just seen how we need to have a grasp of the whole body of Scripture and doctrine. A view of the whole of Scripture keeps our ministry in balance, for it is when we blow up a passage or doctrine out of proportion that truth can become distorted and, like cancerous cells, turn into the heresy that threatens to strangle and destroy the Church. Thus we need not only a view of total revelation, but also a consistency in our handling of, and obedience to, God's Word. Imbalance creeps in very easily.

Whilst it is profoundly true that the general revelation of Scripture must check our interpretation of the particular text or passage, it is equally vital that the particular must shape the general. In other words, we must beware of building an entire doctrine on one text, particularly if there is any uncertainty or controversy over that text. Whatever our general position may be on a particular issue, we may not have the whole thing in place and it is dangerous therefore to take one verse and make it into an absolute that no other text can then challenge.

5. TAKE ACCOUNT OF GRAMMATICAL RULES

Earlier in Step Four we considered the role of grammatical analysis. Grammar rules do affect our interpretation of biblical texts and our approaches in this area will depend on such factors as our grasp of English grammar and our level of understanding of the original biblical languages. For most expositors, points of grammar can usefully be checked by reference to good commentaries and especially so if an issue of actual meaning and interpretation is at stake.

As we have already discovered, however, grammar points cannot be treated in isolation. Context is always significant. Strict grammatical rules must always allow room for the ancient cultural setting of a biblical text. The need to go beyond the mere meanings of individual words and to tackle the cultural, linguistic and literary contexts of phrases, sentences and whole passages, can be seen in the case of Luke 15:13. Regarding the younger son, RSV offers 'gathered all he had' and NIV states 'got together all he had'. A literal rendering of the Greek text would read 'having collected together all things'. Even this, however, does not fully reflect the ancient usage which involved the realization of the younger son's estate and his turning that estate into ready money. Thus in its cultural and linguistic context, the phrase is probably best expressed by the NEB translators: 'turned the whole of his share into cash.'

6. TAKE ACCOUNT OF LINGUISTIC ISSUES

We need to be aware as preachers that all individuals come to a biblical text with their own experiences, cultures and prior understandings of words, concepts and ideas. Thus for example the Greek word *sarx* could be translated as 'flesh' or 'body', but Paul extensively though not exclusively renders it in the sense of 'sinful nature' in the context of his theological arguments. Detailed word-study can be of immense help in our understanding of a passage, but ultimately it is the context that puts limits on meaning and restricts our interpretation of a word. A number of guidelines need to be borne in mind when we consider the meaning of words used in the Bible.

We must not think that words appearing in the Bible had a special kind of magical, spiritual or allegorical significance that they did not possess in ordinary, everyday ancient usage. Sometimes, however, Bible writers did take words out of their ancient settings and give them a new and fuller significance. Thus for example *Christos* referred originally to an anointed king but gained the biblical sense of 'the Lord's anointed one'.

Checking the root derivation of a word can fill in the details of its historical development and changes in meaning, but again ultimately it is actual current usage that decides present meaning. Much has been made, for example, of the Greek word *ekklesia* ('church' or 'gathering' or 'congregation'). The derivation is from *ek* meaning 'out' and *kaleo* meaning 'I call', thus the 'called-out people'. Biblical authors, however, would simply have taken the word in its general, ancient sense of 'assembly', often referring in fact to political gatherings.

Words must always be finally evaluated in their original context and sense, rather than in their modern setting and significance. The New Testament Greek term *hoi hagioi* (lit. the holy ones) simply refers to all Christian believers. It cannot therefore be given the shades of meaning that modern secularists would give it, and it is certainly different from the interpretation that would be understood in Roman Catholic circles.

7. TAKE ACCOUNT OF TEXT TRANSLATION ISSUES

Any preacher who uses an English translation of the Bible is already involved in the act of interpretation. A few examples will serve to show the challenges facing Bible translators and all who use translations.

Cultural considerations affect translation and therefore potentially affect interpretation. Should the 'holy kiss' be translated as 'a handshake of Christian love' in cultures that evaluate visible public kissing as offensive and socially unacceptable?

The grammar of Greek is sometimes readily understandable when taken into English. Thus a Greek genitive can indicate the idea of possession in our English equivalent usage. Hence 'my book' is readily seen as indicating possession. However, the Greek phrases 'the grace of God' or 'the joy of the Holy Spirit' do not really show possession. In this case, the NASB translation 'joy of the Holy Spirit' (I Thess. 1:6) is not as good as 'joy given by the Holy Spirit' (NIV).

When translators are faced by a textual variant in a biblical text, usually the majority choice appears in the main body of the translation, while the minority choice is put into the margin. Thus for example we have the case of 1 Corinthians 13:3 NIV text 'surrender my body to the flames' NIV margin 'surrender my body that I may boast'. In Greek the difference is merely a single letter – *kauthesomai* and *kauchesomai*. In this case both variants have good early manuscript support and both carry problems of interpretation. 1 Corinthians was written well before Christians suffered martyrdom by burning but equally difficult to understand is the idea of boasting. The overall context however concerns the futility of sacrifice if love is lacking. Thus in this case the textual choice does not really affect the actual overall meaning of the verse within its context.

As a general rule, these variations in translation act as an incentive to use more than one English translation. In the event of significant textual variants that might affect meaning and interpretation, a good commentary will shed light on the available options.

8. TAKE ACCOUNT OF LITERARY FORM AND GENRE

Although the basic procedure for preparing an expository sermon is the same for all passages of Scripture, nevertheless we do need to take account of the type of literature with which we are dealing, for this will have a definite bearing on the way in which we handle a particular passage.

(a) *Historical narrative.* There is a profound historical dimension to the Christian faith as God worked in historical events and people, but it does need to be said that the writers of Scripture were not consistently concerned for precision in giving numbers and sequences of events. Their concern was for theological interpretation rather than strict historical accuracy. Thus, for example, genealogies in showing descent from a particular ancestor are not necessarily complete, but rather selective. The three sets of 'fourteen generations' (Matt. 1:1ff.) show Jesus' descent from Abraham and David, possibly related to the numerical value of the Hebrew word 'David' which was fourteen and would thereby emphasize the royalty of Jesus. The Gospels themselves do not give full biographical details of Jesus' childhood and young adulthood since their writers were theological in motivation. King Omri was a wealthy and powerful historical figure but he receives only scant reference in I Kings 16:16-28 because of his evil behaviour. Again theological appraisal overrides historical detail.

(b) *Wisdom literature.* The book of Job deals with conflicting arguments revolving around the issue of innocent suffering and we need to exercise a careful distinction between valid and invalid arguments. Some of the claims made by Job's friends were humanly devised (Job 42:7-9). Ecclesiastes records the struggle of a man over the issue of life's meaning and care needs to be taken in handling a text that is not a straightforward expression of philosophy. Proverbs often consist of observations on life rather than conditions and promises that demanded strict obedience. Thus the proverbs are not to be treated as Christian instruction comparable with that found in the New Testament epistles. The Proverbs often use the device of personification by which a personality is attributed to an abstract idea. Thus for example in Proverbs 8:1ff. wisdom is presented as shouting out her advice by the town gates.

(c) *Hebrew poetry.* Extensive poetic sections are found in the books of Job, Psalms, Proverbs, Song of Solomon and the Prophets. Hebrew poetry uses figurative language and parallelism in which two or more lines of verse are set together and the first one is then echoed or contrasted by the following line(s). Two synonyms may display slight differences but we need to beware of attributing great significance to those differences (Ps. 85:2-3). Another feature of the Psalms in particular is that of anthropomorphism in which a human form is attributed to a non-human being or form. This helps us to understand God's nature, as for example God's hands in Psalm 119:73.

(d) *Prophecy.* It is true that the Old Testament prophets were given divine insight regarding the future, but it is vital to realize that they had much to say about God's dealings with his people both past and present. Indeed we need to realize that God's initial and immediate purpose involved the prophet and his contemporary readers and hearers. We must grasp these historical settings as of prime importance. The prophets gave extensive utterance about God's coming judgment and yet at the same time the hope of restoration. The prophets spoke from time to time of a coming deliverer, fulfilled in the life and ministry of Christ (Matt. 21:4f; Acts 13:32-41). Prophecy of course cannot always be understood in advance nor can we say that the prophets understood what God was saying through them. All biblical prophecy is moral, not speculative, in purpose. New Testament prophecies of Jesus' Second Coming were designed to affect present living as preparation for the future Coming. The prophets sometimes employed similes using the words 'like' or 'as'. For example the prediction of the Servant as being 'like a lamb led to the slaughter' (Isa. 53:7). Metaphors are also to be found in the prophets, such as in Jeremiah's description of Jerusalem as a 'bride' (Jer. 2:2). This is a New Testament form as well, in which descriptive words are transferred to objects to which they are not literally applicable. Thus, Christ as 'cornerstone' (Eph. 2:19-20) or as vine (John 15:1). Such figurative language helps us to grasp unfamiliar truth with our finite minds.

(e) Epistles. A number of particular factors need to be realized in preparing sermons on the New Testament epistles. Firstly, the apostolic writers were not laying out their communication in the form of a systematic theological or doctrinal treatise. Secondly, these writers generally were addressing concrete and particular historical situations and church problems. Because of this we cannot assume that any single letter in the New Testament offers a definitive and absolute treatment of a specific issue. These writers were giving practical advice in particular circumstances. Thus, for example, a theology of marriage ought not to be built on I Corinthians 7 alone, but after due contextual consideration of all relevant passages, including such texts as Ephesians 5 and I Timothy 4:1-4. Sometimes, Paul wrote his letters as a response to enquiring letters, as in I Corinthians 7:1; 8:1; 12:1 and 16:1. There are similarities in Paul's openings and closings of his letters and at times he added his own personal signature to the text he had dictated to a scribe.

(f) Apocalyptic writings. This type of literature can be found in Daniel, Zechariah and Revelation and is typically concerned with trends and patterns in history, alongside the expectation of God's cosmic and final triumph over all the forces of evil. These writings contain future visions, supernatural angelic revelations and symbolic language about such concepts as stars, numbers and beasts. Jesus employed apocalyptic language in Matthew 24 and Mark 13 but it is important

that we remember his own warnings against fruitless speculation (Matt. 24:26-31; Mark 13:4-37). Because of this we need to be very careful in handling apocalyptic passages – its material is not to be viewed and interpreted on the basis of literalism.

(g) *Parables and allegory.* Typology involves an author's use of a parallel between Old Testament and New Testament revelation, but an allegory is a story to illustrate the truth that an author is trying to communicate. Thus an Old Testament story or saying is taken to refer to an actual Christian experience. For example, in Galatians 4:21-31, Hagar and Sarah, alongside Ishmael and Isaac, are viewed as a picture of two covenants of law and promise. Paul himself describes this as an allegory. Parables are of varying length and complexity. Matthew 13:33 'The kingdom of heaven is like yeast ...' is extremely short, but in the same chapter the Parable of the Weeds (Matt. 13:24-30) is then explained in some detail (13:36-43). Of paramount importance for interpretation is our need to be guided by Scripture's own interpretation of Scripture. Traditionally some have claimed that Jesus' parables made a single point only, but the interpretation of the Sower in Matthew 13:18-23, for example, makes more than one point. Our best strategy will be to search out the main point of the teaching. Unless the text itself draws out and explains the smaller, secondary details, we ought not to engage in idle speculation and certainly need to avoid like the plague obsessive attempts at wild interpretation.

9. TAKE ACCOUNT OF COMMON SENSE

This may seem to be a strange consideration but is actually of great importance in our interpretation of biblical texts. Thus, for example, as a general rule, we should not look for magical or allegorical meanings behind plain ones. History is plain narrative and must not be allegorized. Conversely the figurative elements of poetry should not be taken literally. No one would dream of doing that with Song of Songs 7:2: 'Your waist is a mound of wheat encircled by lilies.' We must never make Scripture say those things that are plainly absurd. Thus we must never make illogical applications that would lead us into the absurd, such as the idea that God wants us literally to throw children against walls, or in other ways sacrifice them. The 'absurd' is not so rare as we might think, for there are cults in recent years that have actively taken on board the view that we should commit suicide so that we can reach God's presence in heaven more quickly.

We must never make the Bible say what it does not plainly say. Steps One to Five of our sermon preparation constitute the best way to ensure a careful and considered interpretation of the biblical passage, starting and continuing with an emphasis on the author's intention. This process of serious study will be our best route to the avoidance of errors of interpretation. Scripture is thoroughly consistent as long as we follow all the steps of sermon preparation in a spirit of sanctified common sense, depending on the help of the very Spirit who caused the Scriptures to be written.

10. TAKE ACCOUNT OF THE MYSTERIOUS AND THE UNFATHOMABLE

Scripture has clearly revealed God as Creator and humankind as fallen. The Old Testament, Gospels, Epistles and Revelation all centre on Christ himself. He is the entire focus of all Scriptural revelation and our relationship to him dominates God's Word. The overall purpose of the Bible is to give us a full and adequate understanding of the truth as it is in Christ. In Scripture we see Christ and his fullness. Having said that, we must also face the truth that:

a) God has not planned to reveal the totality of knowledge (Deut. 29:29; Mark 13:32; Acts 1:7; I Cor. 13:12). There are about thirty-nine theories in biblical scholarship regarding the meaning of 'baptism for the dead' in I Corinthians 15:29 but that fact does not actually affect our overall interpretation of Paul's argument.

b) Infinite truth does involve a real dimension of paradox. Thus for example the humanity and divinity of Christ is a paradox, as is the issue of divine predestination and the responsibility of human beings. The least we can do, as well as the most, is to give serious consideration to the whole of biblical teaching on any subject. We must never restrict ourselves to a few texts that happen to suit our own personal position or preconception. That is extremely dangerous! The truth lies not in the middle, nor at one end of the spectrum but in totality of biblical revelation.

c) Our human understanding is limited. Scripture itself reveals that we need to grow in both understanding and discernment (Mark 4:33; John 13:7, 16:12). It is our own moral weakness and spiritual state that set limits on God's interaction with us. There are limits to our ability to grasp God's revealed truth. Because of that, it is crucial that we do not try to fix our own individual understanding as a universal standard for deciding the meaning, significance and value of the biblical revelation as a whole. The fact that some parts of the Bible may never touch our own personal need, understanding or experience does not make Scripture invalid. It is our very weakness and limitation that should make us willing to listen to other voices and especially those writers of faith and sanctified scholarship. We must always evaluate the viewpoints of others, but on some issues there may be multiple and equally feasible positions that we need to value and respect. On other issues, though, we may meet difficulties or contradictions that we may only be able to solve later in life or in eternity. The Holy Spirit is our great assurance of being led into all the truth, knowledge and discernment that we frail humans need for this short life and for the glorious eternity that lies before us by the grace of Christ.

TOOLS FOR INTERPRETATION

G. D. Fee and D. Stuart, *How to Read the Bible for All its Worth* (Grand Rapids: Zondervan, 1982)

L. Berkhof, *Principles of Biblical Interpretation: Sacred Hermeneutics*, 2ⁿᵈ ed. (Grand Rapids: Eerdmans, 1952)

A. Berkeley Mickelson, *Interpreting the Bible: A Book of Basic Principles for Understanding the Scriptures* (Grand Rapids: Eerdmans, 1963)

W. G. Doty, *Contemporary New Testament Interpretation* (New York: Prentice-Hall, 1972)

D. J. Harrington, *Interpreting the New Testament: A Practical Guide* (Wilmington: M. Glazier Inc., 1979)

I. Howard Marshall, (ed.) *New Testament Interpretation: Essays on Principles and Methods* (Grand Rapids: Eerdmans, 1977)

6. Practical Steps:
Step Five
The Issue of Application to Life

THE PRIORITY OF APPLICATION

The English word 'application' derives from two Latin words *ap* meaning 'to' and *plico* meaning 'to fold', in other words, to join something to something else. Thus in a preacher's vocabulary, application involves the process by which the preacher brings scriptural truth so relevantly to the listeners' minds that they can see the ways in which they must change and are empowered to make those very changes. It is quite feasible that a sermon can be precise and thorough in its technical, exegetical content and approach. It can be wonderfully structured, aesthetically presented and even attractively illustrated. Yet if application is deficient, defective, inappropriate or absent, then that sermon will fail to hit the target and fail to accomplish the divine intention for it. Application is not actually Step Five in the preparation of an expository sermon. It requires serious thought and involvement at every step of the way. So application is not actually a step at all – it should be constantly processed in the preacher's mind. I shall argue that true expository preaching is profoundly applicatory and as such makes an impact in its work of changing human lives. Application in a real sense is the bridge between our work of exegesis on the original meaning of a biblical passage and our work of exposition as we apply the text into the lives of our twenty-first century listeners. We are thus now moving through the transition between biblical exegesis and expository preaching. Ultimately we must confront our audience with the fundamental challenge: 'What are you going to do about it?'

THE PROBLEM OF APPLICATION

The problem of application is simply its absence, paucity or inadequacy in much of modern evangelical preaching. Several reasons can be offered for this state of affairs.

In the relative absence of a commitment to expository preaching, there has come a reluctance for, or ignorance over, serious work with the biblical text. This has inevitably strangled the emergence of, and engagement with, biblical principles of application.

Some preachers take the position that application is God's work, not the preacher's responsibility. The argument here is that preachers must not meddle or interfere with the work of the Holy Spirit in human lives.

Others have maintained that the issue of application lies at various points along a spectrum between difficult and impossible. Such preaching becomes a dry, academic exercise that revolves around the 'then and there', with little or no relevance to the lives of twenty-first century people.

A particular temptation for the modern, or rather postmodern, Western preacher is to succumb to the spirit of the age in which we are encouraged to be tolerant of everything except dogmatism, authority and absolute values. The result is that many preachers are fearful of coming across to their hearers as arrogant or holier-than-thou.

That leaves a substantial number of preachers who long to make a connection, between the 'then and there' and the 'here and now', but who are genuinely ignorant or fearful of misapplying biblical texts and passages. They are simply unsure how to proceed with the application step.

The principles of application

If we consider for a moment the above attitudes of preachers toward the challenge of application, it will become apparent that there is a common thread that runs through them all. It is however more than a common thread: it is a fatal flaw. The flaw is the feeling among preachers that somehow it is up to the preacher to create, invent or think out some possible applications of a biblical passage for living. In other words, it is felt that suddenly the preacher must jump from the world of the text into the world of real people. Faced with such a prospect, small wonder that preachers feel they face a difficult, haphazard, uncertain or even impossible task. Such fear is not surprising because it involves the idea that we are somehow moving away from the biblical text in order to construct by our own efforts a bridge of application between the ancient text and the contemporary sermon listener.

It is precisely here, I suggest, that the problem lies. To view application as being unconnected with the text – or merely marginally linked with it – is to fail to understand the actual nature of application. Traditionally the application has tended to be left until the final stage of the sermon, forcing the listeners patiently to await an answer to their recurring question regarding the preached passage, namely 'So what?' In the minds of many preachers has been the idea that preaching involves researching ancient contexts and contents and then seeking and struggling to latch on to an up-to-date application for contemporary listeners. Such a view of application puts the onus on the preacher to discover or concoct applications that are in some way related to the ancient Scripture. No wonder many preachers are reluctant to swim in the unpredictable waters of guesswork, speculation, approximation and humanly designed construction.

On the contrary, the power to change lives today lies in the Word God revealed in times past. The crux of this whole issue is that Scripture was originally given by God as an applied message into specific contexts and for specific reasons. Thus application should be the backbone and tenor of the entire sermon, not just the concluding section.

Our task in exposition is to discover and draw out applications from the text and then to seek suitable contemporary materials to illustrate those applications that are already embedded in the ancient biblical texts. In other words, just as our work on main theme, sub-themes, contexts and content is rooted in the text of the biblical passage itself, so also is our work on application. It is not a question of conjecturing or constructing a possible application scenario, but rather of identifying the way in which the Spirit of God has already incorporated in the biblical text his application for the original readers. In short, the real challenge for us is not to rack our brains to come up with a possible application, for that is to confuse the work of application with the work of illustration. The basic application is embedded in the received text of Scripture and is inseparably linked to the divine intention and purpose of that Scripture. The application of a passage will emerge as we faithfully do the work of biblical exegesis under the overarching control of the divine purpose and intention of that passage.

Fundamental to our preaching of application is our need to ask the question 'What was God's purpose in His revelation of this particular passage of Scripture?' God desires to accomplish his purposes in and through Scripture and we as preachers must seek to discover those purposes. Why? Because the truth God gave in Scripture came to men and women in applied form and that application needs to be identified, extracted and reapplied for the same basic purpose for which it was originally given. The entire expository sermon should thus be applicatory.

A very helpful illustration of this mechanism comes from the work of Jay Adams.[1] He compares traditional application method with the model of a tree. From one trunk, the sermon develops many branches, then sub-branches and then 'application blossoms' are hung onto every available branch end. Application is thus scattered everywhere and lacks cohesion and clarity. Each part of the sermon becomes an end in itself. By contrast, Adams proposes the 'river method'. In other words, if we turn the tree upside down, we now see small tributaries flowing upwards from the bottom of the picture and joining larger tributaries until the whole river becomes one and flows in a single direction, carrying its power in one main stream. This river is like a sermon that gathers material from its tributaries and surges forward with one great application of biblical truth as the preacher expounds sub-themes and relates them to the main theme. In short, everything in the sermon makes a contribution to a unified purpose and the one central application derives from the overall purpose of the passage. This, I find, is a helpful strategy, though we need to be open to the possibility of more than one single purpose and application in any passage.

I. J. E. Adams, *Truth Applied: Application in Preaching* (London: The Wakeman Trust, 1990), pp. 39-47.

Adams then offers a useful example of extracting and reapplying an existing applicatory principle. I Corinthians 10:11 indicates Paul's belief that God's warnings to Israel in their idolatrous wilderness wanderings applied also to the Corinthian church of his own day in the mid first century AD. The text of I Corinthians 9:7-11 'Who serves as a soldier at his own expense...' is connected by Paul to another text, Deuteronomy 25:4, 'Do not muzzle an ox while it is treading out the grain.' In the latter text lies the principle that the labourer should reap the fruit of his labour. Paul thus reapplies that text to argue his own right to material support, which in fact he then actually refuses (I Cor. 9:12, 15). Paul has therefore identified the applicatory principle of Deuteronomy 25:4 based on the purpose of the biblical text. He has then identified similarities in his own contemporary situation that relate to the former biblical setting. Thus he reapplies Scripture on the basis of the purpose of the Deuteronomy text and its similarity to his own contemporary circumstances.

Admittedly, we are not constructing Scripture today in the way that Paul was doing. Nevertheless the relationship between purpose and application is crucial for expository preaching. The circumstances and cultures are different, but the basic purpose and application of a biblical truth are already embedded in the unchanging text of the biblical passage. God has already revealed truth in applied form – we are simply called to identify, extract and reapply that existing application, bearing in mind the purpose for which the Holy Spirit inspired the writing of that passage.

THE PROCEDURE OF APPLICATION

Diligent work on Steps One to Four will give us all the raw material for the final sermon: reading, meditation, prayer, main theme, sub-themes, contexts and content. Through this study and preparation, we will be able to discern the original purpose of the passage, for it is that purpose which will reveal to us the applicatory principle(s) within the text of the passage. In order to identify such an emerging application principle, a number of specific steps will be helpful to us, as we prepare a passage for expository preaching. We need to review the work we have done in the major Steps One to Four. Pay special attention to the main and sub-themes in their contexts as this will help us discover the overriding purpose(s) of the passage. At this point we need to write down in a sentence or two the purpose of the passage we have been studying. That will constitute the main purpose and application for our expository sermon. There may of course be 'sub-applications' as well and we should now spend some time working through these applicatory principles on rough paper as follows.

First, write down a list of all the applicatory issues raised in the passage. Some of these will be explicitly stated, others will be implicit and still others can be logically inferred from the passage. Caution and care will need to be exercised in ensuring that the biblical text remains our constant measuring-stick for life application. Do these issues involve relationships, spirituality, behaviour, ethics?

Second, determine to whom these application principles are applied in the text, whether they are aimed at individuals, corporate groups, leaders, unbelievers, parents, arrogant people, nations, or social groups. How are these people involved in the situation being addressed by the biblical passage?

Third, decide what the passage teaches about the divine perspective on the situation(s) being addressed. Is God pleased or displeased with the situation? What response is the Spirit of God wanting? In other words, is the passage providing information, direction, comfort, challenge, encouragement or rebuke? Is the truth of the passage seeking to initiate, develop or strengthen our trust in God? Is the passage demanding specific action on the part of believers or unbelievers? Such questions will enable us to complete our work of discerning the purpose and application principle(s) of the passage.

Thorough exegesis is the essential foundation for sound application. Having discovered the purpose and application principle(s) of the passage, we now need some practical guidelines so that we can present those applications, not as the vague or woolly concoctions of our own minds, but as the purpose and application revealed by the Spirit of God to his original readers and now powerfully proclaimed into the lives of men and women today.

The practicalities of application

There is a real sense in which application must appear right at the very introduction of an expository sermon. Somehow we must employ or create a verbal situation right at the outset of our sermon that will engage the attention by involving the listener. Whatever situation we present in our introduction must be related to our contemporary hearers. We have to convince our listeners that the biblical passage will be applied to them. Otherwise they will switch off and their attention will be difficult or impossible to retrieve.

As we prepare the main body of the sermon (Step 7), based on our structure and outline (Step 6), we need to make sure that application is entering every stage and that all the application is based on, and intimately related to, the overall purpose of the passage. We frequently need to check whether in our application, we are producing Jay Adams' rushing river or his disunified tree. The difference will be enormous. Our listeners, during all parts of the sermon, must feel themselves to be a part of the sermon. Therefore, our applicatory style must be warm, personal, concrete and directed constantly toward our hearers.

If we leave all our application until the conclusion, we may already have exhausted the patience of our listeners and the conclusion itself may be forced to become overlong by a repetitive summary as a prelude to the hanging of applicatory blossoms! The question 'What are you going to do about it?' need not be reserved till the conclusion. Throughout the sermon we must offer practical guidance on how to implement the message of the biblical passage.

Steps One to Five of the sermon preparation process have underlined the absolute requirement that the preacher live, eat and breathe within the biblical passage. Without that work, an expository sermon will never be born. That accepted, it is also profoundly true that effective expository preachers must know their listeners. They must work hard not only in their studies, but also in the business of getting to grips with current affairs, community issues and the personal lives and changing circumstances of their listeners. This is especially crucial in the work of sermon application and demands time invested in reading, listening, talking, observing the media and interacting socially, not only in the church but in the world as well. The preacher must seek to know and understand the listeners in order to apply biblical exposition effectively. Increasingly in the global village of East and West, expository preaching will be carried out in a cross-cultural context. In Greater London alone, 275 languages are in daily use. Preachers can learn much about applying truth cross-culturally if they are willing to travel, study and interact with other cultures, as opportunities arise.

Finally it needs to be said that the meaning and application of a biblical text must become a part of a preacher's life through prayer, reflection and obedience.

Case Study – Application: Luke 4:1-13

Luke's immediate purpose in this passage is clearly to record the three temptations experienced by Jesus in the wilderness. However, when we read this passage in its wider literary context, we observe such key issues as Jesus' baptism, the descent of the Spirit upon Jesus, the Sonship of Christ and the love that exists between Father and Son. All these themes emerge in the section 3:21-38 and the Sonship of Jesus is mentioned again in 4:3 and 9. Luke's deeper purpose thus seems to revolve round Satan's effort to discredit God by accusing Jesus to distrust his Father's care for him. It is the divine Father-Son relationship that is under attack in the wilderness testing. Trust in a loving heavenly Father is total anathema to the devil. In exposing the goals and tactics of the devil, Luke goes on to show the overriding power of God's Spirit and Word, not only to limit the assaults of the devil (4:1) but also to portray Jesus as victorious through that very Word and Spirit (4:4, 8, 12, 13, 14).

The main theme of Luke 4:1-13 is the temptations from the devil faced by Jesus in the wilderness. Underlying this theme we can trace the devil's attempt to discredit God and to destroy the mission of God's Son. The power of God's Word and God's Spirit, however, are seen in the victory of Jesus over the devil's attacks. These themes are very much in line with Luke's stated purpose in assembling his account, namely, to give certainty of the things that had been taught (Luke 1:4). The ultimate triumph of Christ and believer over the powers of darkness is a great source of assurance for faith.

(1) A number of applicatory issues can be identified in the text of our sermon passage:

(a) Jesus entered this wilderness experience under the leading of God's Spirit (4:1). God himself, in sovereign power, sets limits to the assaults of the devil upon Jesus and upon Jesus' followers.

(b) Jesus demonstrates the power of the divine Word to oppose temptations inflicted by the devil.

(c) The devil's challenge to Jesus' ministry and mission was launched right at the outset and sometimes it is the case that a new work for God is opposed in its early stages.

(d) The devil attacks Jesus at the point of his hunger and possible loneliness. Temptation often strikes us at our most vulnerable as the devil seeks to damage or, if possible, destroy our communion and fellowship with the Father.

(e) 4:4 indicates the importance of a believer's feeding on the Word of God. In any case, God the Father is perfectly capable of supplying our material needs in his time and way.

(f) The devil is trying to persuade Jesus to act independently of his Father. If successful, the devil would thereby break the filial dependence and obedience between the divine Father and Son.

(g) Sovereignty belongs to God alone and he alone is worthy of our worship (4:5-8).

(h) The devil will always seek to encourage us to seek worldly possessions, honour and glory (4:6-7).

(i) Our calling as believers is to trust in God, not to test God by abusing our privileged position as his children (4:12). We cannot dictate terms to God or make deals with him.

(j) The devil cannot compel action; he can only make suggestions. We have the final responsibility for moral attitudes and actions (4:9). God has equipped us by Word and Spirit to deal with temptation, even though the devil is stubborn, persistent and strategic in his planned assaults (4:13).

(2) Luke directs this divine application to Theophilus (1:3) but not to him alone. The message is for all those who would read and hear this circulated gospel. It was aimed to strengthen the faith of

all believers and to answer those who sought to doubt and to damage faith in Christ. The application is for all men and women, including Gentiles.

(3) The passage reveals spiritual truth of cosmic proportions concerning the person and work of Christ and of the devil. It offers practical instruction for dealing with the devil, information about the devil's tactics, assurance about available divine resources for the battle, and encouragement to persevere in life and ministry by submission, dependence and obedience to our loving Lord.

6. Practical Steps
Step Six
Method and Outline

Let us remind ourselves at this point that everything we have achieved in gathering our materials on rough paper or index cards has been the result of our analysis of the biblical text itself. We have identified the main theme and sub-themes, engaged in contexts and contents research, and found application principles based on the purpose and original intention of the biblical author. It is this absolute adherence to the text of Scripture that is the prime hallmark of expository preaching. If we fail to live in and to live out the teachings of Scripture then our preaching will be founded merely on our own ideas and inclinations. Such preaching will be devoid of divine authority and will certainly lack the divine power to change human lives and destinies.

By now you may well be feeling that you are drowning in the ocean of raw material that you have accumulated during the preparation of Steps One to Five. That is very understandable and is precisely why we need to bring together the order, organization and simplicity that will come during Step Six. We now have large amounts of flesh from our work on Steps One to Five. What we must now seek is a skeleton, so that we have a set of bones on which we can hang the flesh. We are now moving strongly from biblical exegesis to expository sermon, but in a real sense we must never leave the biblical text behind. Exposition needs the foundation of biblical exegesis as much as human beings need to breathe oxygen – it is as important as that! The exegetical work of Steps One to Five is hard work and as a general rule, if I am preparing a brand new sermon, the preparation of Steps One to Five absorbs four to six hours of my time. The production of the written sermon in Steps Six to Ten takes a further three to five hours.

Our goal in Step Six is twofold: (1) to establish a method for sermon development; (2) to establish a structural outline for sermon development.

A METHOD FOR SERMON DEVELOPMENT

At this stage of transition into the written form of the expository sermon, we need to give some thought to the variety of methods that we might use to expand the main and sub-themes, in line with the purpose of our passage, into the full and final body of the sermon. There are a number of different styles and methods by which we can structure and develop our material to form the central body of the sermon. Every method has the same ultimate goal: to expand the main and sub-themes of the passage into a sermon whose purpose is in line with the purpose of the biblical passage. These methods are not mutually exclusive for they often overlap and sometimes we will use a combination of them even within the same sermon. They are ways in which we can handle our exegetical material as we develop and present that material in the final body of the expository sermon. Let us look briefly at ten possible ways of processing our information. Our choice of a method or mixture of methods will be determined by the type and purpose of the passage, the preacher's goal and the nature and needs of the listening congregation. Above all, from our perspective as preachers, we need to select whatever way will lead to maximum clarity for our listeners.

1. ASKING AND ANSWERING A QUESTION

This is as simple as the title suggests and yet can produce profoundly powerful pulpit communication. Some passages lend themselves to our setting up a question and then seeking to answer it from the preaching passage. Thus for example in James 3:13-17 the term 'wisdom' dominates the whole passage. According to James, the outworking of the life of faith depends on our possession of wisdom. The passage gives no instantly recognizable definition of 'wisdom', so in this situation, we can set up the question 'What is this wisdom?' and expound the passage with that question uppermost in our minds as we lead the listeners to a biblical answer, based on the context and content of the passage.

2. POSING AND SOLVING A PROBLEM

Sometimes a biblical passage presents a problem issue to which there seems to be no obvious, immediate or clear solution. In such a situation, we might set up a problem and then lead our listeners through a gradual investigation until the picture comes into sharp focus. This can generate a helpful sense of expectancy as the listeners are led through a series of clues in the biblical text. One passage that lends itself to such treatment is Revelation 2:12-17. Verse 13 shows God's approval of this martyr church in Pergamum. Yet God reveals that he expects repentance of such urgency that without it, the church will come under fierce and immediate divine judgment (2:14-16). What on earth was the problem?

As preachers we can then investigate the two areas of teaching – Balaam and the Nicolaitans – that must surely be the source of the problem at Pergamum. The problem must be traced to its Old Testament context in Numbers 22–24, 25, 31. Balaam's doctrine seems to have been that Israel, as God's covenant people, was guaranteed protection and preservation against all its enemies. Israel thought it was safe enough in God's hands to be able to mix with surrounding nations and even be drawn into idolatrous liaisons with pagans without damaging consequences. The believers at Pergamum held sound doctrine – that wasn't the problem – but they felt they were so secure in the name and faith of Christ that their conduct didn't actually matter. The results were excessive tolerance towards pagans, over-accommodation, compromise and the flooding of the church with worldly paganism. The message for the Pergamum believers, and for the contemporary church, is that real love involves upholding truth and living it out whatever the cost.

Problem posing can be very powerful in preaching for it involves a sense of the unknown, even mysterious, and invites the listeners to open their Bibles and follow the preacher on a treasure trail of discovery.

3. DEALING WITH A DILEMMA

Few sermons have greater potential for powerful impact than those which expose real dilemmas faced by believers in ancient times and experienced in tangibly similar ways by Christians today. Thus the scattered believers of Peter's day touch the hearts of many believers today for they encapsulate a real dilemma (1 Peter 1:13–2:3). Why is it that in seeking to serve God wholeheartedly, he still allows suffering and persecution to strike the followers of Christ? What response does God expect us to make in such situations of severe trial and pain? In our preaching of such passages, we can set up the dilemma and perhaps try out a few human solutions before applying our zoom lens to shed light on the biblical text. Peter provides weapons and resources for the people of God in I Peter 1:13–2:3. A number of them can immediately be identified as application principles based on the overall purpose of the author in this passage, namely, how to survive under stressful circumstances:

a) Holiness in living must be maintained (1:13-16);

b) Assurance from the sovereign God who showed the extent of his care by the shed blood of Christ (1:17-21);

c) Love the brethren in the midst of trials (1:22);

d) Sustain yourselves into maturity by feeding on the Word of God (1:23–2:3).

The expounded passage thus takes God's encouragement to the believers addressed by Peter and applies it to all believers facing dilemmas and difficulties. Therein we see the sheer power and contemporary relevance of exposition.

4. DOCTRINAL/TOPICAL EXPLANATION

Sometimes our biblical exposition will take the form of a straightforward explanation of a doctrine or a topic of Scripture. In this method the main and sub-themes will simply be explained systematically and applied for the listeners. An example of this approach might be from Ephesians 4:1-16 in which we systematically explain the main theme of how believers can maintain and show forth the Spirit's unity in the Body of Christ, namely through Christian living and relating (vv. 1-3), through the exercise of various spiritual gifts (vv. 4-12) and through sustained growth to maturity (vv. 13-16).

5. ARGUING A CASE

Emotions must have been running high when Paul wrote his urgent appeal to the Galatians, as they wrestled with threats to the very nature and survival of the gospel itself. Devoid of his customary introductory remarks of gratitude for faith and love, along with assurance of his prayers for the believers, Paul launches straight into the offensive. Even in Galatians 1:1-5 the gospel is uppermost in his mind and in 1:6-10 the apostle expresses his personal devastation over the Galatians' stunning abandonment of the gospel of grace. The whole letter is one of devastating challenge to the faltering believers in the Galatian church but 3:1-14 is particularly vehement and powerful as Paul sets faith in collision with works and sets law in contradiction to Spirit. The force of his argument is palpable, as Paul spares no effort to drive home his case. The main theme – the basis for our justification – is clearly present and a number of sub-themes relate to, and expand upon, this main theme. Paul is direct to the point of labelling his readers 'foolish' (3:1, 3)! I am not suggesting that we insult those who hear our sermons but such a passage does lend itself to a sustained and energetic presentation of arguments.

6. DEFENDING A CLAIM

On occasion the biblical authors set up a specific proposition and then present a series of proofs for their readers.[1] The apostle Paul was a master of this method. As expository preachers, we need to beware of offering our hearers strings of proof texts without adequate contextual consideration. However, there is sometimes a real case for expounding Scripture as a systematic proving of a particular proposition. One of the best known applications of this method occurs in Paul's concern to argue for the bodily resurrection of Christian believers in I Corinthians 15. Having set up his main theme as a proposition – '...How can some of you say that there is no resurrection of the dead?' (I Cor. 15:12) – he then proceeds to draw in a number of sub-themes as arguments that prove how foolish is this denial of the bodily resurrection of believers. Indeed he tries to show how absurd this position is by listing the consequences of the non-resurrection of believers: (a) Christ has not even been raised (vv. 13,

---

1. For this particular approach, I am indebted to Haddon Robinson (1980:119-120). Robinson offers other helpful types of sermon development method on pp.116-127 of his book. I am most grateful to him for shaping and stimulating my own thining about that vital stage.

16); (b) Christian preaching and faith are useless (vv. 14, 17); (c) our witness as apostles amounts to a pack of lies (v. 15); (d) believers are stuck with their sins (v. 17); (e) believers have no hope beyond the grave (v. 18). This method of proving a case can be powerful for our listening believers and unbelievers.

7. DEDUCTIVE UNRAVELLING

If we are preaching regular sermons to the same congregation, the saying 'Variety is the spice of life' becomes especially meaningful. We need to be constantly aware of our need to offer variety in our sermon development method. Our hearers need stimulation not sedation. That requires our conscious and frequent attention to variety of method and particularly so because much of our expository preaching will rightly fall into the category of deduction. In this method, the goal, purpose and even conclusion of the sermon are stated at the beginning and the congregation is then shown all the stages that led to the conclusion. In other words, the main theme is stated at the outset and the sub-themes are then our framework for unravelling all our expository material. Such a method, by its very nature, can become all too predictable if employed to excess! Some years ago I preached Psalm 95 along the following deductive lines –

Main Theme: The greatens of God and the reasons we should worship him.

Sub-themes: 1: Call to worship in song, joy, shouting and thankfulness because he is creator (vv. 1-5).
2: Call to humility because he is personal Lord and Shepherd (vv. 6-7b).
3: Call to hear and obey God's Word (vv. 7c-11).

8. USE OF STORIES AND NARRATIVE

Storytelling was extensively used by Jesus in his preaching and teaching ministry and Western preachers in particular need to rediscover this valuable method. This approach lends itself to the use of ideas and imagination but the details should nevertheless be worked together towards specific points and always under the strict control of the biblical text. Our listeners should be able to identify with the thinking, feeling and reactions of the people portrayed in the biblical stories. In that way, we can impact our hearers as they see themselves writ large in the preaching material. Narratives such as Joseph, David, the Prodigal Son and many other such parables invite greater use of this method of expounding Scripture.

9. INDUCTIVE REASONING

This method is virtually the reverse of deductive preaching, for by induction, the sermon opens with the first point but, instead of exposing the way the sermon will progress, the preacher instead strongly links points in such a way that the punch line or main theme emerges only at the end. In this way, there is a sense of suspense as the listeners are forced to wait for the main theme to be revealed. This method is particularly appropriate for hostile hearers who might switch off quickly if the sermon seemed too predictable in its direction. Peter used this method to great effect in Acts 2:14-36. Twenty years ago I heard a preacher address a very nominally Christian gathering. He spoke from Matthew 7:15-23 in an inductive fashion as he examined and eliminated various types of people who we would expect to have no problems in their standing before God. Only at the very end of the sermon did he reveal what was necessary to secure our right and acceptable standing in the presence of God. Over the space of half an hour I watched 300 people shift from their usual semi-horizontal slouch to a desperate, palpable straining on the very edge of their pews! He had used the inductive method to devastating effect. It was an unforgettable sermon.

10. EVANGELISTIC CHALLENGE

Some preachers feel that the expository preaching method is unsuitable for evangelistic sermons. I suspect that they have misunderstood the nature of exposition, confusing it with verse-by-verse heavy, technical exegesis of the sort that features in some academic papers. Make no mistake. Biblical exegesis is crucial to expository preaching and is indispensable. Our goal is to move our listeners in their minds, hearts and wills – not to send them to sleep in utter boredom. In evangelistic preaching from a biblical text, we should still employ all the steps of expository preparation, but we need to be flexible in terms of illustration, length, organization and presentation as we expound the Word of God to an unbelieving audience. All the rules, steps and guidelines for handling biblical texts do not suddenly change when we engage with the unregenerate mind and will. Much can be learned about the strategy of cross-cultural evangelistic preaching from the Mars Hill sermon of the apostle Paul in Acts 17:22-31, especially in Paul's attempt to identify with the world of his hearers (17:22-3) and in his approach to the nature of God and creation for listeners of Gentile philosophical background (17:24-9). Paul was flexible in his preaching style and approach. We should be too.

AN OUTLINE FOR SERMON DEVELOPMENT

We are almost ready to put the body of the sermon together in its final written form. One thing more is needed: a framework of bones onto which we will hang the flesh that we must select from all of our prepared material. Unless we give the sermon a basic framework, the flesh will collapse in an amorphous, tangled and meaningless heap. We must have an outline. At this point we should return to our Step Two themes, Step Three contexts and Step Four column analysis and re-examine the right-hand column, checking main theme, sub-themes, contrasts, similarities, causes, effects, conditions, commands etc. Column analysis will be a major help in constructing our Step Six sermon outline. Indeed, before deciding our Step Six outline, it will be helpful to read through all the raw material gathered during our preparation of Steps One to Five.

AIMS OF OUTLINE

(1) to enable us to see how the whole and the parts fit together and relate to one another;

(2) to establish the most appropriate order for the presentation of our points of exposition;

(3) to enable us to see what materials we shall need in order to turn the skeleton into the fully fleshed body;

(4) to encourage clarity in the final form and presentation.

FORM OF OUTLINE

Basically we need to review the main theme and sub-themes established in Step Two in light of the work we have done during Steps Three to Six and we also need to examine again our column analysis from Step Four to help us formulate an outline. These refined, and if necessary modified, themes will form the basic framework of the sermon outline. In other words, our main and sub-themes will bear a close correspondence to the points of our outline. A number of factors should be borne in mind in constructing the sermon outline.

First, the outline is for the help and guidance of the preacher. We shall need to lead our listeners through the points of the outline once they are finally enfleshed in the sermon, but I personally seldom announce the outline to the congregation in advance. If our preaching is clear, logical and systematic, the listeners ought to be able to remember our outline without ever having actually seen it! If our outline is heavy and detailed, it will not be helpful or encouraging for our hearers to see it in advance! Better to maintain an element of surprise, suspense and wakefulness by a little secrecy in our sermon plan.

Second, the main theme and sub-themes of the passage will form the basic structure and framework around which the whole sermon will be built. Thus the outline does not necessarily have to follow the order of the biblical passage. Our guiding light in this is the thought of the biblical author. There is room for flexibility in the outline.

Third, every passage of Scripture is unique and some will be easier to outline than others. The identification of main and sub-themes, and thereby the fixing of a sermon outline, is generally speaking easier in my experience for New Testament letters and theological arguments than it is for prophetic oracles, poetic sections or Gospel narratives. Patience, persistence and adaptability are the needed attitudes.

Fourth, the outline should consist of three basic elements: *introduction*: this opens up the topic, main theme and/or first section of the sermon; *body*: this is the core of the entire sermon in which the main and sub-themes are elaborated and developed. This will incorporate their explanation, application and illustration, all based on the overriding purpose of the passage; *conclusion*: the main theme can be summarized, repeated or further applied, thus ending the sermon.

Fifth, the outline should not be complicated by multiple or confusing points. Clarity is the greatest concern, along with faithfulness to the biblical text itself. Avoid ending up with more than half a dozen sub-themes – it can be very discouraging to a congregation.

Sixth, beware of being sidetracked and deflected by additional issues or ideas that are not directly related to the sermon passage itself. Stick to the main and sub-themes and think through how you will eventually make smooth and helpful transitions from one point to the next.

CASE STUDY– OUTLINE: LUKE 4:1-13

Bearing in mind what we have identified as main and sub-themes in Step Two and conscious also of our context work in Step Three, we must now look down the Step Four right-hand column analysis for patterns, similarities, contrasts, recurring thoughts and groups of related features. All these observations in Steps Two, Three, Four and Five will help us to formulate our Step Six Outline.

INTRODUCTION – Let us begin by asking the question 'Why?' Why does the devil decide to tempt Jesus? What is the devil's ultimate goal? Clues in the context include:

1. Timing – Jesus was starting a Spirit-anointed ministry (Luke 3:22; 4:1). He was physically weak and therefore vulnerable.
2. Motive – God had just affirmed his love for and pleasure in Jesus (3:22).
3. Method – The devil is challenging Jesus' Sonship (3:22, 23-38; 4:3, 9)
4. Goal – To divert Jesus from an attitude of trusting submission to God's Will (4:6-7, 9-10).

BODY – Let us now ask the question 'How?' How did the devil seek to divert Jesus? How did Jesus respond to each temptation?

1. Luke 4:3-4: *the devil's strategy*: that Jesus use his Messianic power to provide for his own needs, thus satisfying his own physical needs outside of his Father's ability to provide (4:3).

Jesus' response: God will provide all our needs in his own way and material needs are not the only ones (4:4).

2. Luke 4:5-8: *the devil's strategy*: that Jesus should gain worldly power and glory by worshipping the devil (4:5-7).

Jesus' response: sovereignty and worship belong to God alone, not to the devil (4:8).

3. Luke 4:9-12: *the devil's strategy*: that Jesus test the miraculous power and love of his Father and proves His Messiahship (4:9-11).

Jesus' response: we are called to submit obediently to God's Ways, God's Word and God's Will. We must not put God on trial (4:12).

Conclusion – Let us finally ask the question 'What?'

What should be our response to the devil's temptations?

1. Rest in divine Sovereignty – Satan is limited in power (Luke 4:13; Job 1:12; 2:6). In Matthew 4:10, Jesus commands Satan to depart.
2. Employ the divine Word (Luke 4:4, 8, 12).
3. Trust in the power of God's Holy Spirit (Luke 3:22; 4:1, 14, 18).
4. Experience the care of God in the midst of the spiritual battle (Matt. 4:11; Mark 1:13).

The temptation after all was within the purposes of God for Jesus (Luke 4:1). God will bring us to victory and maturity even through trials and testings.

6. Practical Steps:
Step Seven
Write Out the Body of the Sermon

Rejoice and relax! Rejoice because you have carefully and systematically worked your way through six steps of sermon preparation and you now have all the raw material – indeed more than enough – with which to construct your expository sermon. Relax before you move into the final four stages of actual sermon writing. Often I take time out at this stage and play a game of soccer with my two sons or set off on a fishing trip with them. The completion of Step Six normally brings me not only a sense of rejoicing and relaxation but also one of relief. The hard slog of preparation – as well as its joy – is past and we are now ready to assemble our raw material ingredients into the final version of an expository sermon.

Having said that the hard work of preparation is now behind us, I must quickly admit that Step Seven is always a challenge and calls for a fresh dependence on the Spirit of God to anoint us physically, mentally and spiritually. Step Seven is not a single isolated step. It means drawing on all the ingredients of Steps One to Six and deciding how to mix the right balance of material into the final sermon. Usually preparation of Steps One to Six takes me anything from four to eight hours of study, sometimes more, sometimes less, yet the work is still not finished. For most of us the greatest challenge of expository preaching will lie in one or more of three areas:

(1) Willingness to make time for rigorous work on Step Three (Contexts), Step Four (Content) and Step Five (Application).

(2) Ability to think analytically and critically by constantly firing questions focused both at the biblical passage and at the world being addressed by the passage.

(3) Knowing how to select the most suitable and necessary raw materials, knowing what to leave out and knowing how actually to assemble the whole body from the multiple parts. This stage is not only challenging to do but also difficult to demonstrate to others. It

is an art that gradually develops with time, practice and accumulated experience. Although Steps One to Six set very clear boundaries to our sermon, nevertheless within Step Seven there is considerable scope for personality, flare, creativity and imagination to be applied to the actual method of writing the sermon body. Just as there is scope for some degree of variation in our fixing of main and sub-themes in any single passage, so also it is true that no two preachers will preach an identical sermon on the same passage – unless one has copied the other! There is freedom for individual approach within Step Seven.

In all of this matter of sermon assembly, bear in mind that I am a Westerner. My temperament also leads me in the direction of planning, structure and organization. Two decades in Asia have helped me to gain needed flexibility. I do not want to push you towards excessive organization but what we all need is clear, powerful, applicatory exposition. Any structure that aids clarity is to be welcomed.

Some years ago, a Western missionary to the Philippines proudly told me that he had just preached his first sermon in Tagalog, the national language of that land. Very quickly, however, his smile disappeared and he admitted to me that he had been forced by his language limitation to write out his sermon in full. Further conversation unearthed a commonly held view among many preachers, namely that a written sermon is indicative of the beginner and that as we become more mature, we reduce the sermon to a few notes or headings on a postcard or the back of an envelope. I went on to share with my colleague my own fundamental unease with that popular misconception. I am not suggesting that preachers should mindlessly, with head bowed and buried in the pulpit, read out the full text of their written sermon. I am however strongly advising a fully written out version and for a number of reasons.

(1) The Holy Spirit is not restricted in our preaching to the thirty minutes during which we occupy a pulpit. He is active and helping us through the entire process of preparation.

(2) The regular discipline of writing a full version will enable us to time our sermons more predictably. Indeed those who preach with a

few brief notes only may well become sidetracked and long-winded in their presentation.

(3) A full version gives us the freedom to add, subtract or change material just prior to or during the actual presentation. Good preparation allows for flexibility.

(4) In the event of disturbance or interference during preaching, either from within or from outside ourselves, a full version will save us if we suddenly lose our train of thought.

(5) A full version greatly reduces the chances of kicking ourselves, after preaching, for failing to include some vital point, application or illustration. We will be able to avoid that sinking feeling of leaving an examination room, then checking our study notes and realizing that we have made a major mistake or left out a vital piece of information.

In short there are great benefits from a fully written out form of your sermon and that is my own personal policy in sermon preparation. Let me therefore now attempt to show you how I assemble my raw material into an expository sermon, emphasizing again that this is not an inflexible concrete sequence of stages. Flexibility is not only allowed; it is to be expected and encouraged.

Procedure for assembly of body
Stage I
Surrender yourself and your raw material to the scrutiny and help of the Holy Spirit, preferably on a Monday morning! The pastor who married my wife and me took several hours every morning for sermon study and preparation, informing his elders that, except for emergencies, they ought to avoid phoning him during such times. Sometimes preparation time is unavoidably cut short. Sometimes pastoral problems overwhelm our ministry and change our plans and timetables drastically. Accident, sickness and death can seldom be predicted or arranged for the preacher's convenience! For all these reasons, and for others, weekly sermon preparation should begin on a Monday and definitely not on the Saturday evening before Sunday preaching! A sense of utter and absolute dependence on the power and leading of the Holy Spirit is indispensable for every expository preacher.

The following stages describe the process of writing out a sermon after the preparation work has been done.

Stage 2

Select some suitably sized sheets of paper on which to write out your sermon body or alternatively use your own personal computer or typewriter. What on earth is the relevance of paper size to expository preaching? Simply this: large sheets of paper prominently displayed on a pulpit surface can be very discouraging to a congregation, especially if there are many of them and they look well filled with text. Don't let your audience see how much material you have! I try to use paper, generally A5 size, that is small enough to be concealed inside the pages of my preaching Bible or on the pulpit surface itself. Some use index cards and this can be helpful and acceptable for the final written form. During preaching, by the way, if a sheet of paper falls to the ground or, as in tropical Manila, is blown off by a whirring fan, I suggest you pick up the sheet immediately. If you don't, someone in the congregation will spend the rest of the sermon wondering whether or not you will pick it up during the course of your preaching!

Stage 3

Decide how much time you have for your message and measure your material according to the limitations of time. This is in fact a very real consideration. In some churches I am told that fifteen minutes is the most that a congregation can tolerate. A Chinese church once told me that it was entirely up to me and I should feel free to follow the Spirit's leading, the only condition being a minimum of forty-five minutes! I recently prepared a thirty to thirty-five minute sermon and was then informed by the minister that the service would incorporate a celebration of the Lord's Supper, thus limiting the sermon to twenty minutes maximum. I quickly but carefully eliminated some material and preached the sermon on Luke 4:1-13 in seventeen minutes precisely! Pressure of time sometimes actually improves our presentation by forcing us to concentrate on the real essentials and eliminate the minor items.

The advantage of regular use of a certain paper size is that we can be fairly certain of our sermon length. Each written side of A5 paper will yield about five minutes of my preaching time.

Stage 4

At this stage, don't worry about introduction, illustrations or conclusion, unless ideas or suitable materials suddenly occur to you. During this Step Seven you should concentrate on writing out the whole body of your sermon. I try to do this in a quiet place if at all possible, and preferably in one continuous sitting or at most two or three. The writing-up of a thirty-minute sermon body tends to take me four to five hours to achieve, because of the degree of thinking, as well as writing, that is required. The expository preacher never stops thinking.

Stage 5

Before you begin to write or type a single word of the body of your sermon, you must spend time looking through all the raw material you have gathered together during Steps One to Six of the preparation process. By now you should have accumulated rough notes in the following ten areas:

Main and sub-themes statement
Historical setting
Sociocultural and religious background
Literary context
Column Analysis
Grammatical Analysis
Exegetical Analysis
Biblical/ Theological Reflection
Applicatory Principles and Issues
Method of Development and Outline

The whole aim of Step Seven is to take our outline and add to it supporting material that will actually function like flesh and skin covering the bare bones of the outline. In other words, the outline is a necessary but not sufficient requirement for the expository sermon.

Without flesh our sermons will lack power. Indeed they will not live at all. Our guideline in this process of transferring flesh from rough paper to the final form of the body is basically threefold. In short, having reviewed the material, we must select thoughtfully, carefully and prayerfully only that material which (a) develops the main and sub-themes of the passage, (b) fulfils the purpose of the passage, and (c) explains the meaning and application of the passage.

The selected material will then be used to put flesh on the various bones of our outline. The skeletal framework of this outline will gradually be expanded into a body. This transition from outline to body is absolutely vital but often frustrating and needs much prayer, thinking and rethinking. It is to this challenging task of expansion that we must now turn in some detail.

Stage 6

In a nutshell we need to use an appropriate method of expansion, working systematically through each point of the outline and sticking at all times to the biblical text. For every theme or point of the outline, we need to review all that we have discovered about it during our work on Steps One to Six of preparation. For each point, we then need to include the following approaches in varying degrees.

Highlight it. One of the marks of expository preaching is that we should be continually using the biblical text and frequently referring our listeners to it as we expound the sermon passage. At each treatment of a new point, we should call attention to its location in the passage, so that our hearers are ready to follow the imminent exposition. This should not be done in a stereotyped, wooden or predictable fashion but with interest, flow and variety. Sometimes we will need to read aloud the relevant verse or section during the sermon but at other times, we may simply summarize its content and theme for our listeners.

Explain it. Having indicated a particular point from the passage, we must explain its meaning in light of our study in contexts (Step Three) and content (Step Four). This explanation will be intimately tied to the overall purpose of the writer in both the surrounding literary context and in the sermon passage itself. We must draw on that raw material from our preparation that will illuminate and elucidate the meaning of this particular point as intended by the original author. The ancient author and readers must be constantly at the front of our thinking.

Apply it. As we expose the meaning of each point and refer to our notes on the purpose we will be able to see its significance as applicatory principle. We must then clearly identify and draw out for our listeners the application that lies in the biblical text.

Illustrate it. Some applications may be obvious and self-evident to our listeners. Others may need more concrete and contemporary application through an appropriate illustration. A sermon must not be dominated by the excessive use of illustrations, but an illustration is valid if it makes a definite contribution to clarity, emphasis or re-enforcement of audience understanding.

Check it. We must always do this before moving on to treat the next point. Right at the beginning of our preparation in Step Two, we decided the main and sub-themes of the passage. Then in Steps Five and Six we discerned the purpose and application of the passage. Failure to decide these issues will raise the real danger that we will consciously or unconsciously try to bend, force or manipulate the passage to fit our own personal aims and agendas. Our goal in exposition is to discover the message that is there in the passage and to deal with, and include, material that uncovers the meaning and significance of that message in a way that is related and relevant to the overall purpose of the passage. It may be that some of the material in the passage will be left out if it is not directly relevant to the main aim. Certainly it is only a portion of the raw material we have derived from preparation that will actually find its way into the final form of the sermon. All that we include must serve the goal of creating a response in the minds, hearts and wills of our listeners. Yet again therefore we need to check every point and ensure that each is utterly rooted in the biblical text and that each has been explained and applied in line with the main theme and purpose of the passage in particular and the whole biblical book in general.

Just as it is vital to treat each and every point individually, so it is equally crucial to pay attention to the relationships to each other of the points in our outline. To this we now turn.

STAGE 7

We must show how each point fits into the overall aim and purpose of the sermon. To help us achieve this, we must clearly link the points of our outline so that our listeners know where we are taking them. The points themselves should be so clearly expressed that the clarity will communicate the themes in a thoroughly understandable fashion. If that is the case, then our hearers ought to be able to remember the main and sub-themes and their application well after hearing the sermon. In achieving memorable points, alliteration can be helpful but becomes predictable and even painful with excessive use, especially if the same letter of the alphabet is used week after week. Likewise preachers ought to avoid forcing unnatural or bizarre headings onto points. The main issue in linking points is that of relationship. All the themes in a sermon must be clearly related both to the text of the passage and to each other. Here we need to make allowances for flexibility based on the different cultural backgrounds of preachers. Western thought tends to be linear, progressive and logical, moving in a straight line and building up to a climax. Thus deductive methods may be the more natural environment for the Western preacher. Eastern thinking tends to build blocks into a total holistic picture. Whereas the Westerner might deal with three truths each individually illustrated, the Eastern approach might take one truth and approach it from three different angles. The essence in all approaches is faithfulness to the biblical text and clarity of communication. The guiding light in our linking of points is that the whole thing must move in the direction of the overall purpose of the passage. The Spirit of God is waiting to apply the text that he gave to his first readers. That is where the power of expository preaching lies.

We must remember to give adequate treatment to each point . If we have an excessively long introduction or first point, our hearers may become restless as they try to predict the length of the whole exposition! The length of exposition of each point may not always be equal but will always be appropriate, depending on points that may require careful explanation and points that are especially significant in relation to purpose and application.

STAGE 8

Limit your material for each point to that which explains meaning clearly, develops purpose and reveals the application. This means that we must be determined to exclude everything that fails to fulfil those three goals. That is always a painful process, especially if the eliminated material is new, interesting or unusual. If we try to include too much material in the sermon body, we might easily lose the sense of direction of the sermon or confuse our listeners or perhaps both. Expository preachers can give their listeners indigestion through information overload! We would all do well to heed Denis Lane's warning: 'Our hearers' ability to receive is far less than our enthusiasm to give.'[1]

STAGE 9

We must make a conscious effort in our elaboration of the outline to maintain a healthy balance between the overall direction and purpose of the sermon and the detailed, developmental material. If the balance slips excessively in one direction, then we must make changes. We need enough detail to establish the purpose, meaning and application of the passage, but we do not want so much detail that these aims are obscured, deflected or confused. Practice may not make us perfect but it will certainly improve us enormously.

STAGE 10

As we move through each point in a sermon, it can be helpful briefly to restate in a nutshell the previous point. The main theme needs to be repeated and reinforced a number of times in the course of a sermon. The main problem facing our listeners is that they only get one opportunity to grasp our points, unless of course the message is tape-recorded. If one of our points is unclear, the listeners may well miss the next one or even more, as they wrestle in their minds to unravel that foggy point. This can be a disaster. If we can restate a point in different words, we are actually underlining the issue and the truth will be reinforced for our hearers. The secret lies in not making it obvious to the congregation that we are actually repeating ourselves.

1. Denis Lane, *Preach the Word* (Welwyn: Evangelical Press, 1979), p. 29.

The only exceptions to the benefit of repetition in a sermon are excessive repetition or repetition caused by our laziness in preparation such that we are searching for something to say! One of the best ways to check ourselves is to reread the body to ourselves or to a friend in order to appraise such issues as flow, links, direction, application and clarity. Rereading is needed for greater familiarity with our final product, but we should not put ourselves into bondage by trying to memorize the contents of our sermon.

Some special pleas

During the expansion of an outline into a sermon there are, in my opinion and experience, three overwhelming characteristics that should be visible in the final product.

I. Clarity

Whether we come from a Western or Eastern cultural background with associated differences in patterns of thought, our goal must be clarity of communication. Clarity comes through two necessary processes:

(a) *Thinking.* If we have given much serious thought to our passage and worked our way through the steps of sermon preparation, then we ought to be able to state something clearly and simply. That is why serious preparation is so vital and is never a waste of time. It not only produces a sound expository sermon; it trains our mind at the same time.

(b) *Understanding.* The discipline of a clear outline and a full written body are crucial aids to our own comprehension of a passage. Make no mistake, if we ourselves are unclear in our understanding, and therefore unclear in our communication, this will guarantee even greater lack of clarity for our hearers. Whenever we seek to define or explain something, we must be completely sure about the material in our own minds before we dare try to explain it to others. If it is clear to us, then there is a strong chance it will be clear to our hearers.

Clarity is of paramount importance. Without it we are simply wasting our time and our listeners' time. Effective communication means taking that which at times is complex, analysing it and presenting it in an understandable way. The challenge to be clear is an awesome responsibility because its presence or absence will mean that our preaching either draws people nearer to the Lord God or it drives them away from him. It is that important. Clarity enables hearers to move in tune with the preacher.

In achieving clarity, there are certain aids available to us, though this will vary with our different cultural and linguistic backgrounds. In English, it is generally a good idea for the preacher to stick to short, written sentences. This helps to clarify communication, but again, in terms of oral sentence length, variety can add spice. Simple words and simple sentence structures aid clarity, as does the avoidance of unnecessary jargon or technical terms. We must use language that is comprehensible to our hearers and we must not assume that all our hearers understand such words as 'eschatology' or 'justification', or even such 'obvious' words as 'sin', 'redemption' or 'God'.

2. ACCURACY

As preachers we are ultimately responsible to the living Lord for the way that we handle and present his Word to the church and the world. The very steps that we have trodden in our sermon preparation are designed to ensure accuracy in handling the biblical text. When we then use additional material to build the outline into the body, we will also seek accuracy. Thus for example factual information, examples, illustrations or statistics should be carefully screened for accuracy, especially if we use medical examples with doctors in our congregation or economic data with a businessman in the third row! Evangelicals in many ways are a minority group and we must beware of the temptation to exaggerate in order to encourage or impress our listeners. Accuracy applies also to the acknowledging of brief references or quotations from other sources.

3. RELEVANCE

Accuracy in handling texts and clarity in communicating those texts are essential features of expository preaching. Both however will lose their impact if we fail in the third area of expertise: relevance to the hearer. Having discovered the applicatory principle(s) in the passage, we must drive the message home to our listeners. We are called to preach so that every hearer knows we are preaching to him or to her. This is the great beauty of preaching – we can be direct and sometimes God's Word will cause offence, yet through our preaching the Spirit of God can convict people deeply without exposing them publicly. In many societies, concern to avoid loss of face is of paramount importance and this often generates a subtle, indirect, circling-the-issue kind of communication. Preaching can be direct, devastating and yet in a sense considerate of the feelings of the listeners.

If we are to reach into the minds of our hearers and expect the Spirit of God to touch their minds, hearts and wills in response to the expounded Word, then we must use language that communicates relevantly. Concrete, down-to-earth words must be selected. It cannot be denied that as preachers we ourselves ought to read more frequently and more widely than we do. That in itself will enrich our pulpit speech. We must learn to shed the skins of our ecclesiastical vocabulary and style if they have been reducing our relevance and impact on twenty-first century audiences. There are ways of being personal and intimate without losing reverence. We are convinced that God's Word is totally relevant in the twenty-first century but we cannot assume that our hearers share that view – we must work ceaselessly to convince them!

AN EXAMPLE OF BODY-BUILDING – EPHESIANS 4:1-16

Enough has been said about the method of expanding an outline into a sermon. We need to examine a passage to see what it looks like. The following sermon body on Ephesians 4:1-16 will be set out, with my text on the left and a coded system on the right, related to the key below.[2] This should help us to see how, in this passage, the pieces of the jigsaw puzzle make up the whole picture. For each section of the sermon in the left-hand column, the specific raw material source behind that section can be traced in the corresponding right-

---

2. The Coded Key system will help you see how I have assembled the ingredients of the sermon. This idea was suggested to me during a helpful conversation with Denis Lane.

hand column. This sermon is designed to show a range of Steps One to Six ingredients and methods of expansion. The result is a longer-than-usual sermon, especially in its introductory material.

KEY 1 Purpose of the passage

    2A Main Theme

    2B Sub Theme

    3A Historical setting

    3B Sociocultural and religious background

    3C Literary context

    4A Column Analysis

    4B Grammatical issue

    4C Exegetical point

    4D Biblical Theological Reflection

    5 Applicatory principle(s) of the passage

    6 Structure and outline of the passage

Method of expansion from outline to body:

  (a) Asking and answering a question

  (b) Posing and solving a problem

  (c) Dealing with a Dilemma

  (d) Doctrinal/topical explanation

  (e) Arguing a Case

  (f) Defending a claim

  (g) Deductive Unravelling

  (h) Use of stories and narratives

  (i) Inductive Reasoning

  (j) Evangelistic Challenge

Some observations on this sermon body

First, I have deliberately made this sermon body extensive and detailed so as to show a wide range of materials and methods. In many churches, this sermon would need to be shorter, especially the opening introduction to the main theme.

Second, I have omitted a number of coded keys from this example for the sake of clarity and simplicity. My expansion method involves a mixture of approaches rather than one only. At a number of points

I have also made reference to wider biblical and theological issues. My overall approach has combined asking questions, doctrinal explanation and deductive unravelling of the main theme through its sub-themes. Each sub-theme carries an illustration of the application.

Third, my basic strategy has been to use an inductive investigation to establish the main theme of the passage – the need to maintain and demonstrate the unity of Christ's Body. Having set that up, I then switched to a deductive unravelling of that main theme. For each sub-theme, I followed the same basic sequence of treatment: locate the verses, explain the point in its contexts, identify the applicatory principle(s), illustrate the application. This process operates throughout the entire sermon body. In reality, the symbol 4C (Exegesis) is the basis of every section of the whole sermon.

Fourth, notice how the code for purpose (1) recurs frequently through the text of the body. The purpose of the passage is central to our entire exposition.

Fifth, closely tied to the references to purpose are the constantly exposed principles of application (5). It is the Spirit's purpose in a biblical passage that profoundly determines the applicatory principle(s) that are already built into the text of the passage.

Sixth, notice the frequent occurrence of the main theme code (2A) and the way that the theme of unity runs like a thread through the text, appearing at a number of places. The relationship between main and sub-themes must be apparent in our exposition.

Seventh, in this particular sermon, much attention was paid to the literary context of the biblical passage. This is crucial for all passages, but particularly so when we are expounding doctrinal arguments that have practical consequences for Christian living. Chapter and verse divisions did not exist in the original documents of the Bible. Lines of thought frequently cross the boundaries of chapter and verse.

Eighth, be encouraged that there is very little reference in this sermon to grammatical and textual issues. Though such matters can be significant, we must not depress ourselves by feeling that as expositors we need to be world-class grammarians and linguists. That would not be fair and God in his wisdom has not set that down as an entry requirement for preaching.

Ninth, be encouraged that very little reference has been made in this sermon to secondary sources and commentaries. Heavy dependence on verse-by-verse commentaries can produce an overweight sermon and one that is liable to be deficient in its grasp of themes, contexts, purpose and application. If the preacher only and the text only are put together into the same room, then that preacher can achieve a huge amount by the Spirit's help!

Tenth, all the steps of preparation are necessary but there is no concrete formula that can be programmed into the preacher such that out pops an automatic sermon! The preacher and the listeners are not robots. The ten steps of preparation are always needed and the text and contexts are our unchanging foundation, but there is room for variation, flexibility and personal choice in the actual mix of ingredients for our expository sermon. The sense of consistency lies in the need to deal adequately, for every verse/ topic/ theme, with the key issues of explaining meaning in context, relating each point to the overall purpose and main theme and identifying the applicatory principles in the text. That is my basic structure for every sub-theme of the sermon body.

A word of encouragement

In Steps One to Seven, I have sought to present the ideal scenario for preparation. You know that you will not always have time and energy for such detailed work on the text. Don't get discouraged. Be flexible and realistic in your preparation. Think CAMELOT! Think of the seven letters of that word and make sure that each ingredient gets some serious attention in your sermon preparation, however great or small the time available:

Column analysis
Application
Meaning
Exegesis
Literary context
Outline
Themes

TEXT OF SERMON BODY	CODED KEY (source of material in Steps 1-6 Preparation)

TITLE   THE UNITY OF CHRIST'S BODY

Why did Paul write this letter to the Ephesian Church?	(a)
The reason is not immediately obvious. Let us do some detective work together. First clue – the letter *may* have been a circular letter to a number of house churches in the city of Ephesus, which was originally Greek but became capital of the Roman province of Asia. A busy commercial port – multi ethnic, multi religious. Therefore it had potential for complex interpersonal relationships e.g. Kosovo in the Balkans or Indonesian conflicts in 1999.	(b) (i) 3A 3B

EXTENDED INTRODUCTION THROUGH CONTEXT	6
Let us look at this Ephesian letter in general terms.	3C (i)
Ch. 1–3 God's initiative in reconciling people to God and people to people. The indicative of God's act in Christ to build a new community of His people i.e. the indicative of doctrine.	6 I 5
Ch. 4–6 The responsibility of God's people to live in such a way that the new life of Christ is shown forth in action i.e. the imperative of duty.	6 I 5
What was Paul trying to convey in this central section Ephesians 4:1-16?	(a) (b) (i)
The surrounding text has strong clues about Paul's intention.	3 C (i) I

I.I0 God's overall purpose is to bring all things in heaven and earth under one Head, Christ.	3C (i) I
1:22-23 God appointed Christ head over everything for the Church, which is His Body.	3C (i) I
2:16 Christ reconciled both Jew and Gentile to be that one body.	3C (i) I
The key theme of chapter 3 centres on the fact that Christ by His Gospel has brought Jews and Gentiles together to become members of one body – the Church.	(i) 2A I 3C
Paul's plea in chapter 4 is for Christian living that will prove and show the reality of a united church – prove to the world, pleads Paul, that you are as new people, united in the one Body of Christ which is the Church.	2A I 3C 5 (i)
The whole of God's eternal purpose and goal for this cosmos is centred on His concern for this body. Let us look more closely at the concept if it is that central! What is the nature of the body and how was it formed in the first place?	I 2A (a) (b) (i)
NATURE OF THE BODY The key section here is Ephesians 4:4-6 where we are simply told that 'there is one body'. In fact Paul tells us about oneness regarding the components that make up vv. 4-6:	6 2A
The One Father creates the one family of believers.	(d) (g) 4C
The One Lord Jesus Christ creates the one faith, hope and baptism and Christ is the one object of our faith, hope and baptism.	(d) (g) 4C

The One Spirit creates the one body and indwells it.	(d) (g) 4C
All of this is by grace. We have no part in the process of the establishment of the Body of Christ. This is God's sovereign work set in plan before the foundation of the world.	(d) (e) (g)
Who makes up this Body of Christ? Answer: Rebel sinners who have returned to the One Father through faith and repentance towards the one Son, the Lord Jesus Christ. When that happens, the believer is baptized by the Holy Spirit into the one Body of Christ – I Corinthians 12:13. We become permanent members of that body by Spirit baptism.	(a) (d) (g) 4C 4D 5
The one Body of Christ finds its unity and cohesion because of the One Spirit who indwells that body. The invisible unity of the Church cannot be destroyed because it is the work of the Godhead which itself cannot be destroyed.	2A (d) (e) (g)
If it is true that the invisible unity of the body is indestructible, then is it acceptable to ignore the visible disunity within the body?	(a) (g) (I) 2A
Paul's answer is an emphatic 'No'. The believers are to take the invisible unity given by the Spirit and to demonstrate that unity visibly in each local church.	(e) 2A I (g) 5
RESTATEMENT OF MAIN THEME How exactly is that unity to be eagerly maintained as Paul demands in Ephesians 4:3? Let us bear in mind that 'eager' is a Greek emphatic participle meaning 'spare no effort'. Work, labour and strive continually to demonstrate the visible unity of the Body.	2A 5 I (a) 4B 4C 2A I

DEVELOPMENT OF SUB-THEMES	2B 6
Paul shows the Ephesian believers three ways to attain this goal.	(d) (e) (g) I

I. *Showing unity through Christian living 4:1-3.*   2B 4C 6

In 3:14-21 we see the 'tail-end' of Paul's doctrinal   3C (g)
arguments in Ephesians 1–3, yet it is not merely a
'tail-end'. It is a highly significant transition in
which Paul prays earnestly that the Ephesians will
understand and experience in full measure the love
of Christ. Then in 4:1-3, he calls for a   5 4C
demonstration of that love in practice. Our love
for the brethren is the evidence of the reality of
our having been called to Christ and baptized   I
by His Spirit into His Body.

Church unity is maintained through a cluster of   5 I 4C
qualities, like the five fingers of a hand. These   2A
Pauline requirements are listed in Ephesians 4:2:

    a) *Humility* – the Greeks despised humility as
a weakness, which is one reason they had challenged   3B 4B 4C
Paul's apostleship in the Corinthian letters. Pride
lurks behind all disunity. We need to value our
brethren and exercise humble attitudes towards each   5
other.

    Some years ago I visited a church which had   Story
four organs at the front of the worship area – the
four organists had failed to agree on the most
suitable organ for the church! Each one had insisted
on his own personal choice.

    b) *Meekness* – involves gentleness and lack of   4B 4C
insistence on personal rights.

    c) *Patience* – an attitude of tolerance and long   4B 4C
suffering toward irritating people.   5

    d) *Forbearance* – mutual tolerance of other   4B 4C
people.   5

    e) *Love* – is the source and root of all the other   4B 4C
virtues and involves seeking the welfare of others.
It is all about interpersonal relationships – getting
on with one another.   5

Many years ago, an Anglican bishop in the UK was asked 'What is the evidence that a person is filled with the Holy Spirit?' His answer: 'When a person writes the address on an envelope, then if he or she writes the town clearly and legibly, that person is filled with the Holy Spirit!'

Meaning that it is in the small details of life that we reveal our consideration for others, even for the postman's ability to read an address easily! The bishop's answer was not theologically complete but it scored a vital point.

Story

The Spirit-filled life is new and distinct. Unity in the Body of Christ can only be maintained by the active presence of these five virtues. They are manifestations of the love of Christ in the Body of Christ.

4C 5 I 2A

For example, how do Christian believers, who are sick and suffering, know that Christ still loves them? Answer: The love of Christ is made visible through the practical love of church members towards those in need. Christ loves us through other believers in His earthly body.

(a) 5

5

For example, in Summer 1999, whilst teaching at Asian Theological Seminary, Manila and retraining the pastors of the renewed Worldwide Church of God, I fell ill with double pneumonia and my wife and two sons contracted tropical dengue. This happened precisely at the time when our niece and her friend arrived from the UK for a two-week vacation for which they had saved money for a very long time! Members of our local Filipino Church quickly set up a rota of couples to take these two English girls for meals and whole-day trips out. A disaster was averted! The love of Christ in action was palpable and greatly affected those two girls. The unified body showed forth love.

Story

2. *Showing unity through diverse spiritual gifting 4:7-12*	2B 4C 6
Let us look briefly at the nature of the gifts and then the purpose of the gifts.	I (g) (d)
Unity does not mean uniformity in all things. 'Charismata' or 'spiritual gifts' are given in diversity to the whole Body of Christ. Every church in this sense is 'charismatic'!	4C 4B
Where do these gifts come from? Answer: The whole Godhead!	(a) (g) (b)
Ephesians 4:7-9 parallels Psalm 68 where God leads His people after the Exodus. The stress is on Christ's descent through the humiliation of His incarnation and/or death and on His subsequent ascent. The twin ideas are Christ's receiving of all power and authority, followed by His giving of the Holy Spirit to the Church.	3C 4D 4C (d) (e) 4B 4D
Limited time requires that we deal only briefly with the five gifts listed by Paul. In this original sense and function, apostles were the first leaders of the early church, having seen Christ personally. Prophets revealed Scripture directly..	(d) (g) 3A 4C
All believers are under obligation to bear witness to Christ as opportunities arise, but some are specially gifted in this. These roles alongside pastors and teachers are all related to the ministry of teaching, through which the body is built up. Indeed Paul tells us in 4:12 that the gifts are ultimately given for the building up of the Body of Christ. Their immediate purpose is to equip every member of that body for works of service. Every one of us is called by God to discover, develop and exercise our gift or gifts. Church leaders have a special part in helping members to achieve those goals.	5 5 4C I 2A 5 I

In the Philippines, jeepneys are extended American jeeps in which passengers sit facing each other on two long benches. Some churches practise 'jeepney theology': one pastor in the driving seat and 20 passengers sitting, talking or watching the world go by. This is not the model demanded by Paul or other New Testament writers. All members of the Body are called to be actively involved in ministry, employing their various spiritual gifts.

Story

3. *Showing unity through sustained growth 4:13-16*
Just as there are rules of diet and lifestyle which control the growth of the human body to maturity, so also there are necessary ingredients which promote growth into maturity and unity in the Body of Christ.

2B 4C 6 (g) I 5

a) God will use the spiritual gifts of the Church to bring the members of the body to fullness, maturity and unity of faith in Christ, to knowledge of Christ, and to the experience of the fullness of Christ (4:13). We have already seen that the Church's teaching ministry is the common thread of the gifts mentioned by Paul.

5 I 4C 2A

5

The fact that sustained growth comes through this teaching ministry is made clear by Paul in 4:14. Well-taught believers will not be easy prey for false teachers.

b) The ministry of teaching will not by itself produce sustained growth. It must be accompanied by practical love. See 4:15 where the Greek verb does not actually say 'speaking'. Rather, it means 'maintaining, living and doing the truth in love'.

5 I 4C 2B

4B

4C

Here we need to seek a healthy balance. Some churches are so concerned with the particulars of correct doctrine — which of course is needed — that they lack practical care/compassion.

5

Other churches are so concerned to display wide social involvement that they ignore or relegate the issue of truth.

c) Paul now brings in the truth he began with in 4:1, having come full circle in his argument. Sustained growth is based on taught truth and practical loving but it only works if every member is working within the Body of Christ.

5 1 4C
3C
2A
4D

The spine is a highly complex part of the human body. In 1999 I had many months of back pain and disability. The doctor assured me that one of the reasons for the problem was that for many years I had not forced some of the connecting muscles and ligaments to do their work. The result: bodily weakness. Likewise, the Body of Christ will not achieve balanced, mature growth if certain of its members are spiritually unemployed, under-employed or mis-employed in their service of Christ and one another. A healthy church is one in which every member has found his or her vital ministry.

Story

LUKE 4:1-13
CASE STUDY: WRITE OUT THE MAIN BODY

Not every sermon has three points. This one does, but my three points are not the ones you might expect in a story of three temptations. I want us to ask three questions as a framework for unpacking this passage.

Those questions are simply 'Why?' 'How?' and 'What?'   (a)

1). WHY?   6 (a)

Why did he do it? Why did the devil assault Jesus   (i)
with a prolonged and intensive period of severe temptation?

It is not often in Scripture that we find glimpses   3C 4D
into the mind of the devil but occasionally the curtain is pulled back to reveal what makes the devil tick. The clues are not only in our sermon passage but also in its wider context. Let us trace the evidence in the text that will help us to answer
the question 'Why temptation?'   2A (i) (a)

   a). *Timing* – Luke 3:23 signals the opening of   3C 4C 6
Jesus' public, Spirit-anointed ministry that would
lead to His final triumph through death. Satan's   3A
opposition to Jesus emerged again as the Lord   4D
approached the agony of Gethsemane and Calvary.
In the desert, Jesus in His human nature felt weak, desperately hungry and perhaps lonely. In short, He was vulnerable.

   b). *Motive* – Luke 3:22 tells us that a heavenly   3C 4D
voice had just declared that Jesus was a much-loved
Son who delighted His Father's heart. Is that
significant? We need to go even wider in Scripture   4D
to seek an answer. Buried deep in the Old Testament
in the book of Job, God reveals Job's devastating   4C
experience of personal tragedy in his loss of health,   5
property and family members.

Job 1:8-11 and 2:3-5 record God's presentation of Job as blameless and God fearing, to which Satan responds in effect 'You must be joking! You cannot be serious!' Satan denies that Job truly fears God. In Satan's opinion, Job fears God only for what he gains from it. 'You mess up Job's life and then just watch him. He'll curse you to your face,' says Satan.

Satan is exposed in Scripture as arrogant, disobedient, deceitful but also loveless. He is devoid of compassion. He cannot understand love and that God is love. He cannot conceive of Job, or any human being for that matter, actually and genuinely responding to the love of God by trusting and loving a heavenly Father.

4D

4C

5

c). *Method* – Luke 3:22 testifies to a loving relationship between Father and Son. Significantly the devil picks the issue up and taunts Jesus with it in 4:3 and 9 – 'If you are the Son of God...' Satan detests it. He hates the very idea that God the Father actually loves His Son, Jesus, and loves the Church that Jesus will establish. Sonship is a dominant theme in the entire section 3:21–4:13 and it is that Sonship which angered the devil and triggered his attacks on Jesus.

3C 6

4C
3C

d). *Goal* – On this evidence, let me suggest that the devil sought to smash the Father-Son relationship of love, dependence and obedience. Satan longed to discredit God and to destroy the Messianic ministry of Jesus. Is that aim detectable in the devil's challenge to Jesus?

1 6
4C
2A

a

2). *HOW?*

How did he do it? How did the devil tempt Jesus? How is Satan's mindset revealed by his strategy?

(a) 6
(g)

a). *4:3-4*

6 (g) (d)
2B 4C

This was a profound temptation. The prospect of a meal for a desperately hungry man. After all, Jesus was one day going to feed 5000. A meal for one surely wasn't an unreasonable suggestion for a miracle worker.

God's people of old had struggled over food in the wilderness. They had been unwilling to trust God for His provision and here Jesus tells the devil from Deuteronomy 8:3 that physical need is not the prime one – it is the Word of God that is the source and sustainer of our lives.

4D
3C

4C
5

How does the devil seek to infiltrate Jesus' mind? Satan, as the master of slander and deceit, tries to sell one of his dominant lies – 'God cannot be trusted. You cannot depend on the Lord for his sustenance and provision for all your needs.' Satan's line to Jesus seems to be something like this – 'Your Father has forgotten to be gracious to you. He either cannot or will not provide that which you need. Therefore it is better to take things into your own hands. Act independently of your Father, for He is not reliable. Go on, turn stone into bread!'

(a)

4C

5
4C

Surely the root of all temptation lies precisely here. The devil's dominant lie to human beings is that God the Father either cannot or will not take care of us, whether it is materially in terms of our need for shelter, food, work, income, or emotionally in providing friends, spouse, guidance, self-worth. The Tempter argues 'Take things into your own hands. Work things out your way, with your resources and according to your plans and times. Don't lean on God; He is not reliable. You cannot put your trust in him.'

5

I recall a young Christian woman say to me 'I've waited long enough for a Christian husband. I can wait no longer. I will marry this unbeliever.' She lived to regret yielding to the Tempter's voice.

5 (h)

In the year 2000 residents in Manchester, England were shocked to discover that the family doctor along the street proved to be a serial killer of his patients. The country reeled at the name of Dr Harold Shipman and one lady interviewed by the media was heard to say 'Who then can we trust?' That is a question we must all ask.

5 (h)

Our trust is in Christ, the living Word of God. Our own circumstances are different from the specific threefold struggle of Jesus in the wilderness, yet in a real sense, nothing has changed.
Satan's tactics remain unchanged:

5

    to doubt Jesus' Sonship;

1 2A

    to doubt the Father's provision;

4C

    to cause Jesus to use power independently.

In short, Satan tries to undermine Jesus' obedient submission to the Will and Word of His Father.

1 2A
5

Christ's tactics remain unchanged:

1 3C

    Jesus, in Luke 4:4 and Matthew 4:4, reaffirms His trust in His Father's power and provision and care. Lies can only be countered with truth: the truth of God's Words. In the face of devilish lies, Jesus proclaims truth. He underlines absolute trust in God's provision, in God's way and according to God's Word (Deut. 8:1-6).

4C

2B

4C

    We resist Satan by living in the Word of God: we are called to guard it, protect it, proclaim it, explain it and obey it. That is how evil is defeated and lives changed: by the unchanging power of the Word. 'It is written,' said Jesus. That means it was written in the past and still stands valid in Jesus' day and beyond.

5

4B

b). 4:5-8

6 (g) (d)
2B 4C

The devil cannot stop lying, but this time it is a triple lie. He claims in 4:6 that he owns the authority and glory of all the world's kingdoms. He follows this up by stating that he possesses the right to dispense that glory. Then in 4:7 he offers this glory and power to Jesus in return for the Messiah's service and worship. Actually the devil had nothing to offer.

The devil wanted Jesus to seek worldly glory instead of the glory that would come through His obedience as Son. Satan's old strategy again! Satan offered Jesus an alternative route to glory: a worldly crown instead of a criminal's cross. Christ would receive a crown but He would receive it only in God's way and in God's time and in God's place on a hill called Calvary. Jesus' devastating response in 4:8 is that His goal was to do what His Father wanted Him to do and to serve no one else.

4C

2A
4D
I

5

It was Jesus' dependence on, and obedience to, His Father's Word and Will, that terrified Satan. He wanted to smash that relationship.

I 2A

Satan claimed for himself the final authority and sovereignty that belonged to God alone. It was God who was sovereign, not Satan. It was Jesus who was anointed by the Spirit ready for battle (3:22); it was Jesus who was filled with the Spirit as battle commenced (4:1) and it was Jesus who was led and empowered by the Spirit of Almighty God (4:1,14). None of this was by accident: the Sovereign Power of God had ordained it.

I 4D

4C 2A

3C

5

Sovereignty is the umbrella that covers all doctrines. It is God, not His enemy, who has the last word in our lives.

I 2A
5

c). *4:9-12*

'If at first you don't succeed, try, try again.' Satan does precisely that: he tries a third time, but on this attempt, he demonstrates that, if Jesus can quote Scripture to him, then he can do the same to Jesus. The scene is set in Jerusalem and the devil invites Jesus to take a 'bungie jump' but with a difference: no rope!

6 (g) (d)
2B 4C

The likely location is the highest point of the Jerusalem temple as it overlooks the Kidron Valley and the devil's idea does sound reasonable. After all, says the devil, even the Word of God in Psalm 91:11-12, promises the protection of guardian angels. And surely no one deserves that protection more than Jesus: 'You are the Son of God, aren't you?' The devil quotes Psalm 91:11-12 to include the phrase 'to guard you carefully'. In actual fact, the original text of Psalm 91:11 contains the phrase 'to keep you in all your ways'. If we examine Psalm 91 as a whole it quickly becomes apparent that it concerns taking refuge in God and being found in constant dependence on Him. Those who know, hope and trust in God will receive His protection, listening ear, presence and deliverance. There is however a condition: these promises and assurances are for those who walk in obedience and trust within the will of God. They need not fear even the evil spirit (v. 6). The devil carefully avoids quoting that promise to Jesus in the wilderness! Indeed Satan fails to include scriptural quotations about foolishness and interference with divine providence. So the context of Psalm 91 involves divine protection but set clearly in the condition of a trusting and obedient walk in God's Will. Satan is skilled in misquoting Scripture and taking it out of context. The devil seeks continually to keep us away from God's Word. His success rate in pulpits is very high in that respect. If he fails in

3A 3B

3C

4D 4C

4B

5

4C

4D

5

that venture, however, he has a second option: to persuade us to detach Scripture from its rightful context. The result: distortion of truth.

The devil's goal once again is to raise doubts in Jesus' mind about his filial relationship with the Father and to push Jesus to operate outside the Will of that Father. Jesus was not willing to test His Father by presuming on His power to protect. There can be no deals with God, no dictating to God, for we are called like Jesus to trust, not to test.

Israel, God's ancient people, had struggled in the same way. In their wilderness experience they had lived in gross disobedience and yet had the nerve to expect and demand water (Deut. 6:16; Exod. 17:1-7), thus presuming on God rather than trusting in God and living responsibly and humbly in His presence.

It is rather like a believer, praying for healing or good health, yet breaking every basic rule of healthy living. Or again, similar to our expecting and asking God for His protection on our children's lives, whilst we ourselves fail to invest time in their lives or fail to speak out when our children are heading into trouble.

So Jesus refuses to test his Father by forcing Him to give protection on Jesus' own terms and demands. Satan was pressing hard for Jesus to be delivered from suffering, weakness and death. Jesus was prepared for all three, within His Father's Will, and for the glory that would accrue not by deliverance from them, but rather through them.

Margin notes:
I 2A
4C
5

4D 3A
4C
3B

5 (h)

I 2A
I 2A
5

As we leave 4:9-12, I find myself reflecting on our strange tendency as Christians. When all is well and going our way and the sun seems to be shining on us, then we are quick to say 'God is good' and 'God is at work' and 'He is in control.' But as soon as we encounter problems, we change our tune and readily begin to blame all our frustrations and difficulties on Satan. We immediately give Satan the credit for messing things up. The reality is surely that the battle is going on all the time and it is impossible at times to distinguish between God's overruling and Satan's intervention. Even Jesus in the desert was apparently led at the same time by the Spirit (4:1) and in a sense, 'led' by the devil (4:9). God by his Spirit was, of course, in total control but Satan was actively at work. The issue for us is to realize the absolute power of Christ and to trust Him to intervene on our behalf. Jesus was going through deep trials but His Father had the upper hand.	5 4D

3). *WHAT?*
Our final question concerns what response we should make to the devil's temptations to doubt our status as sons of God and to question His purposes, sufficiency and faithfulness.
What must we do in order to deal with the devil's attacks?
The resources available to us are both passive and active.

(a) 6
(g)
5

I
(a) (d) (g)

a). Jesus rested in His knowledge and assurance of the supreme power, absolute authority and total sovereignty of the Godhead. So should we likewise rest. Satan is limited by God in what he can actually do to us (Job 1:12 and 2:6) but he will try to influence our response to trials by damaging our sense of trust in God as our loving Father. God is in control (Luke 4:1).

4C 5

4D
3C

I

b). Jesus delivered three devastating hammer blows, one for each of the devil's temptations and all three directly from God's Word in the Old Testament. Jesus used Scripture to establish that God can and will supply all our needs in His way (Luke 4:4), that He does so because He, not Satan, is sovereign ruler of the universe (4:8), and that God demands our trusting obedience to His plan, His will, His way. God is sovereign and sufficient, but demands the submissive trust and obedience of His children. | 4C 5

I 2A
2B
I
2B
2B
I

The truth of God's Word will hold us firm when Satan's voice whispers to us that God does not really love us, that God is not really dependable, that God does not really have our interests at heart and that our own trust in God is a pointless illusion. We must feed on that Word (4:4) and use it. Satan knows no mercy: he will come again and again (4:13). | 5

5

c). Jesus trusted in the power of the Holy Spirit who anointed Him (3:22). It comes as no surprise that He who was full of the Spirit at the Jordan River (4:1) and who was led by the Spirit in the desert (4:1) was then serving in Galilee in the power of that same Spirit of God (4:14). Satan's temptations, handled rightly, become God's preparations. | 4C

3C

5

d). Jesus resisted the devil (Matt. 4:10). We are called to do the same (Jas. 4:7; I Pet. 5:9) in a spirit of persevering and aggressive prayer (Eph. 6:18) | 4C
3C
4D

e). Jesus lived a responsible and holy life. So must we! Satan can only make suggestions. He suggested that Jesus throw Himself down from the Temple (Luke 4:9). The devil cannot compel action on our part, nor can we heap all the blame on Satan when we ourselves choose to yield to his seductive temptations.

4C

f). Jesus received angelic ministry (Matt. 4:11; Mark 1:13). Perhaps there is irony here. In Luke 4:10, the devil promised angelic help if Jesus would test it out by jumping. Once Jesus had resisted that temptation, the angels are actually sent to help him! We too will experience the care and encouragement of God in the midst of intense spiritual warfare. Lies, slander, accusations and deceit are the tools of Satan's trade, but in Christ we have all the resources we need to enter combat and witness the triumph of truth.

4C 5

3C 4D

5

4D 5

Practical Steps:
Step Eight
Insert Illustrations

It would be easy to think that for these final three steps we shall at last depart from the biblical passage. Nothing could be further from the truth. To depart from the biblical text is to court disaster for the expository preacher. The work that we do in these closing stages gains value only in the degree to which it serves the interest of the biblical text. The revealed, inspired and authoritative text always holds priority for the preacher – we never leave it behind. To do so is to desert our only powerbase.

Just as the completion of Step Six brings a sense of relief at having gathered together all the raw material needed for the construction of an expository sermon, so also the assembly of the sermon body in Step Seven signals major progress in the task of preparation. In a real sense we are now into the downhill section of the journey. Nevertheless the importance of the final three steps must not be minimized, for they have their own special roles in contributing to an effective and powerful expository sermon.

THE PURPOSE OF AN ILLUSTRATION

The goal of an illustration is not to introduce new themes, points or teaching into a sermon body. An illustration has value only in so far as it makes truth clearer or simpler to understand. One test of this function is that our hearers should not remember an illustration at the expense of the truth it was intended to illustrate. This would be to defeat the primary intention of using an illustration which is to simplify and clarify truth by bringing it down to earth, into the arena of our hearers' lives and into the realms of credibility and comprehension. The secondary values of using illustrations are that they can help break down any barriers between preacher and listener, stimulate attention span, affect emotions and wills and make our main and sub-themes literally more memorable.

GUIDELINES FOR USAGE

1. Limit your use of illustrations. We have already highlighted the perils of producing a 'skyscraper sermon' that consists of 'one storey on top of another'. A patchwork quilt of stories may seem entertaining but can all too easily ignore, exclude or severely restrict actual biblical exposition. Our illustrations must not be allowed to dictate or dominate the sermon – they must be our servant, not our master. I hesitate even to suggest a maximum or minimum number of illustrations for any individual sermon, for it really depends on what truths require clarification or simplification. Generally I tend to use just one or two to illustrate each main and sub-themes. Above all we must remember that ultimately it is not illustrations that change lives. It is the Word of God applied by the Spirit of God that convicts unbelievers and builds up believers into a mature church.

2. Concentrate an illustration on a single truth. An illustration is of value and validity only if it focuses attention on the biblical theme or point. There will always be a temptation in public ministry for preachers to draw attention to themselves by throwing out a series of amusing anecdotes. The preacher is not a stand-up comedian and whilst I do not agree with one preacher who argued for the total exclusion of humour from the pulpit, neither do I condone the use of humour to promote the ego or reputation of the preacher. An illustration should be brief and to the point, and detailed explanation or elucidation of a story should not be necessary. In any case, no illustration is a perfect tool for our use and we must avoid pressing every detail of an illustration, for that will rob the illustration of its specific and relevant impact.

3. Check the accuracy and authenticity of a story. This means that even an illustration needs to be thoroughly prepared in advance and perhaps written out in full, otherwise the preacher may forget some key element or even the punch line itself. This would be acutely embarrassing if it were to happen in the pulpit in mid-flight. The telling of bizarre or unlikely stories will not help the credibility of the preacher. Unusual stories may need some additional back-up material. Personal stories of the preacher's experiences may be high in accuracy and authenticity but should be used sparingly lest our audience question or doubt our motives for using them. In particular preachers to regular congregations need to avoid the public parading of the exploits, failures, weaknesses, or even strengths of their own family members!

4. *Check the suitability of an illustration.* The better we know our congregation, the less likely are we to make mistakes in our choice of illustration. If we are preaching to an unfamiliar group or in a cross-cultural setting, we must check, modify and even replace our examples. During our nine years of ministry in Indonesia I befriended two or three local pastors and having gained their confidence, I sometimes surrendered my sermons to them for their opinion on language and illustrations. That was another advantage of producing a written sermon that could be discussed among friends.

5. *Choose comprehensible illustrations.* Whilst teaching a group of church members in Manila, I asked them to prepare material to illustrate the meaning of repentance. One particular student produced a confusing illustration. Reluctant to embarrass him in this Asian context, I sat quietly until the student's close friend rose to his feet and graciously but firmly put forward an unusually direct observation: 'That illustration was so confusing that it would require a second illustration to explain the first!' Examples are designed to clarify the complex, abstract or unfamiliar by using the simple, concrete or familiar. Any illustration that fails to achieve this goal must immediately be discarded. We must never make confusion even more confusing.

In some contexts, often rural areas, storytelling may well be the most comprehensible medium for conveying biblical truth. Stories, in and of themselves, must not dominate the sermon structure in case our hearers lose their concentration on the progress of the message itself. The value of stories can be to present living concrete illustrations for those unfamiliar with abstract concepts.

The ability of our listeners to comprehend an illustration will tend to decline if our story is too long. Short, direct illustrations will not only clarify or simplify truth for the mind but ought to make an impact on the emotions and will as well. The best and most comprehensible illustrations are likely to arise from situations that press as close as possible to the lives, circumstances and experiences of our listeners. Yet even then, we must never forget that ultimately it is not our illustrations but the truth and power of God's Word and Spirit that will make our preaching effective and bring lasting change into our listeners' lives.

SOURCES FOR ILLUSTRATIONS

In my own pastoral and preaching experience, I have tended to draw sermon illustrations from four main sources:

1. READING. The range of literature available to many of us is vast – magazines, newspapers, novels, textbooks, advertisements. As we read, so we encounter texts that strike us as having potential for the pulpit. There are a number of ways in which we can use paper or PC disc to record and store suggested information. Of course, we need to record not only the content of an illustration but its context as well.

(a) Large, letter-sized file for sermon notes, divided up according to subjects and books of the Bible. These notes will incorporate illustrations in their sermon contexts.

(b) Card index systems. For example one set could be for Bible books arranged according to chapter and verse, whilst another set could be reserved for Bible themes and subjects. You could keep sets also for stories, illustrations, bibliography, quotations, exegetical notes, ideas for visual aids to accompany illustrations. The latter are not only for children's talks. Visual helps often bring great benefit to adult understanding. Cards can be arranged in alphabetical sequence if appropriate.

(c) Preachers should keep one small notebook in their coat pocket and another by their bedside. Illustrations have a habit of occurring to us at odd times and in odd places.

2. EVERYDAY LIFE. Life itself is a vast ocean of illustration and even those things that we ourselves don't see directly are swiftly brought to our attention by TV, radio, e-mail and Internet. Increasingly we all inhabit a global village. That might deceive us into thinking that anything goes in the communication arena. Much care, however, is still required in our choice of life illustrations.

Material drawn from the fields of history or politics needs wise handling, especially in cross-cultural preaching contexts, both in terms of comprehension and personal or group sensitivity. We need to be especially careful not to make sweeping generalizations about people groups and jokes about national characteristics.

Preachers benefit enormously from visiting their church members but must exercise extreme caution in the pulpit, lest they are tempted to betray personal, pastoral secrets. The results of such indiscretion can be devastating and lasting.

3. *BIBLICAL EXAMPLES*. There is a real sense in which the biblical writers themselves used illustrative material in their own writings. Jeremiah's visit to the potter's wheel in chapter 18 of his prophecy constitutes an extended illustration, as does the waist girdle, symbol of judgment (Jer. 13:1-7). The Old Testament itself is a fund of great illustrations for New Testament truth. The apostle Paul made extensive use of the wilderness wanderings narrative for his exhortation to the Corinthians regarding the perils of idolatry (1 Cor. 10:1-13). Jesus' parabolic material functioned as illustrative of theological points and propositions. Biblical illustrations should be used carefully and with due consideration for their various contexts.

4. *PERSONAL EXPERIENCE*. This can come through our observation of life around us, our involvement in life's experiences and the lessons we might draw from those events. Such experiences often give analogies and applications of spiritual truth that can be formed into sermon illustrations. Even as I write this section, for example, I am in the Eye Department of a hospital, awaiting drops in my eye that will distort my vision in preparation for examination behind the eyes. The visual distortion, I am told, will last up to six hours. Sin, by contrast, distorts our view of God, the world and its people for a lifetime unless God himself corrects it. Personal illustrations do require careful handling and real humility, as well as accurate telling. The very last thing we want is glory for ourselves rather than for God.

EXAMPLES OF THE USE OF ILLUSTRATIONS

The goal of using an illustration is to make expounded truth clearer or simpler to grasp. All illustrations should serve that end. In order to check that we are on target for that goal, it is a helpful exercise actually to write out the purpose and point that we are trying to illustrate before we choose or construct the illustration itself. In this way, the biblical text, theme or point will occupy centre stage while the illustration will function as a spotlight.

PURPOSE: to define and explain what the biblical writers meant by the word 'repentance' and to distinguish it from mere regret, apology or even remorse.

ILLUSTRATION: Imagine a couple living in South London who are excitedly awaiting their annual holiday in Scotland. The morning of departure dawns but in the rush to start the long drive north, a window is left wide open at the rear of the house. After driving thirty miles the couple suddenly begin to wonder whether they have in fact secured both doors and shut all the windows. Both husband and wife begin to regret their failure to check security carefully before leaving in such a hurry. Maybe they did shut that window after all and they certainly didn't want to drive back through London and waste the advantage of their early start!

So although they seriously regret their negligence, they speed on to Scotland where a day later, the hotel gives them the shattering news that their London home has been entered by thieves, thoroughly ransacked and considerably damaged. Though they had regretted their carelessness, they had pushed on with their journey rather than turn round and return to London to check the house. Repentance involves sincere sorrow for, and regret over, the sin and sinful nature of our lives. It also requires, however, a 180 degree turning away from sin and a leaning on Christ alone for forgiveness and new life. Regret is a necessary, but not sufficient, part of repentance. Our lives in their entirety must be surrendered to the lordship of Christ as we repent toward Christ and trust in his death on the cross as our sinless substitute. It is a total turnabout, as God by his grace makes each of us a new creation in Christ.

PURPOSE: To attempt to explain the grace of God as revealed in the undeserved love received by the Prodigal Son in Luke 15.

ILLUSTRATION: Two small boys grew up in the same town, enjoying together fishing, sports and computer games. As they grew up they went their separate ways, one into the legal profession, the other into the world of business and finance. After some years, the businessman got himself into deep trouble through corrupt and illegal practices. He was eventually arrested, detained and taken to court. His trial day arrived and he found himself facing the very judge who had been his close friend. After a lengthy court case, the businessman was found guilty and the judge imposed the maximum fine possible. As soon as he had pronounced sentence the judge stunned the court by removing his robes and walking across the courtroom. Standing face to face with his old friend, the judge took out his cheque book and paid the fine on behalf of the convicted and crooked businessman. The seriousness of sin is such that it has condemned every human being to a verdict of guilty in the sight of God. All people everywhere stand under divine judgment and in His holiness, God must punish sin. He has no option, that is the requirement of His justice. Yet in His great mercy and because of His overwhelming compassion for sinful men and women, God chose to punish our sin in His own Son on the Cross. The punishment due to us was laid on the sinless Christ and He was the one who died in our place, so that we might be forgiven and set free. This is the grace of God: God's Riches at Christ's Expense. The grace of God defies and demolishes all human ideas of logic, justice, fairness and common sense. We can never earn or deserve God's grace.

PURPOSE: to show Christians that they should follow the injunctions of Romans 12:9-21 to demonstrate visibly godly living in attitudes, deeds and relationships.

ILLUSTRATION: two gold prospectors searching in the western USA in the nineteenth century made an unexpected and sudden discovery of large gold deposits in a remote desert area. They made their way to a distant town in order to register their find and protect their ownership of it from the threat of competing prospectors. They agreed that whatever happened in the town, they would not say a word to anyone about their gold discovery. They duly registered their claim in the town but when they arrived back in the desert a few days later, were shocked and devastated to find several hundred townspeople rushing around their precious site with shovels and pickaxes. In reporting the bizarre story several days later, the town newspaper was headed: 'Though they said not a single word, their faces told the whole story.' When a believer's life is changed by Christ, the difference to lifestyle should be tangible, palpable and visible. Christian action should manifestly speak louder than words. The transformation in our living should be unmistakable to the observing eye.

Case study – Illustrations: Luke 4:1-13

In addition to the stories already included in the Sermon Body (Section 7), the following might also be helpful.

Purpose: to illustrate how the devil seeks strategic opportunities to attack the people of God at their points of vulnerability. (Part 1: *Why?* Section a – Timing).

Illustration: Etched deeply into my mind is the experience in 1989 of being strapped onto a stretcher and flown from Singapore to Manchester. At the end of nine years in Indonesia, it was a serious back problem that terminated our service in that land at the very stage where spiritual fruit was appearing. Why, Lord? The rollercoaster ride of apparent healing only to be dashed by further deterioration; the laying on of hands and anointing with oil by OMF Directors in Singapore; the loss of ministry, home, church and friends in Indonesia; the man in the nearby plane seat who refused to stop smoking as I struggled on the stretcher with crippling back pain and a bronchial infection. It was a battle all the way home, followed by four further months until I could walk again. Repeatedly the devil assaulted me with his suggestions. Was I really sure that my God was the God of all compassion? Was I sure that God was sovereign and would finally have the last word? Was I sure that God was actually supplying all that I needed? In my great physical, emotional and spiritual weakness, the devil multiplied his assaults. As in the experience of the Son of God, attacks are launched with special ferocity during our times of vulnerability.

Purpose: to illustrate the influence of the devil in the realm of personal relationships (Part 2: *How?* Section B: 4:5-8).

ILLUSTRATION: the devil consistently sought to question the relationship of Son to Father. In the 1970s the American nation was shocked by the mass suicide of 900 church members in a South American jungle. Those believers had been convinced by their pastor, Rev. Jim Jones, of the rightness of suicide by poisoning. Jim Jones was clearly a deceived and power-seeking man. His own deceit of his elders and members was slow, subtle but very sure. Mutual suspicions crept into that church as the pastor began to dominate his elders and abuse their wives. Fear and distrust spread into that congregation. One of the devil's primary tactics lies in the area of infiltrating personal relationships in church and society. He liberally scatters seeds of suspicion, doubt, fear and a critical spirit, resulting in the division and, if possible, destruction of communities. The devil knows that healthy relationships are crucial within the church, so he concentrates his attacks in that area.

PURPOSE: to illustrate the devil's lie that ease and comfort should be our goals as believers (Part 2: *How?* Section C: 4:9-12).

ILLUSTRATION: the overall strategy of the devil seems to be that Jesus had the right to be delivered from suffering, weakness and death. This mind set has been promoted especially in the postmodern Western world and has substantially infected the church. Many believers have become convinced by their enemy that they have a right to be pain free, to rise to the top of their career ladder, to expect sustained health, but if sick, to expect immediate healing. The result is that many believers are unwilling to move outside their comfort zone in their service to the Lord. There is now a strong temptation that if anything goes wrong in our lives or circumstances, then it cannot be God's will for us, so we back out or delay or move on to the greener pastures we think exist on the other side of the fence. God is in control of all our circumstances; that is the testimony of the Scriptures and of the people of God in all ages. It was the devil who sought to deflect Jesus from the paths of suffering, weakness and death.

6. Practical Steps
Step Nine
Prepare an Introduction

The last thing I did before submitting my PhD thesis was to write a three page introduction to it. Now that might seem a very strange way to organize things, but it was only after knowing where I had been in my research that I could actually state in an introduction just where I was heading. It is the same with an expository sermon. Once we have worked through the main theme, sub-themes, contexts, content, application, purpose, outline and body development, we are then in a position to know how best to open our sermon.

GOALS OF THE INTRODUCTION

My own preaching experience, as well as that of others I have helped to train, tells me that there are three major purposes in deliberately and thoughtfully preparing an introduction.

1. To gain our hearers' attention. Times of preparation for expository preaching are times of hard work, challenge, joy and emotion as we live in and live out our own sermons. Yet we must never make the mistake of assuming that our hearers await our sermons with bated breath or frenzied anticipation. We must never feel they are bound to be as excited as we are when we walk into the pulpit. Our task as preachers is to tackle the minds of our hearers even in the first thirty seconds and force them to pay attention to us. If we fail to do this, we risk losing our audience for the next thirty minutes. If we succeed, we have won ourselves a listening ear and all our work of preparation will prove worthwhile. There is a real sense in which an effective introduction is more important than the illustrations and conclusion, for it is during the introduction that our hearers will evaluate the preacher and decide whether or not the sermon is likely to be worth the effort of listening and serious concentration after a busy week.

2. To touch our hearers' lives. The heart of this issue lies in the applicatory principle(s) of the biblical passage and here we need to recall the point of Step Five – the application starts in the introduction, not in the conclusion of a sermon. Somehow in the introduction we need to convey relevance by bringing together the two worlds of the biblical text and everyday living. We need to tackle the sort of questions, problems and longings that are running through our hearers' minds and lives. If we do this well, we will be opening up felt needs and the desires for love, value, self-worth and assurance that all human beings crave. If our hearers get the feeling, right from the outset of a sermon, that the message may turn out to be for them, then ears will be open. If that happens, then we have an open channel through which to expound Scripture and trust God to impact the minds, emotions and wills of our hearers. This of course brings the spiritual maturity and life experiences of the preacher right to the fore. If we are to be effective preachers, we must be ready to stand where our hearers stand, feel what our hearers feel and hurt where our hearers hurt. If we open a sermon with the question 'How should I respond to news of my terminal illness?', then we have touched our hearers' lives in ten words. 'Should a believer tell lies?' may trigger a felt concern in just five words? 'Why me?' will do the job in just two, as will the phrase 'If only'. If we cannot in some way touch our hearers' lives, then we cannot expect their attention.

3. To introduce the body of the sermon. In the same way that we wrote out a full version of the body, so we ought to write out the introduction. A failure to do this might produce a shaky or confusing start that will tend to unsettle the confidence and concentration of our listeners. This can be disastrous because the introduction has to serve as a link into the main subject or theme of the sermon. As with illustrations, an introduction gains validity only as it serves the interests of the sermon body's themes.

In constructing an introduction, we shall need to ask ourselves just what our goal is, what point we are trying to make, what method of expansion we have used from outline to body and how much of the message we want to reveal at the outset. These will be key considerations. The following three examples of an introduction can be compared, in terms of their embodiment of our three goals for an introduction to a sermon. These examples are possible introductions to Mark 10:32-45.

(a) 'The prediction of the death of Jesus is followed by evidence that James and John had misunderstood the true nature of servanthood.' This introduction is true and accurate, but obvious and boring!

(b) 'If only Christians in churches were willing to exercise a servant spirit in their relationships with others, there would be much greater harmony and far fewer problems.' The introduction is again true and relevant, but boring and rather predictable.

(c) '2 p.m. is not the best time to teach New Testament Greek in the scorching heat of tropical Manila. One student sat bolt upright, smiling and constantly nodding his head, yet when I asked him a question, he betrayed his total ignorance of what I'd been teaching. A few minutes later, I watched the eyes of another student rolling violently as he struggled to maintain consciousness. Yet as I deliberately fired a complex question at his vacant face, he shot back a correct and accurate six-point reply! I realized that you can never predict who is really understanding. The one group that ought to have had total comprehension was that little group completing a three-year honours degree course in "Discipleship" under the finest teacher this world has ever produced. They all failed miserably. They revealed major areas of misunderstanding which we now need to uncover, as we study this encounter between Jesus and his failing followers.' This story sets up the problem, but keeps the investigation, symptoms and solution to be gradually revealed through our exposition. We have tried to draw attention to the theme whilst at the same time creating a sense of anticipation and expectancy.

METHODS OF INTRODUCTION

A wide range of strategies is available to us as we seek to fulfil the three goals of introduction. Once again, it is crucial that we do not become boringly predictable in our choice of method. Variety is the spice of life, especially to help an audience that listens to us regularly, year in, year out.

I. Familiar situation. This method takes serious account of our hearers' background and experience because unless our introduction is familiar and relevant to our hearers, then we are wasting our time and may lose the audience right at the critical opening stage. As a broad working principle, we ought to begin with the familiar and known, and then move into the realm of the unfamiliar and unknown. Paul did this skilfully in Acts 17:22-31 when he drew attention to the religious objects in Athens and then, having gained attention, he highlighted the altar inscription 'To an Unknown God'.

2. *Shock statement.* Some years ago, I watched a tall preacher wearing a black gown enter the pulpit and in a very loud voice of authority, he bellowed 'There is no God...' He then waited in silence and after a lengthy pause, added in a quieter tone '...says the fool.' He then preached from Psalm 53. The impact was such that I still recall that introduction vividly. A similar shock approach might be the challenge of Psalm 74:1 'Why have you rejected us forever, O God?' These introductions stimulate interest, arouse attention and leave the audience demanding further explanation, clarification or information.

Jesus sometimes used a stunning introductory statement to arouse the interest of his hearers. In the middle of a group of tax collectors, sinners, Pharisees and teachers of the law, the Lord suddenly said, 'Suppose one of you has a hundred sheep and loses one of them' (Luke 15:3). Again, on leaving the temple, Jesus shocked his disciples by saying, 'Do you see all these things? I tell you the truth, not one stone here will be left on another; every one will be thrown down.' The impact was so powerful that it opened up an entire discourse by way of explanation (Matt. 24–25).

One caution does merit our attention however. We should never make a shock statement which cannot be handled in the body of the sermon. In other words, our stunning introduction must be such that we can develop, justify and substantiate it during the rest of the sermon. If not, then our hearers will feel cheated.

3. *Ask a question.* Questions can be used to set up a problem or pose a dilemma or add a sense of direct involvement for the hearers. A question can be used to add tension and excitement that will then be gradually resolved as the exposition proceeds. A question certainly creates a sense of expectancy because inevitably there must be more to come in the form of an answer. To be avoided in an introductory section is the excessive listing of questions or the use of long or complex questions. If we ask our audience a specific introductory

question, we ought to make clear whether we are expecting a reply or whether our question is merely rhetorical. Cultural sensitivity should always be observed in our questions.

4. Tell a story. Stories, both fictional and true, can be taken up in order to gain our hearers' attention, touch our hearers' lives and introduce the theme of the sermon body. The main requirements are simplicity, brevity and direct relevance. Again factual information should be checked for accuracy and if we ourselves are in any way personally involved in the story, then we should ensure that it is not for our glory that we recount the tale. In particular we should never present as our own experience that which actually belongs to someone else. Once again, don't offer a half-finished story in an introduction, unless you are intentionally planning to reveal the full story during the course of the sermon exposition. Use of language needs careful checking and especially so if we are including idioms, sayings or colloquial expressions in a cross-cultural situation. Take time to think through the backgrounds, mind sets and cultures of your congregation. Then go through your story several times at the preparation stage so you can weed out any actual or potential weaknesses in its oral communication.

5. Act a drama. The effectiveness of this approach may depend in part on our personality and whilst our aim must never be to put ourselves at centre stage, drama can be a powerful tool for introducing a sermon. Sometimes it might take the form of acting out the dialogue of a story. I have seen a preacher acting out a dialogue between two imaginary people. Dramatic reading with planned pauses can be exceptionally powerful.

Occasionally dramatic effect can be introduced at the start of a sermon and developed to a climax. Jesus' tale of the man who built fresh barns to store his produce, until the night that his soul was demanded of him, was once enacted to brilliant effect by a preacher. He embellished the story of Luke 12:13-21 somewhat and on each of four occasions when the barns were rebuilt into bigger ones, he produced a small balloon, blew it up a few degrees larger and took a pin out of his coat pocket, pretending to burst the balloon but then changing his mind at the last split second. As the story reached its climax and the enormous balloon exploded, the punch line of the parable was driven home as the farmer's soul was demanded. The effect on the congregation was devastating, the atmosphere electric, the noise of both children and parents deafening. It was a powerfully dramatic introduction and development to climax. Above all it was made relevant and rendered memorable. I heard and saw that sermon in 1977!

As a general rule the only caution to the use of drama in an introduction is that if the drama is excessively spectacular, the body of the sermon may come across as relatively dull by comparison and may even seem like an anticlimax. If this causes our hearers to ignore or marginalize the biblical exposition, then we have failed in our task. Another caution is that humour of any sort, especially in the introduction, should be used sparingly. It can be effective but we don't want to be labelled a comedian and treated as a joke!

GUIDELINES FOR USING AN INTRODUCTION

First, an introduction should last only as long as it takes to gain our hearers' attention, touch their lives with relevance and connect with the main theme or first point of the sermon body. In short, it should be short! In a half hour sermon, we ought not to take more than two or three minutes for an introduction and the absolute limit would be five minutes.

Second, in addition to the purposes of an introduction already outlined, one of the reasons for serious, advanced preparation of an introduction is to give confidence and assurance to the nervous preacher. Thorough thinking through and writing down of an introduction are the currencies that buy peace of mind for the preacher. If nerves confuse our minds at the outset, the written text is at hand and will settle us into the sermon right from the start.

Third, one technique that I first encountered in Manila is that of delivering the introduction first and then reading the biblical passage to the congregation. This is feasible with a short passage and can be effective if we have just stirred a sense of relevance and need in our introduction. Some preachers even interrupt their sermon three or four times to read the next section of the Scripture. The danger here is the possible loss of continuity, of a sense of unity and of the role of literary context.

Fourth, we need to avoid two weaknesses that in a sense are at opposite ends of the spectrum. The first is that of over-confidence in the introduction, in the sense that sometimes preachers promise more in the introduction than they can possibly fulfil in the body of the sermon. At the other extreme, however, some preachers are under-confident. In expounding the Scriptures we have no reason to make apology for the Word or for our exposition. If we are unprepared because of a series of unavoidable interruptions, better to say nothing by way of excuses but rather quietly and confidently trust the Holy Spirit for special enabling. If of course we are under-confident and inadequate through sheer lack of preparation, then we should rightly feel ashamed!

CASE STUDY – INTRODUCTION: LUKE 4:1-13

Whenever trouble or temptation struck our lives, one of our OMF Directors came up with the same consistent response 'The Lord knows.' But does he? How can Jesus possibly know or understand the intensity and ferocity of the temptations that invade my life – and yours? The temptation to lie, to lust, to steal, to criticize, to deceive. The strength of a temptation does not lie in the sin being proposed but in the advantage connected with it. Jesus was not subject to temptations from within, for he had a sinless nature. He did however feel temptation from outside in a very powerful way. A weak person falls quickly, maybe without seeing the full attractiveness of the advantage. We are all too familiar with sin; Jesus was not. A strong person, or a sinless one, is highly sensitive to the advantage and has a greater battle on his or her hands. Jesus felt temptation intensely. 'Because he himself suffered when he was tempted, he is able to help those who are being tempted' (Heb. 2:18). Can it really be true that the Lord Jesus does know and does understand and does feel for us in our temptations?

6. Practical Steps
Step Ten
Prepare a Conclusion

As is the case with an introduction, so also with a conclusion – careful preparation is required. Some preachers prepare the conclusion first of all so that the whole sermon moves in the direction of the conclusion. I myself have seldom adopted that method. Usually I write the conclusion as the final stage and logical consequence of the sermon body because only then is my work of exposition complete and I can view the sermon in its entirety. My writing of the conclusion always precedes my assembly of the introduction. I tend to insert my illustrations during or after my writing of the sermon body in Step Seven. Preachers vary in their method here.

PURPOSE OF THE CONCLUSION
In our conclusion, the main theme should be clarified, summarized or repeated. Our listeners should be able to grasp in a nutshell the fundamental purpose and application of the passage. They should have realized what practical response the passage demands from them. The conclusion should reinforce and challenge our audience to live out the main theme, purpose and application. In the conclusion, our listeners must not be left hanging in mid air with the question 'So what?' running through their minds. We must spell out through the entire sermon the details of the 'what must be done'! It is too late to start that in the conclusion. We must remember that application should run through the whole sermon.

FEATURES OF A GOOD CONCLUSION
1. Short. A long-winded and wandering introduction can be damaging to the whole sermon. So can a lengthy conclusion. Two or three minutes should be enough and five at the very most. Excessive length in a conclusion sometimes happens because the preacher opens up a fresh train of thought or injects new material or repeats the themes in too much detail. At the conclusion stage, we must avoid opening up

new avenues for our hearers to walk along. That will deflect them from our main theme, purpose and application, thereby inflicting confusion and conflict. It will also greatly reduce or remove the final impact. The secret as ever is to prepare the conclusion in advance, even though we might suddenly feel the need to change, adjust or even abandon it at the last moment. Careful preparation will help us avoid the tortuous stretching out of the conclusion that can be so irritating to our congregation. Indeed a short, sharp abrupt ending can often be powerful and memorable.

2. Complete. One of the functions of a conclusion is to summarize the whole sermon by repeating the main and sub-themes so that the congregation can see in a nutshell how the conclusion has been reached. As long as all the details of the sermon are not repeated in the conclusion, then the conclusion will function to reinforce the themes, connections between the themes, purpose and application of the biblical passage. Repetition must not be excessive, otherwise it can be boring to the listeners. Rightly executed, repetition not only reinforces applied truth but enables the hearers to recall the details of the sermon well after the preacher has left the pulpit.

3. Clear. The conclusion is our last chance to ensure that we have clearly communicated the truths of the passage. It is our last chance to show our listeners the way we have produced the conclusion as the final stage of a procedure that began in the introduction. If every step of our preparation has been thorough and we have understood the passage in its themes, contexts, content, purpose and application, then we can have the assurance that we have fulfilled the prerequisite for clear communication, namely, our own thorough grasp of the passage. The conclusion is our final opportunity not to weave a new tapestry but rather to draw together the threads of the sermon as clearly as we possibly can.

4. Relevant. Whilst it is true that the whole sermon should embody and display applied truth, the conclusion is a useful place where application needs to be reinforced and illustrated. We must leave our audience convinced in their minds, hearts and wills that Scripture speaks as powerfully into twenty-first century life as it did for its original readers and listeners.

MATERIALS FOR CONCLUDING A SERMON

A wide range of choice is available to us for the conclusion, in terms of method and materials. Yet again, it is good not to become predictable in the way we conclude our sermons, especially if we minister regularly within a single congregation. Here are a number of ways in which over the years I have sought to bring my sermons to a close.

1. Challenge through story. This could be an event, experience or even a potential future scenario which serves to show just how crucial the main theme is found to be. The focus should be on highlighting the main theme of the sermon and because the illustration occurs in the conclusion, there will be no time for explanation. The story must get straight to the heart of the main point of the sermon and it must bring the whole sermon to a very definite and decisive closure. The criteria for the choice of story are that it must illuminate the main theme being taught and it must be understandable to the hearers. Thus for example a sermon on the church's experience of, and response to, the suffering that stems from persecution, such as that addressed in I Peter, could helpfully be concluded by an example taken from the Cambodian Church. Seldom if ever has the world witnessed the virtual annihilation that was the lot of the Cambodian believers in the decade of the 1970s. A short but suitable quotation, if it can hit the mark better than we can, often has a very moving and powerful effect. Likewise a well chosen Bible verse can underline and reinforce the main point being made in the sermon body.

2. Challenge by question. My personal preference is to set up questions in the introduction and/or body of the sermon and to take the audience through a detailed exposition of the text in order to let them observe just how Scripture contains applied answers to those questions. It is entirely possible, however, to use a question or two in the conclusion, depending on the purpose and application of the biblical passage. Thus a sermon on Philippians 2:1-11, which challenges the church to unity through humility, might conclude with a series of questions to the congregation about particular areas of weak relationships that need to be corrected.

3. Challenge to live differently. We have just noted that a conclusion can take the form of posing the sort of questions that encourage serious thinking in our listeners. It may be that some sermons have the aim of inspiring and building our faith and the conclusion may take the form of an encouragement to perseverance and consistency. It is sometimes the case, however, that the preacher ought to make specific directives for changes in the hearers' living. Thus for example in the numerous situations where Paul commands the believers to love one another, we can make practical suggestions such as the need to visit one another more often, invite one another for times of fellowship over a meal, offer to baby-sit for a weary young couple and offer to tidy up the garden of an elderly widow. If the biblical writer is challenging his readers to a practical obedience, then we should offer some concrete steps of obedience for our sermon listeners.

CASE STUDY – CONCLUSION: LUKE 4:1-13

We have asked and answered three questions, Why? How? and What? There remains a fourth and final question: Where? Where did this battle take place – for Jesus and for us?

In the wilderness? Yes. In Gethsemane? Yes. On Calvary? Yes. Yet the real battle – the centre of the battle – lies in our minds. This is where battles with the devil are found and it is here that they are won or lost. If Satan can control our thoughts, he can control our behaviour (Rom. 7:23; 8:5-7). We have two invincible weapons:

We have the *power* of God. Behind the resurrection of Christ lies the mightiest work of power ever recorded in God's Word. That same power which raised Christ and seated him in glory is available to us (Eph. 1:19-23).

We have the *truth* of God. It is that truth which exposes the devil and all his schemes. Deliverance and freedom from bondage are won in our minds and they are won, not through a power encounter, but through a truth encounter. Liberation comes by the truth of the Word: believing it, proclaiming it and living it. The devil hears and sees and is rendered totally impotent. He has no answer and no weapon against the most potent force in God's universe. That truth is ours in Christ and His Word.

6. Practical Steps
Summary of Steps

STEP 1

Read and reread passage and immediate context.

    Initial *seed-thoughts* regarding:

        1. author's purpose

        2. circumstances

        3. clues to main theme.

Note down ideas that occur. Any initial thoughts or *application?*

STEP 2: THEMES

1. Are there words in the passage that link clearly to a previous or following context?

2. What is the *overall* issue being dealt with?

3. Are there any reasons, results, consequences, contrasts or developments pertaining to that main issue? These are the sub-themes. They must be related to the main theme and *all* themes must arise from the passage.

    Step 2 requires *some* initial work on context that will be deepened in Step 3.

STEP 3: CONTEXTS

HISTORICAL

1. Date and place of writing. Look for historical events, details, etc.

2. What caused the author to write? Who wrote? Why? Author's method.

3. Recipients of the biblical passage? Who? Relation to author? Behaviour? Doctrine?

4. Write one or two paragraphs to express the *nature* of historical context in a nutshell.

SOCIOCULTURAL AND RELIGIOUS

1. Sociocultural environment of author and readers. Overlap of religion, society, culture.

2. Customs and practices of author and readers – dates and locations. Universal or local?

3. Thought – worlds of author and readers.

Literary
Three goals:
1. What is the point of the passage?
2. How does it fit into its immediate surrounding context?
3. Why located here in the overall scheme of the biblical book?

Method for study:
1. Content.
2. Wider Context – several chapters.
3. Immediate context – 6-10 verses or 1 chapter before and after.
4. Content in Context. How do the two affect each other?

STEP 4: Contents Analysis
Stage 1: Column Analysis
Left-hand side – biblical text.

Right-hand side – express briefly, in your own words, the main points being made on the left-hand side. Right side comments must arise from the text of the passage.

Begin to look for patterns, reasons, results, causes, statements, commands, questions and doctrines.

Themes, similar ideas, connected thoughts, contrasting units. Use numbers/codes.

This is the basis for *outline*.

Stage 2: Grammatical Analysis
Four levels of approach will help us to decide what grammatical issues might need to be treated in our sermon passage:

A. *Whole Text*
   Are there any textual variants in the passage?
   Do they affect meaning and interpretation?
B. *The Individual Sentence*
   Check Main Subject, Verb, Object.

Identify Subordinate Clauses.

Select key sentences (or all sentences, depending on the passage and time available) for this diagramming process.

C. *The Structural Indicators*

Conjunctions— but, and, nor, if, although, because, that, lest, since, until.

Therefore, so, however, since.

In order that – purpose.

Because – a reason.

But – continuation or contrast.

Therefore – draws conclusion or inference.

Relative Pronouns – who, which, that, whose, whom.

Demonstrative Pronouns – this, that, these, those.

D. *Key Work Analysis*

1. *Select significant words*

words whose meanings are not obvious, e.g. grace.

words of theological significance, e.g. sin, God, justification.

words that could be culturally ambiguous, e.g. 'touch' in I Corinthians 7:1.

words that are repeated motifs, e.g. 'love' in I Corinthians 13.

2. *Establish their range of meaning*

changes in use over time.

usage elsewhere by the same author.

usage elsewhere by other authors.

3. *Decide the meaning in the Present Context*

Flow and context of an argument are vital influences on meaning.

Identify and treat those issues that affect meaning.

STAGE 3: EXEGETICAL ANALYSIS

Examination. Read and examine each verse in light of the results from Steps 1–5 of preparation.

Evaluation. Think through what is happening and being taught in each verse, especially in relation to the overall purpose of the passage.

Explanation. State the meaning of each verse in 1–3 sentences.

Extraction. The applicatory principle lies in the text and must be identified and extracted.

STAGE 4: BIBLICAL/THEOLOGICAL REFLECTION

Not necessarily a written stage, but a stage of checking results of exegesis/interpretation against the total revelation of Scripture. This can be done by asking two sets of three questions each.

Check Biblical Context

1. What is the relationship between the passage and the section, book, testament, Bible, of which it is a part?
2. Are you dealing adequately with the multiple contexts of a sermon topic?
3. How does a topic in one passage compare with other passages on the same topic, both by the same author and by others?

Check Theological Context

1. How does the biblical passage treat theological problems, issues or misunderstanding?
2. How does the passage seek to strengthen or challenge certain doctrines and deal with deviation?
3. How does the theology contained in the passage relate to the general revelation of Christian theology?

STEP 5: APPLICATION

CRUX:

1. What is the purpose of the passage?
2. What is the application embedded in the text?
3. How is this applied truth to be identified, extracted and reapplied?

METHOD

Review the main and sub-themes especially in light of their literary context. This will help us discover the purpose(s) of the passage.

1. List the applicatory issues raised in the passage – explicit, implicit, inferred (ethics? behaviour? spirituality?).
2. To whom is the application addressed? Unbelievers? Nations? Groups? Leaders? How does the text address these people?
3. How does God feel about the situation? Pleased or displeased? Does the passage give information, direction, comfort, encouragement, rebuke/action required? Aimed to stimulate faith?

STEP 6: METHOD AND OUTLINE

AIMS:

1. Establish a method for sermon development.
2. Establish a structural outline for sermon development.

1. Select a method(s) to expand the main and sub-themes, *in line with the purpose of the passage,* into the final sermon. A combination of methods can be used:

    1. Asking and answering a question.
    2. Posing and solving a problem.
    3. Dealing with a dilemma.
    4. Doctrinal/topical explanation.
    5. Arguing a case.
    6. Defending a Claim.
    7. Deductive unravelling.
    8. Use of stories and narratives.
    9. Inductive reasoning.
    10. Evangelistic challenge.

2. Outline for Sermon Development

Go back to Step 2 – main and sub-themes.
Go back to Step 4 – column analysis.
Use these to construct an Outline.

METHOD

1. Check Step 2 – main theme/sub-themes.
2. Check Step 4 – column analysis.
3. Formulate:

    Introduction: Opens topic, main theme, and/or first point of sermon.

    Body: All themes explained, applied and illustrated, based on the overall purpose of the passage.

    Conclusion: Main theme summarized, repeated or further applied.

STEP 7: Write out the Sermon Body

Stages:

1. Utter dependence on the Holy Spirit.
2. Suitable and concealable paper.
3. Decide a suitable length of sermon.
4. Concentrate on the Sermon Body.
5. Review all of Steps 1-6 material.
6. For each point/theme in Outline:

    Highlight it.

    Explain it

    Apply it

    Illustrate it

    Check it — is it related to the text? explanatory? applicatory?
7. Good transitions, so the hearers can see how each point/verse/theme fits into the total *purpose* of the passage and sermon. The sub-themes must be related to the main theme and to each other. This is crucial to your exposition.
8. Limit material to that which a) explains meaning clearly, b) develops purpose and c) reveals application.
9. Get the right balance between the general and the detailed.
10. Reinforce main theme by careful repetition in different ways. As you flesh out the skeleton, and thereby develop your Step 6 Outline into your Step 7 Sermon Body, you need clarity, accuracy and relevance.

STEP 8: Insert Illustrations

1. Must serve the interests of the biblical text.
2. Make truth clearer and simpler to understand.
3. Must be earthed in the lives of hearers.

Guidelines

1. Limit use of illustrations — usually two or three.
2. Concentrate an illustration on a single truth.
3. Check accuracy of an illustration.
4. Check suitability.
5. Choose comprehensible illustrations — simple, short and sharp.

SOURCES OF ILLUSTRATIONS

1. Reading
2. Everyday life
3. Biblical examples
4. Personal experience

STEP 9: PREPARE AN INTRODUCTION

GOALS:

1. to gain hearers' attention;
2. to touch hearers' lives;
3. to introduce the main theme of the sermon.

METHOD OF INTRODUCTION:

1. Familiar situation. Begin with the familiar and known, and move to the unfamiliar and unknown e.g. current affairs issues.
2. Shock Statement. e.g. 'There is no God,' followed by a long pause and then 'says the fool' (Ps. 53). Must then be handled in the body.
3. Ask a question. Then unfold the answer by exposition.
4. Tell a story. Simplicity, brevity and relevance.
5. Act a drama. But not too spectacular, artificial or contrived.

Guidelines for Use:

1. Short enough to make relevant contact and introduce the main theme. Two or three minutes should be enough.
2. A written introduction settles your nerves.
3. Could give an introduction first, followed by the actual reading of the passage. This can be effective as long as continuity is kept up.
4. Don't promise too much in the introduction.
5. Don't be apologetic in the introduction.

STEP 10: PREPARE A CONCLUSION

AIM:

Clarify, summarize or repeat the Main Theme. The purpose and application of a passage should be clear. Listeners should know what steps must be taken by them as a result of hearing the sermon.

FEATURES:

1. Short – Two or three minutes. Sharp and abrupt can be powerful.
2. Complete – repetition of main theme and sub-themes.
3. Clear – draw together the threads of the sermon.
4. Relevant – reinforce applied truth in a final thrust.

MATERIALS:

1. Challenge through a story – to reinforce the main theme of the sermon.
2. Challenge by question – applied to particular areas of our hearers' lives.
3. Challenge to live differently – concrete steps for changed living.

7

The Act of Preaching

*O*nce the writing of the expository sermon has been completed, there are still a number of issues that we need to be aware of, and to follow through in practice, during the period between preparation and delivery of the message.

(A) THE PREPARATION WE NEED AS PREACHERS

The time-lapse between preparation and delivery of our sermon will vary according to circumstances. However long or short that period, we must seek to implement the following three necessities.

1. Review. As the time for delivery of the sermon approaches, it is essential to go through the material again, so as to refamiliarize yourself with it. If you have already trusted the Spirit of God to guide and direct your preparation, be very cautious about making radical additions, subtractions or amendments at a late stage just before delivery of the message. It is very unlikely that your sermon will be short of material, so you should tend to be reluctant to add to the length of the sermon by inserting new material. On the other hand all of us must remain open to the possibility that the Holy Spirit *may* direct us into a new or modified approach to some aspect of the sermon. The need to review the message and ask the Spirit for fresh light is also important if you preach the same sermon more than once. Someone once said that if a sermon isn't worth preaching twice, then we have to wonder whether it was worth preaching once! Indeed C. H. Spurgeon once disclosed without any embarrassment that he had preached at least one of his sermons well over a hundred times! When I review a sermon, it is not with a view to memorization, but increased familiarity with our message is certainly a positive preparation for the pulpit.

2. *Pray.* Just as we prayed during the ten preparation steps of the sermon, so we need to pray consistently and regularly during the interval between preparation and delivery. Indeed we ought to pray even beyond D-day (Delivery Day). Prayer should be concentrated on the message of the sermon, the listeners to it and for ourselves as preachers. Contrary even to what many evangelicals realize, the expository preaching of biblical truth will trigger spiritual opposition that can take a whole variety of forms. Paul's teaching in Ephesians 6:10-20 must be taken with utmost practical seriousness, for the enemy of our souls is profoundly opposed to the life-changing power of exposition. Satan will try any and every means at his limited disposal to distract the preacher and detract from truth. As OMF International missionaries, my family and I are required to have a circle of at least thirty prayer supporters who have committed themselves to regular prayer for our life and ministry. Regular expository preachers ought to set some similar target for the protection, sustenance and divine fruitfulness of their preaching life and ministry.

3. *Live in and live out the sermon.* Expository preachers must live in constant dependence on the Lord and exercise an attitude of practical obedience to the Word they are seeking to expound. The personal, spiritual life of the preacher is absolutely inseparable from the passage being preached. That is true for all places, all times and all circumstances. We must prepare ourselves as seriously as we prepare the message. The business of expository preaching requires not only personal preparation but also preparation of our church leadership and membership. They must likewise treat the preaching ministry seriously. For example, they ought to be sensitive to the preacher's needs, not only for adequate sermon preparation time but also for freedom from unnecessary or non-urgent interruptions by people, just prior to the ministry of the Word. After all it is in everyone's interests to provide the preacher with some time for quietness, meditation and prayer, as both preacher and listeners look to God to come down in power upon his preached and life-changing Word.

A word of advice: following the emotion, exhilaration, excitement or despondency of delivering our sermon, we should avoid the temptation for immediate self-evaluation of our own preaching. After the elapse of some time, it can certainly be helpful to listen to positive and negative comments from those with maturity and discernment who may offer advice. Even here, however, we must be careful; our listeners will bring a mixed bag of moods and motives, even with the best intentions. Accountability to a group of fellow-preachers is probably even more helpful. Balance is needed. Excessive praise can lead to pride; total failure ever to give praise can bring deep despondency; regular negative criticism can drag us into discouragement. Every sermon I preach fails in some respect and a feeling of self-dissatisfaction is the norm rather than the exception in my own case. Ultimately our responsibility begins, continues and ends in adequate preparation of sermon and self. Beyond that, we must consciously remember that the ability of the Lord to use his own precious and powerful Word does not depend on our own positive or negative feelings about our performance in the pulpit. Such an awareness ought to produce that combined fruit of deep assurance and deep humility in the expository preacher.

(B) THE PRESENTATION SKILLS WE NEED AS PREACHERS

In so far as we are able to influence the effectiveness of an expository sermon, there are three avenues through which we can work: (a) the written form of our finished sermon; (b) our verbal communication style; and (c) our use of non-verbal communication skills.

Thus far our overwhelming preoccupation has rightly focused on producing the final written form of an expository sermon. In other words we have emphasized what we say rather than how we say it. We have spent much time in thinking about a passage, organizing the material and expressing it in the written form of a sermon manuscript. It is now time for us to turn to the whole area of *how* we actually communicate our sermon material. However adequate and well-prepared our written sermon may be, its impact and effectiveness do still depend heavily on the skill with which we put the material across to our hearers. The use of these skills will have a major effect on our preaching, either to enhance our communication or to exasperate our listeners. We must avoid anything that will distract our audience and divert its attention from what we are saying.

I. VERBAL SKILLS

The impact of the words we utter in a sermon can be enhanced by the way we use our voices. In a number of ways, preachers can improve their verbal skills and thereby communicate more effectively with their listeners.

(a) *Voice Volume.* Changes in the volume of our voice can be used for two main reasons. Firstly, voice variation can be effective for the purpose of emphasis. Thus certain words, phrases or even sentences can be stressed so as to produce a varying emphasis. A range of emphases can be created, for example, by putting varying stresses on each of the following words: 'God so loved the world.' Secondly, voice volume can be varied simply to produce interest in our listeners. They will be more interested if we keep their attention by appropriate volume fluctuations. A word of warning – there are preachers around who seem to be convinced that the louder they raise their voice, the greater will be their spiritual impact. That sort of sermon, especially in some cultures, can be both irritating and embarrassing to listen to. My suspicion, sometimes confirmed by actual disasters, is that such shouting can be a sign of personal insecurity, spiritual weakness or plain vindictiveness in the preacher. Shouting preachers sound alarm bells in our minds.

(b) *Voice Movement.* Some preachers speak in a constant voice level with no variation in pitch. In other words they fail to vary the inflection, tone or sound quality of their voice by moving it up and down the scale of variation. Some mistakenly feel that a high voice volume must be accomplished by a high pitch level to match the volume. Failure to vary voice movement will result in a monotone that will be boring and very tedious to listen to, however good the quality of the material might be. The monotone effect will be even worse if preachers fail to open their mouths adequately during delivery or if they breathe too heavily in pushing words out. Not only will there be monotony, but there will also be unclarity. Generally speaking when we ask a question, we raise the pitch of our voice whilst a negative answer will be given a falling pitch. We need to be guided in this by the cultural, linguistic norms into which we preach. Monotone preaching is not only boring and tedious to listen to, but it makes it harder for our hearers to recognize emphasis, question forms and even humour.

(c) *Voice Speed.* Some preachers are so nervous or excited about their message, that their words pour forth at a rate in excess of the ability of the hearers' minds to process and cope with the avalanche. That sort of speed can be very annoying for listeners to grapple with. The secret once again is that variety is the spice of life. Clarity of voice is an absolute necessity but the speed of delivery should be varied. If we are preaching a point with reasonable speed, a sudden slowing can be very effective in emphasizing and underlining a key point. Beware, however, dropping volume and speed to the extent that a key point becomes inaudible in a tailing-off sentence. Missing a vital climax or finale can be extremely frustrating for a congregation. Whispering can be very powerful at certain points but the effect will be lost if it is out of hearing range.

(d) *Voice Pause.* In written material, commas, colons, semi-colons and full stops or periods, function as varying pauses. In our speech, pauses can produce a number of effects. A pause before or after a word, phrase or sentence, serves to isolate and emphasize that point. A pause can also help to demonstrate our own feelings about a particular point and can help the listeners to think, reflect and respond to that point. If we pause for too long, of course, that could give the impression of hesitancy or confusion, but a suitable pause that highlights the point can be a highly potent tool for emphasis and reinforcement. Some preachers find it helpful to practise reading out their sermon with pauses, so they can spot weaknesses and alter them. I used a tape recorder for that purpose when I first began to preach in the Indonesian language. The aim here though is not memorization. I know preachers who even find it useful to write the word 'pause' at relevant places in the actual written manuscript of their sermon. Punch

---

[1] I am grateful to Haddon Robinson for this important point. Readers will benefit by consulting his helpful material on the preacher's voice (1986:202-8).

lines, key themes and climactic statements can be very powerfully communicated by incorporating a pause that will stir the attention of our hearers.

2. NON-VERBAL SKILLS

Written material and oral expression are of paramount importance in preaching, but non-verbal communication also demands serious attention from the preacher. These non-verbal skills can be of major significance in helping or hindering effective exposition.

(a) *Personal Preparation.* Even the act of preparing to enter the pulpit merits consideration and so much of it involves thoughtfulness, awareness and common sense. I recall waiting with the rest of the congregation for a late visiting speaker who had lost his way to the church. He finally arrived an hour late, totally exhausted, flushed, trembling and embarrassed. After half an hour he began to settle down, but the damage had already been done, for his listeners were more preoccupied with the utterly dishevelled state of the speaker than with his message. Some situations are unavoidable but we should allow sufficient, indeed extra, time that will allow a good margin for such problems to arise – we owe it to our listeners. We should aim to arrive early at the appointed place for our expository preaching and we should plan to arrive in such condition that will enhance our preaching and not detract from it.

As well as checking items like order of service, acoustics and other logistical points concerning our preaching venue, it is always worthwhile looking at the pulpit itself and particularly its height. A pastor friend of mine once turned up to preach from an enclosed wooden pulpit in a church. He is a distinctly short person and he discovered to his horror as he entered the pulpit that he was totally invisible to the congregation and that the congregation was completely out of his sight! Embarrassment followed as the leaders looked around for a suitable box on which he could be elevated within the pulpit. I recall my own experience of preaching in a church from a sort of low altar table on which I set my sermon notes, only to realize that the extreme lowness of the table put my notes out of the range of my own vision. In mid-service I asked for a box on which to place my notes and the elders scurried around looking for something suitable. In a corner of the church lay a large cardboard box which was hurriedly brought forward by an elder and turned upside down to act as a supporting surface for my notes. No one realized that the box had been filled by the caretaker with dry autumn leaves which immediately covered the altar table, floating down, scattering and settling onto the knees of the front row listeners!

The point is clear. Let us not be so preoccupied with the stages of sermon preparation that we forget the little, yet significant, details of practical sermon delivery.

(b) Personal Appearance. As a general rule, we ought, as preachers, to aim for dress and general personal appearance that suits the particular audience we are addressing. That will vary greatly, according to sociocultural and economic conditions. In the part of Indonesia where we worked for ten years, I had to wear a suit and tie regardless of the searing temperatures and soaring humidity. In Manila I wear the national Barong Tagalog shirt without suit or tie. Neatness and tidiness are of general relevance, as are cleanliness and personal freshness. Cultural suitability needs to be checked out in advance, so as to avoid giving offence. I recall not too long ago a leadership training seminar led by a speaker who was grossly overweight. Here we need to exercise caution because clearly there could be a number of reasons for that condition. If however the problem is rooted in greed and lack of self control, then such preachers may be found hard to stomach by their listeners. Our approach must be not only to live in line with the Scriptures we profess to expound, but to put ourselves in the position of our hearers and work through in our minds any facets of our appearance that are potential stumbling blocks to those listeners. We must actively remove such hindrances for the sake of our preaching and its effectiveness.

(c) Negative Habits. All of us have blind spots and we need others to identify and inform us of them. My wife is my greatest preaching critic and my two sons are not far behind in that role. If we make ourselves accountable to fellow preachers, that also can be a useful source of insight into those blind spots that really can damage our preaching ministry. I watched a TV interview the other day and the rate of hesitant er ... er ... er sounds was so frequent in the interviewee's

answers that the interviewer eventually took over the conversation herself so as to silence the pathetic performance of the interviewee. It was painful, irritating and embarrassing to listen to the halting, stuttering efforts of that invited TV guest.

A few years ago, during an actual sermon, the preacher's glasses slipped down his nose and were promptly pushed back again a total of fifty-six times in the course of a single sermon delivery. I wonder how much of that sermon was heard by the people listening, let alone by the person counting!

Scratching the nose, stroking the chin, revolving the wedding ring, inserting and withdrawing hands in pockets, the list is endless with infinite variety but the effect, if taken to excess, is the same: our listeners' attention is drawn towards our negative habit and away from the message we preach. Search out and avoid negative, distracting habits.

(d) Body Movement. This consists of a range of gestures designed to complement our oral delivery of the sermon. The effects can be beneficial in two directions. Gestures help to express the thoughts and feelings of the preacher, but they also help to produce interest, maintain attention and stimulate a sympathetic hearing in our listeners. Such finger, hand, arm or body movements ought to occur naturally, decisively and in tune with the point being preached. Again cultural sensitivity is needed. Pointing a finger in much of Asian culture is deemed unacceptable, and even more offensive is the curling of a finger to someone in order to call them toward the speaker. Such directions are offered only to animals in many Asian countries. Physical gestures will partly be limited by the constraints of the pulpit structure that confines us. If we preach on a platform with a roving microphone then our freedom is extended. I once watched a preacher prowl like a tiger backwards and forwards across a ten-metre platform and it was both helpful and stimulating because he spoke with tremendous energy and enthusiasm. On another occasion, I observed a lecturer doing the same prowl for three hours and it became extremely tiresome and boring. Indeed if we are moving around because of nervous feelings, we must control ourselves. If, however, we want to help our hearers to pause or to recognize a fresh point or direction in the sermon, then a short, physical step in a new direction can be effective. The rule is

surely twofold: not only variety of gesture type but also moderation in frequency and intensity. Again we need to be formally or informally accountable to someone who will graciously but firmly and honestly reveal to us our own particular blind spots of pulpit movement and manner.

(e) *Eye Contact.* One of the dangers, alongside the multiple advantages, of a fully written sermon manuscript, is that preachers might be inclined to bury their heads in their notes and mechanically read off the sermon with minimal or non-existent eye contact with their listeners. Eye contact is a vital ingredient in sermon delivery and for three principal reasons: (a) it helps to build a personal relationship between preacher and hearers; (b) it helps to hold the attention of the congregation; (c) it helps the preacher to gain some, though by no means infallible, insight into the listeners' reaction, response and reception of the sermon. In order to establish and maintain effective eye contact, here are a few positives and negatives.

Do's
(a) Check the visibility and facial clarity of the preacher from the audience perspective. My concentration on one preacher's sermon was seriously undermined some years ago by a light above the pulpit which threw the face of the preacher into impenetrable darkness. I spent much of the sermon guessing his true appearance!

(b) Another source of some irritation is the preacher who wears glasses that reflect light, dazzle the listeners or otherwise obscure the congregation's view of the preacher's eyes. Modern technological advances should enable us to choose suitable glasses, even to the point of their being rendered barely detectable on the preacher's face.

(c) In a large congregation, concentrate on looking at small groups of people before looking at another cluster.

(d) Try to pick out individuals for a brief visual encounter. On the evening of my own conversion to Christ, I distinctly recall the evangelistic preacher giving me a piercing look for several seconds before he looked elsewhere.

(e) Look at individuals or small groups just long enough for them to realize that you are focusing on them.

DON'TS

(a) Don't forget to make eye contact from time to time with listeners in every part of the room. Some preachers definitely do have a leftwards, rightwards or central orientation that causes them to ignore large sections of their audience.

(b) Don't repeatedly stare at the same individual. It may send the wrong message to them and even create possible misunderstanding!

(c) Don't stare constantly at the rear ceiling of the room, ignoring the entire congregation. Remember those in the balcony, though.

(d) Don't close your eyes for long periods. I have seen this done and I felt that the preacher was being rude or sleepy or engaging in some sort of strained or contrived appearance of spirituality. The impact was certainly negative. Blinking, however, is acceptable!

(e) Don't stare out of the window whilst preaching. Some years ago, a Chinese colleague and I witnessed the delivery of an entire sermon in this style in a rural church in Britain. Not once did the preacher remove his eyes from that window on his right hand side. Being Asian, my friend was rather hesitant to confront the preacher after the service, but he did write the man a letter, not only pointing out the poor delivery technique but also challenging that preacher concerning the state of his spiritual life and trustworthiness. No reply to that letter was ever received but the point had been made!

(c) THE PURPOSE WE HAVE AS PREACHERS

Just as we earlier discovered the areas of impact of God's Word in Nehemiah 8, so we now examine this again by turning to another example of the three directions in which the Spirit of God works through preaching. Peter's Pentecostal sermon recorded in Acts 2:14-36 hits the audience in three vital areas of their lives. Interestingly he begins where his audience is, by creating and tackling a live issue, namely the apparent drunkenness of those on whom the Spirit had fallen. Peter then immediately proceeds to a biblical explanation of these strange happenings (Acts 2:16ff.). Notice that for most of his message, Peter reasons and argues his case by addressing the following:

The mind. The sermon was packed tightly with clear reasoning regarding Peter's threefold assertion that these disciples were not drunk, that Jesus had indeed lived, died and risen, and that the Holy Spirit had been poured out. Peter presented this detailed evidence to the minds of the listeners (Acts 2:14-35). As expository preachers we must strive to touch the minds and thereby affect the understanding of our hearers. Thorough preparation of themes, contexts, content, purpose and application will enable us to engage the minds of our sermon listeners.

The heart. At two points in his sermon, Peter makes specific mention that the Christ had been crucified by the very same people being addressed through his preaching (Acts 2:23, 36). The impact of this challenge was devastating for we are told that the listeners were cut to the heart (Acts 2:37a). With the reasoned application of truth to the human mind, the Spirit of God moved powerfully in the hearers' hearts. Those listeners of course could have resisted and rejected the truth but on this occasion the Spirit opened blind eyes and shed light into their minds which then moved their hearts. We should not be surprised to see God's Spirit use his expounded Word to move emotions and feelings. We must never try to manipulate or stimulate emotions but neither should we stand in the way of the divine work of moving hearts. Some cultures are afraid to feel and express emotion. In our own private preparation of sermons there is most definitely a place for the shedding of tears and I have been there myself on many occasions. There is certainly also a place for our hearers to weep as they listen and respond to expository preaching. I suspect we ought to see more crying in and around our pulpits than we actually do.

The will. The stirring of mind and heart was so real in Peter's preaching impact that the people actually pleaded for help to act (Acts 2:37b). Peter was able to follow this immediately with specific instructions to repent and be baptized (Acts 2:38). This would result in the gift of forgiveness (Acts 2:38), salvation (Acts 2:21) and the Holy Spirit (Acts 2:38). The message was then intensified with further promises, warnings and pleadings (Acts 2:39-40). Finally the Spirit of God shifted the wills of the audience so radically that three thousand came to faith and baptism (Acts 2:41). The lasting effect of Peter's preaching can be read in the ongoing spiritual life of that church (Acts 2:42-7).

These three vital ingredients – mind, heart and will – are not like choices on a menu. They are all required and the absence of any single item renders deficient the work of God through our preaching. Denis Lane is absolutely right when he argues the following scenarios:

Preaching that only informs the mind produces intellectualism.
Preaching that only moves the heart produces emotionalism.
Preaching that only touches the will produces fanaticism.

Our glorious goal and purpose is that when all three zones are engaged in our exposition of a biblical passage, then the result will be growth, action and changed lives in those who hear our sermons.

(D) THE POWER WE HAVE AS PREACHERS

Underlying the whole of this book from start to finish is the absolute conviction that expository preaching must begin, continue and end with an utter dependence on the enabling of God's Holy Spirit. In this, preachers have three great sources of assurance:

(a) The Scriptures themselves are God-breathed in their inspiration and authority (2 Tim. 3:16). Not only that, but they are powerful to bring salvation through faith (2 Tim. 3:15) and to equip every believer for the whole of Christian life and ministry (2 Tim. 3:17).

(b) Jesus himself on a number of occasions promised the presence, indwelling and enabling of the Holy Spirit. Thus when believers have to live under the pressure of persecution they have the promised inspiration of the Spirit of God in their speaking (Matt. 10:17-20; Mark 13:9-11; Luke 12:11-12, 21:12-19). Indeed the teaching and reminding ministry of the Holy Spirit is promised by Jesus in John 14:26 and 16:12-15.

(c) Not only are the Scriptures inspired truth and the suffering servants of God Spirit-anointed, but the Spirit works through those Scriptures as they are expounded. The Pentecost context of Peter's sermon is an excellent example in this regard for in Acts 2:4 and 14, Luke uses a Greek verb *apophthengomai* meaning 'to speak forth in revealing words by inspiration'. Peter preached his Pentecost sermon

---

[1] Denis Lane *Preach The Word* (Welwyn: Evangelical Press, 1979) pp.91-2.

under that Holy Spirit inspiration, so the massive resulting fruit is not really too surprising. It was also the experience of the early church that the Word inspired by the Spirit continued to bear fruit by that same Spirit. This can easily be traced in such texts as Romans 15:4; I Corinthians 2:6-16; Ephesians 6:17; Colossians 1:6; I Thessalonians 1:4-6; I Timothy 4:16; Hebrews 3:7-11; James 1:21; I Peter 1:10-12; I John 2:20.

As we prepare and preach expository sermons, we have those same great assurances of the ongoing work of the Holy Spirit in our lives and ministries. In particular we have the promised power of God's Spirit in every area that we need him.

Power for our consistency. The Holy Spirit-inspired Scriptures constantly teach and empower consistency between, on the one hand, the words of the passage and the words of the preacher and, on the other hand, the willingness of that preacher to embody those words in personal, practical living. That consistency is impossible without the power of God's Spirit. We need that same consistency in getting the right balance between time spent in the study dealing adequately with the biblical text and time spent getting to know our hearers so as to understand their felt needs and how those needs will be met by the biblical text. As in I Thessalonians 1:4-6, the Holy Spirit is the sole key to this.

Power for our content. The prophets proclaimed God's Word by inspiration of the Holy Spirit (2 Pet. 1:19-21). The apostles either expounded and applied Old Testament truth (I Cor. 10:1-13) or delivered new truth under divine revelation and inspiration (2 Tim. 3:14-17). The Holy Spirit inspired the whole of Scripture and as such is utterly committed to biblical exposition. It is the tool by which he transforms lives and builds the church. The Spirit of God waits in power to come down upon the exposition of the biblical passage. That is our thrilling and overwhelming assurance, anticipation and excitement as preachers.

Power for our communication. Two of the primary qualities needed by the expository preacher are clarity and courage. Every step of our sermon preparation indicated how crucial those two requirements were. Not surprisingly it is for those two qualities of preaching and preachers that the apostles prayed expectantly. Bold proclamation of God's Word was a result of being filled with the Holy Spirit (Acts 4:31). It was for this same Spirit-anointing that Paul pleaded in order that he might preach fearlessly (Eph. 6:19-20) and clearly (Col. 4:3-4). Courage and clarity are completed and complemented by a third great quality. We need to plead that, by God's Spirit, we will preach with passion. Yes, we seek accuracy. Yes, we work from a strong exegetical base. But we desperately need passion. Beware of cold, clinical correctness in the pulpit. People need to hear and see the passion of God in his Word and in us, his messengers. After all Hebrews 4:12 tells us that God's Word is 'living' and 'active'. We need to plead that the sermons we prepare and preach will be truly alive, not only for us and in us, but that the life of our sermons will be seen and felt by our hearers. They need to sense the divine source of our preaching and to feel its impact on their lives.

Power for our contact. The Holy Spirit is our helper (John 14:16, 26). He helps us not only at every step of our preparation of an expository sermon, but also in our choice of biblical passage in the first place and in the preparation of those who will hear the finished sermon. In short, the Spirit of God is sovereign in causing preachers to make contact with listeners at the right time and in the right place. Our task is to pray and trust for the Spirit's sovereign intervention for that vital and timely contact. It was the work of God's Spirit for example which timed the encounter between Philip and the Ethiopian eunuch on the road from Jerusalem to Gaza (Acts 8:26-40). That same Holy Spirit directly opened the way for Philip's exposition of Scripture (8:32-5) and for the fruit of that piece of ministry (8:36-40).

During my early days as an assistant pastor, a church couple plus friend arrived on our doorstep at 9 a.m. one Monday morning. They were incensed that I had paraded all their personal problems and anxieties from the pulpit during my Sunday evening sermon on the previous day. It took me three hours to convince them that I was totally unaware, both before and during that sermon delivery, of the precise nature of their problems. In a remarkable way, the Holy Spirit had brought together the exposition of Scripture and the needs of that couple in the right place and at the right time. Eventually they calmed down and my relationship with them was restored!

Power for our continuation. We said at the outset that the work of expository preaching is hard work. The hours spent in preparation involve hard work. The years spent in regular sermon ministry require perseverance. At times the temptation to take short cuts in preparation will be very keenly felt. Perseverance is of paramount importance for the expository preacher. It is fascinating that perseverance is often portrayed in Scripture in the context of suffering, pressure and difficult circumstances. The obtaining of such grace for perseverance is also linked with asking God in faith, receiving the divine help of the Spirit and experiencing the further blessing of God in response to our present perseverance. As we set our faces towards perseverance in expository preaching, the Holy Spirit will make it all possible as the promise and gift of God. This growth in perseverance, so crucial for the preaching ministry, can be studied in such texts as Romans 5:1-6; 1 Timothy 4:15-16; 2 Timothy 1:13-14, 2:1-13; Hebrews 10:19-39; James 1:2-8, 5:10-11. Though these contexts emphasize suffering and persecution, these are the very situations in which expository preachers will sometimes be called to function. Our perseverance in preaching will be a real part of our perseverance in Christian faith and life.

In the practicalities of sermon preparation and delivery we need to exercise continual dependence on the presence and power of the Holy Spirit.

(a) We need illumination during all the preparation steps as we study the themes, contexts, contents, purpose and application of the passage.

(b) We need to know the Spirit's continuing help during the waiting time just prior to delivery of the sermon, as we review, pray and seek to live in and live out the truths of the biblical passage.

(c) We need the anointing and leading of the Spirit during the actual act of preaching.

(d) We need to plead for the ongoing work of the Spirit in ourselves and in those who have heard the message. As we lean upon the Spirit, we can be expect God's working.

After all, the Word belongs to God, the Spirit produces the change, yet the act of preaching is entrusted to us, his vessels of clay. The Spirit of God effects the transformation in the listeners. Expository preaching that ignores or neglects the role of God's Spirit is a waste of time, both for preacher and listener. It is as serious as that.

(E) THE PRIVILEGE WE HAVE AS PREACHERS

As preachers we have the enormous privilege of bringing the Word of God to the men and women of the twenty-first century. At the same time, this calling puts us under the most awesome responsibility. It has been reported by elders at Charlotte Baptist Chapel in Edinburgh, Scotland, one of my own supporting churches, that a well-known former pastor, Rev. Graham Scroggie, was not infrequently prone to vomiting immediately before leading the worship of that large congregation. Such was the weight of responsibility he felt in the preaching ministry, that his hands could be seen trembling or even shaking as he mounted the steep pulpit steps. As he left the pulpit, however, it is said that it was the listeners who were then trembling and shaking, such was the power of God's Spirit upon the expounded Word. If you are amongst those preachers who feel a desire to be replaced at the last moment by someone else as you prepare to preach and to be anywhere other than the appointed place of preaching, then you are not alone. Sometimes, and strangely, you will want to run away from preaching! That is my own frequent feeling before preaching, even in spite of my love for, and absolute commitment to, expository preaching ministry. I often echo in my own thoughts the words of Moses: 'O Lord, I have never been eloquent, neither in the past nor since you have spoken to your servant. I am slow of speech and tongue' (Exod. 4:10). Often also do I want to say: 'O Lord, please send someone else to do it' (Exod. 4:13). With the apostle Paul we are profoundly aware of our weakness (2 Cor. 4:1-18, 11:16–12:10) and imperfection (Phil. 3:10-14) in life and ministry. If as preachers that ceases to be our own experience, then the alarm bells will be sounding and we will be drifting into the dangerous waters of confidence in our own strength and sufficiency. Here another word of warning needs to be sounded and heeded.

I met a man some years ago who said that his calling from God was to a 'ministry of correcting preachers'. He travelled from church to church fulfilling that ministry which I myself would sum up as 'how to influence people and lose a lot of friends in the process!' Here we need the right balance. There definitely is a need on occasion to challenge and even correct preachers, though of course it must be done in a right spirit and in a right way. The effect of reading and implementing the preaching method of this book might well be that you develop a healthy self-criticism and a sharper discernment when you hear others preach. We must be so careful not to become excessively critical of other preachers, for ultimately we all sit under the Word of God and are accountable for our submission and obedience to that Word. I know preachers who are unwilling to sit under the preaching ministry of others, because they themselves are not the ones standing in the pulpit. Others are unwilling ever to vacate 'their own' pulpits to allow another into their fiercely guarded fortress. That tendency is not only unhealthy; it is actually dangerous and potentially disastrous. Unless we can prepare sermons, preach sermons but also sit under others' sermons, in a spirit of true humility, then we would be wiser to step aside from our ministry of exposition.

The most important balance we will ever need in expository preaching is that between our own proclamation of divine truth and our own practice of that divine truth. It is as simple yet utterly demanding as that. Enormous privilege; overwhelming responsibility. The Word of God reveals what he is still saying to men and women today. Exposition brings God's purpose and application to bear upon the lives of our listeners. Our calling as expository preachers is to be faithful to the biblical text and deliver his message with clarity, humility and compassion for our hearers. Expository preaching ministry will not be welcomed by those opposing powers that hold men and women in spiritual darkness. Expository preachers deal in a commodity that decides temporal and eternal futures. That commodity is hated by the spiritual powers that know and fear its impact. That commodity is called biblical truth. Such ministry will at times be very costly for us and there will undoubtedly be those, both inside and outside the church, who will refuse and reject the biblical message. There will be times of real discouragement and distress for every preacher. My own testimony and that of others, however, is to the great joy of witnessing Almighty God at work by his Spirit and through his Word. He it is who desires biblical exposition far more than we do. He comes alongside, challenges, convicts and changes men and women. He does so supremely through his appointed means, our expository preaching of the biblical text. The cosmic purposes of God for his creation and his church will actually be fulfilled as his Word is proclaimed, explained and applied in the strength and life-changing power of the Holy Spirit. Expository biblical preaching is that important!

Subject Index

Scripture Index

Spirit Empowered Preaching
Involving the Holy Spirit in your Ministry
Arturo G Azurdia III

Art Azurdia's excellent book... will convince you, if your mind and heart is open to God, to get power as well as material... I intend to read it again and again and widely recommend it to pastors the world over.

John H Armstrong

Seldom does a book arise of which one can say, "This should be essential reading for preachers at whatever stage of their ministry!" But I can say this honestly of this book... It has made me wish that I could start all over again.

Derek Prime

You will be delighted by this book... If your praying for the Spirit's power has become formal or thoughtless then this book can change both you and your ministry – by the Spirit's power.

Edmund P Clowney

When you finish reading this book not only will you have a better idea of the role of the Spirit in preaching, but you will also know better how to preach in dependence on the Holy Spirit. Everyone who is preaching, or preparing to preach, needs to read this book.

Joey Pipa

If you desire that your preaching be lifted up to a position in which you are being used by the Spirit as a channel, then Arturo Azurdia can help you.

Arturo G. Azurdia III has been the minister of Christ Community Church in Fairfield, a growing church in Northern California for over 10 years. The insights in this book are gained from his careful study and practical experiences of being used by the Holy Spirit in his ministry.

ISBN I 85792 413 4

Firm Foundations
150 Examples how to structure a Sermon
Peter Grainger

Charlotte Baptist Chapel has a long tradition of expository preaching and in this book, its current pastor, Peter Grainger, passes on some of the method as well as the heart for good biblical preaching.

Firm Foundations includes sermon outlines for over 150 sermons, introductions on preaching a whole book, a verse, a topical series, a psalm, Old and New Testament; and recommended books for further study.

It is designed to help old and new pastors alike, and could also be used in personal bible study.

...a glimpse into the mind and heart of someone who expounds Scripture well in his setting. Like a good sermon illustration, the specificity of this book, with its many introductions and outlines, helps us who preach imagine how we could craft our sermons and sermon series that are equally faithful to Scripture.

Greg R. Scharf, Trinity Evangelical Divinity School

Peter Grainger's Firm Foundations sounds a loud and clear note for lively, imaginative, Bible-based, Christ-centered preaching. These principles and patterns will prove as helpful to the seasoned expositor as they will to the fledgling pastor. I commend it enthusiastically.

Alistair Begg, Parkside Church, Ohio

This is not a volume of instant sermon solutions! Preaching is work. "Firm Foundations" is another valuable tool for the workshop.

Rev Bev E Savage General Secretary FIEC

Peter Grainger spent 20 years working with Wycliffe Bible Translators in India, Pakistan and Nigeria. He has been Senior Pastor of Charlotte Chapel, Edinburgh for 10 years.

ISBN I 85792 678 I

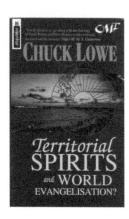

Territorial Spirits and World Evangelism?
Chuck Lowe

A biblical, historical and missiological critique of strategic level spiritual warfare.

I am pleased to commend this careful examination of a controversial subject. You do not have to go along with the theology of Frank Peretti and Peter Wagner to take seriously the devil and his minions.
Nigel M. de S. Cameron.

So eagerly do many accept the new and the novel. Chuck Lowe has given a clarion call to reject that which is built upon a foundation of anecdote, speculation and animism.
George Martin, Billy Graham School of Missions

Clear, admirably lucid and mission-hearted. Strategic level spiritual warfare (seems) uncomfortably closer to contemporary animism than to any biblical understanding of demonology.
Max Turner, London Bible College

The evangelical community at large owes Chuck Lowe a debt of gratitude (for his) dogged insistence that one must not build doctrine on vague texts, assumptions, analogies or inferences, but on clear, solid, biblical evidence.
Richard Mayhue, The Master's Seminary, California

Over the last decade, a new theory and practice of spiritual warfare has taken hold around the world. This teaching proposes the existence of a newly-discovered class of demons, 'territorial spirits', whose function is to rule over specific jurisdictions of different sizes. Along with the theory has come a new practice of spiritual warfare: ruling demons are named, their territories identified, and they are then bound or cursed. Evangelism and mission are then said to proceed rapidly with dramatic results.

CHUCK LOWE examines the full range of biblical, intertestamental, historical and empirical evidence cited in promotion of this new teaching. Lowe, a lecturer at Singapore Bible College, affirms that we need to be involved in spiritual warfare and proposes a more biblically legitimate and effective model.

ISBN I 85792 3995

THE BEGINNER'S GUIDE TO EXPOSITORY PREACHING

STEPHEN MCQUOID

The Beginners Guide to Expository Preaching
Stephen McQuoid

Preaching, that long neglected and much required skill, has two competing the strains. On the one hand preachers need to hold onto the truth of the message, striking the line of truth cleanly, never adding to it or removing from it. On the other hand preachers need to communicate – to reach out, and with the help of the Spirit, grab the heart of listener.

It's not an easy balance to find, but Stephen McQuoid brings a refreshing dose of sensible and thoroughly Biblical advice to help us.

Stephen McQuoid's readily digestible and stimulating new book will help seasoned preachers (and enable them to give themselves a good check-up). Beginners will benefit from the straightforward and sensible counsel he gives. And some, who never preach, may be helped to pray for and encourage those who do. I for one am grateful for the labour of love this little manual represents.

Sinclair B Ferguson

Stephen McQuoid will succeed in making preachers think hard about the passion, preparation, style and development of their preaching gift. I trust it will be a blessing and a challenge to them – it certainly was for me.

Derek Lamont

Its great strength is the emphasis placed on preaching accurately: relaying what is in the text and context rather than bending it to suit the preacher's convenience – a cardinal sin unblushingly committed in many pulpits up and down the land!

Dr Tony Sargent

Stephen McQuoid is the principal of Tilsley College, part of the ministry of Gospel Literature Outreach. He teaches theology and evangelism and exercises a national and international preaching ministry.

ISBN I 85792 769 9

OMF International works in most East Asian countries, and among East Asian peoples around the world. It was founded by James Hudson Taylor in 1865 as the China Inland Mission. Our purpose is to glorify God through the urgent evangelisation of East Asia's billions.

In line with this, OMF Publishing seeks to motivate and equip Christians to make disciples of all peoples. Publications include:

- stories and biographies showing God at work in East Asia
- the biblical basis of mission and mission issues
- the growth and development of the Church in Asia
- studies of Asian culture and religion

Books, booklets, articles and free downloads can be found on our web site at *www.omf.org*

Addresses for OMF English-speaking centres can be found at the back of this book.

English-speaking OMF centres

AUSTRALIA: PO Box 849, Epping, NSW 2121
Freecall 1800 227 154   email: omf-australia@omf.net   *www.au.omf.org*

CANADA: 5759 Coopers Avenue, Mississauga ON, L4Z 1R9
Toll free 1-888-657-8010   email: omfcanada@omf.ca   *www.ca.omf.org*

HONG KONG: P O Box 70505, Kowloon Central Post Office, Hong Kong
email: hk@omf.net   *www.omf.org.hk*

MALAYSIA: 3A Jalan Nipah, off Jalan Ampang, 55000, Kuala Lumpur
email: my@omf.net   *www.omf.org*

NEW ZEALAND: P O Box 10159, Dominion Road, Auckland 1030.
Tel 9-630 5778   email: omfnz@omf.net   *www.nz.omf.org*

PHILIPPINES: 900 Commonwealth Avenue, Diliman, 1101 Quezon City
email: ph-hc@omf.net   *www.omf.org*

SINGAPORE: 2 Cluny Road, Singapore 259570
email: sno@omf.net   *www.omf.org*

SOUTHERN AFRICA: P O Box 3080, Pinegowrie, 2123
email: za@omf.net   *www.za.omf.org*

UK: Station Approach, Borough Green, Sevenoaks, Kent, TN15 8BG
Tel 01732 887299   email: omf@omf.org.uk   *www.omf.org.uk*

USA: 10 West Dry Creek Circle, Littleton, CO 80120-4413
Toll Free 1-800-422-5330 email: omf@omf.org   *www.us.omf.org*

OMF International Headquarters:
2 Cluny Road, Singapore 259570

Christian Focus Publications
publishes books for all ages

Our mission statement –

STAYING FAITHFUL

In dependence upon God we seek to help make His infallible word, the Bible, relevant. Our aim is to ensure that the Lord Jesus Christ is presented as the only hope to obtain forgiveness of sin, live a useful life and look forward to heaven with Him.

REACHING OUT

Christ's last command requires us to reach out to our world with His gospel. We seek to help fulfill that by publishing books that point people towards Jesus and help them develop a Christ-like maturity. We aim to equip all levels of readers for life, work, ministry and mission.

Books in our adult range are published in three imprints.

Christian Focus contains popular works including biographies, commentaries, basic doctrine, and Christian living. Our children's books are also published in this imprint.

Mentor focuses on books written at a level suitable for Bible College and seminary students, pastors, and other serious readers. The imprint includes commentaries, doctrinal studies, examination of current issues, and church history.

Christian Heritage contains classic writings from the past.

For a free catalogue of all our titles, please write to

Christian Focus Publications, Ltd
Geanies House, Fearn,
Ross-shire, IV20 1TW, Scotland, United Kingdom
info@christianfocus.com